MARGARET LAURENCE WRITES AFRICA AND CANADA

MARGARET LAURENCE WRITES AFRICA AND CANADA

LAURA K. DAVIS

For Elaine,
Enjoy!
Laura Davis.

WILFRID LAURIER
UNIVERSITY PRESS

Wilfrid Laurier University Press acknowledges the support of the Canada Council for the Arts for our publishing program. We acknowledge the financial support of the Government of Canada through the Canada Book Fund for our publishing activities. This work was supported by the Research Support Fund.

Library and Archives Canada Cataloguing in Publication

Davis, Laura K., author
    Margaret Laurence writes Africa and Canada / Laura K. Davis.

Includes bibliographical references and index.
Issued in print and electronic formats.
ISBN 978-1-77112-146-0 (hardcover). – ISBN 978-1-77112-147-7 (softcover). –
ISBN 978-1-77112-148-4 (PDF). – ISBN 978-1-77112-149-1 (EPUB)

    1. Laurence, Margaret, 1926–1987 – Criticism and interpretation. 2. Africa – In literature. 3. Canada – In literature. 4. National characteristics, African, in literature. 5. National characteristics, Canadian, in literature. 6. Decolonization in literature. 7. Nationalism in literature. I. Title.

PS8523.A86Z575 2017   C813'.54   C2016-906834-X
                                                C2016-906835-8

Cover image: *Portrait of Margaret Laurence* (acrylic and pastel on canvas, 1978), by Charles Pachter. Used by permission of the artist. Cover design by Daiva Villa, Chris Rowat Design. Text design by Mike Bechthold.

© 2017 Wilfrid Laurier University Press
Waterloo, Ontario, Canada
www.wlupress.wlu.ca

This book is printed on FSC® certified paper and is certified Ecologo. It contains post-consumer fibre, is processed chlorine free, and is manufactured using biogas energy.

Printed in Canada

This book is dedicated to my parents,
Ken and Wendy Strong.

Thank you for believing in me.

Contents

Preface

I was first introduced to the writing of Margaret Laurence many years ago, when her children's book *The Olden Days Coat* was published in 1979. Only eight years old, I was enthralled by the book and the protagonist Sal's travel back in time to meet her own grandmother at her age. What *would* it be like, I thought, to be able to do the same and meet my own grandma when she was my age? Would we be fast friends? It was the first time that I would read a book and feel that the place and characters in it were my own: it took place on the Canadian prairies, and the characters were people who lived there, just like I did. Only two years later, the Canadian Broadcasting Corporation (CBC) film version of the book was released, with Megan Follows, who would later play Anne in *Anne of Green Gables*, in the lead role of Sal. Watching the film on CBC television became a family tradition each Christmas season for many years to come. I remember those evenings, the fireplace crackling and the icy wind blowing outside, much like the cold winters described in the story. In early January of 1987, when I was sixteen years old, my mother sat the family down at the breakfast table and sadly and emotionally announced that Margaret Laurence had died. Profoundly influenced by her writing, she made it known to us how important Canadian literature was, and how significantly Margaret Laurence was a part of it. A few years later, I began to take English courses at the University of British Columbia, and for the first time to read Laurence's corpus of writing. Yet my early introductions to the author's work and her influence on my mother and me always stayed with me.

Laurence's importance as a Canadian writer began, arguably, when she first published with McClelland and Stewart in 1959, and it grew in the years that followed. Clara Thomas wrote the first scholarly work on her writing in 1975, *The Manawaka World of Margaret Laurence*. An English professor at York University who was groundbreaking in terms of her work on Canadian literature and her position as a woman in what was then a male-dominated profession, Thomas also became a lifelong friend of Laurence's. Since then, numerous articles and books have been published on the writer, including three biographies, written by James King, Lyall Powers, and Donez Xiques. Scholarly work in the 1980s and early 1990s often focused on her strong female characters and feminist themes. Such was the case, for instance, in Harriet Blodgett's "The Real Lives of Margaret Laurence's Women" (1981); Gayle Green's "Margaret Laurence's *The Diviners*: Changing the Past" (1991), which she published in a book called *Changing the Story: Feminist Fiction and Tradition*; and Stephanie A. Demetrakopoulos's "Laurence's Fiction: A Revisioning of Feminine Archetypes" (1982). A few scholarly books and articles published in the 1980s addressed her writing about Africa and her Métis characters in her writing about Canada. These include, for instance, Micere Githae Mugo's *Visions of Africa: Fiction of Chinua Achebe, Margaret Laurence, Elspeth Huxley and Ngugi Wa Thiongo* (1981), and Leslie Monkman's "The Tonnerre Family: Mirrors of Suffering" (1980). However, criticism on Laurence's work that addressed post-colonial and national themes became more prominent in the decades to follow. For instance, works such as Sandra Carolan-Brozy and Susanne Hagemann's "'There is such a place' – Is There? Scotland in Margaret Laurence's *The Diviners*" (1996) and Wendy Roy's analysis of Laurence's work in *Maps of Difference: Canada, Women, Travel* (2005) address such themes. From the 1970s to the present, scholars have been writing about Laurence, although the focus of the criticism and the context in which that scholarship was written and published have shifted and changed.

In short, to date, there has been much criticism on Laurence's writing, from biographies to full-length studies that address diverse themes and critique her fiction and non-fiction alike. This book builds upon and is indebted to the work done previous to it. While many have addressed her writing about Africa and Canada, fewer have drawn explicit connections between the two. *Margaret Laurence Writes Africa and Canada* provides a unique contribution to the field of Laurence studies because it considers her work in relation to African philosophies, such as those endorsed by V. Y. Mudimbe and Kwame Anthony Appiah; in relation to Canadian government policies related to immigration and multiculturalism; and in relation to historical events on decolonization. Moreover, I engage in unique analyses of Laurence's individual works of fiction and non-fiction related to both Africa and Canada, and connect them to the context within which they were written. My aim is to draw out the nuances and complexities of the author's varied writings in order to show how she demonstrated a multi-faceted subject position, particularly for the settler subject, and how she did so within and in relation to her own time and place. Throughout the book, I focus on the primary texts, Laurence's writing itself, and on relatively recent scholarly work and theoretical writings related to my analyses. I only occasionally refer to early Laurence criticism, although that important work always stands firmly in the background and informs my writing, as it does at some level, in my opinion, for any contemporary scholar.

I have structured this book around analyses of key texts by the author: three books that she wrote about Africa, drawing from the years she lived in Somaliland and the Gold Coast; and three books that she wrote about Canada, set in the fictional town of Manawaka and based on her hometown of Neepawa, Manitoba. With regard to her writing about Africa, the works I consider include a memoir (*The Prophet's Camel Bell*), a novel (*This Side Jordan*), and a collection of short stories (*The Tomorrow-Tamer*). I do not address all of Laurence's writing about Africa. Indeed, she was the first person ever to translate Somali poetry into English, in a book called *A Tree for Poverty*, first published by the Somaliland Protectorate in 1954, and she wrote a book of criticism on Nigerian literature, *Long Drums and Cannons* (1968), neither of which I discuss here. Yet the memoir, novel, and stories are particularly conducive to a study that considers how Laurence imagined and depicted decolonization. Focusing on these three books enables a consideration of her use of different genres and her settings of various geographical and cultural locales: *The Prophet's Camel Bell* takes places in Somaliland, whereas *This Side Jordan* and *The Tomorrow-Tamer* take place on the Gold Coast. Furthermore, my reading of Laurence's writing about Africa differs from other critics' readings. I argue that despite the male protagonists in these texts, Laurence highlights feminist issues as well as colonial ones, and interrogates the notion of the feminine. My choice of primary texts with regard to her writing about Africa in this book is informed by the extent to which they exemplify intriguing and relevant themes at hand.

Just as I have selected certain works that Laurence wrote about Africa, so too have I selected certain ones she wrote about Canada. Some studies on her writing about Canada, such as Christian Riegel's *Writing Grief: Margaret Laurence and the Work of Mourning* (2003), to name just one example, have considered all five books in the Manawaka cycle. However, I consider only three of the five: *The Stone Angel*, *A Bird in the House*, and *The Diviners*. My choice was determined by the extent to which these works consider nation building and multiculturalism, the focus of this study. *The Fire-Dwellers* and *A Jest of God*, considered "sister novels," are significant texts in the Manawaka cycle. While they take up themes of identity, their focus is more on gender and less on nation and multiculturalism. The three works that I consider, like the Manawaka cycle in its entirety, have been addressed extensively by critics in terms of feminism, but less so with regard to nationalism and multiculturalism. I build upon previous work on nationalism in Laurence's writing, such as Paul Hjartarson's "'Christie's Real Country. Where I Was Born': Story-Telling, Loss and Subjectivity in *The Diviners*" (1988) and Kristina Fagan's "Adoption as National Fantasy in Barbara Kingsolver's *Pigs in Heaven* and Margaret Laurence's *The Diviners*" (2004). Most studies on nationalism in Laurence's writing have considered *The Diviners* as a primary text. An earlier and shorter version of my analysis of *The Diviners* in chapter 4 of this book, with an emphasis on the theme of motherhood, was published in my article "Creating a New Multicultural Canada: Motherhood and Nationalism in Margaret Laurence's *The Diviners*." I extend and widen both other critics' analyses and my own by expanding upon them and by bringing *The Stone Angel* and *A Bird in the House* into that discussion. They too, like *The Diviners*, portray and foreground a divided and multi-faceted settler subject position.

In this book, I use the term "settler" along the same lines that Anna Johnston and Alan Lawson do in their article called "Settler Colonies." They note that "in general, historical definitions of 'settler colonies' have relied on the presence of long-term, majority white racial communities, where indigenous peoples have been outnumbered and removed by colonial policies and practices" (361). The term varies in use according to its context, and can have complicated political implications in places such as South Africa and Israel, as Johnston and Lawson explain. With reference to Laurence's fictional characters, I use the term to refer to Anglo (British, but also Scots and Irish) and French settlement in early Canada, and the descendants of Canadian pioneers. Like Johnston and Lawson, I too use the term "'settler' for reasons of brevity," but agree that "the 'invader' rider should always be kept in mind, as it is in the theory" (362). At times, I use the term "settler-descendant" to refer to those characters in Laurence's work who themselves may have never lived in or even visited Britain, but whose ancestors settled in Canada. The distinction between "settler" and "settler-descendant" is an important one with regard to certain characters and instances in Laurence's writing. My use of the word "settler-descendant" is not meant to deny or efface their complicity with their settler ancestors or, in some aspects, their ongoing oppression of Aboriginals.

Relatedly, throughout this book I use the word "Aboriginal" to refer not only to First Nations peoples, but also to Inuit and Métis peoples, although

Laurence's fictional work primarily takes up the Métis history of the Red River area of Manitoba, which I discuss in more detail in the introduction to this book. A historic ruling by the Supreme Court of Canada in 2016 recognized rights of non-status Indians and Métis peoples. While the discussion regarding who has been and continues to be considered "Indian" by the federal government is historically complex and outside of the scope of this book, it is important to note that there are distinct groups of Aboriginal peoples in Canada, such as First Nations, Métis, and Inuit. I mean to include all of them with the term "Aboriginal," and yet not to deny or conflate the histories and identities particular to each group.

Acknowledgements

This book could not have come to fruition without the support and hard work of many people. First and foremost, my heartfelt gratitude goes to the staff at Wilfrid Laurier University Press, and particularly to Lisa Quinn, the director of the press, who did such excellent work as my editor on this project and believed in it from the outset. Her advice and encouragement have been acute and steadfast, and much appreciated. I give special thanks to the press's managing editor, Rob Kohlmeier, for his work on this book, and to its copy editor, Margaret Crammond, for her insightful comments on the manuscript. I am also grateful to the anonymous reviewers who provided valuable feedback for revisions. I give heartfelt thanks to the Canadian artist Charles Pachter for his permission to publish his wonderful painting of Margaret Laurence on the cover of this book. I owe a debt of gratitude to my research assistant, Meagan Roberts, who was also one of my best students at Red Deer College and a graduate from the English program there. Her work on the research for this manuscript, which included attaining numerous articles and compiling an extensive bibliography, was meticulous. Thank you to the archivists at the Clara Thomas Archives and Special Collections, York University, Toronto, and the William Ready Division of Archives and Research Collections, McMaster University, Hamilton, where Margaret Laurence's papers are held: Michael Moir, Suzanne Dubeau, Anna St. Onge, and Julia Holland (Clara Thomas Archives); and Carl Spadoni and Rick Stapleton (William Ready Division). All of these individuals were welcoming and helpful, and their enthusiasm for my research was greatly appreciated. I will not forget viewing the author's papers in the Margaret Laurence home in Neepawa, Manitoba. I thank Ruth Kaspick for hosting me there and for inviting me for tea on the Laurence home porch.

For guidance on earlier work related to this book, I would like to thank Nora Foster Stovel, a truly wonderful professor whose mentorship throughout graduate school and during the early years of my career as an academic has meant so much to me. I am grateful to Diana Brydon, Paul Hjartarson, and Onookome Okome for thoughtful and insightful feedback on early drafts of this manuscript. I give special acknowledgement to Red Deer College, which provided me with financial assistance for my archival work and research toward this project through extended funding grants and professional development funds. I also thank the Alberta Association of Colleges and Technical Institutes (AACTI), which awarded me a grant to hire a research assistant for work on this book. My colleagues and my students at Red Deer College have been an inspiration to me and have greatly influenced my study of Margaret Laurence. I thank them for their enthusiasm and insights on the author and on Canadian literature. On a personal note, I would like to thank my mom and dad, Ken and Wendy Strong, for nurturing my creative spirit and for their constant and unwavering support; my brother Greg Strong, for his encouragement and lifelong friendship; and my husband, Roger Davis, who has been at my side through thick and thin. Finally, I would like to thank my three children, Rachael, Kai, and Clara Davis, who are an inspiration to me each and every day.

Introduction

Writing and Place

Margaret Laurence has long been known as a prominent figure in Canadian literature, and her name is recognized among literary scholars and the public alike. She is most famous for her five books about life in a small Canadian prairie town, and this writing has been and continues to be celebrated. In 1977, for instance, W. H. New stated that "more than any other writer of her time," Laurence "seemed to have mastered the rhythms and cadences of the Canadian speaking voice" (Introduction 1). Similarly, in 1997, Christian Riegel exclaimed that "Margaret Laurence touched Canadians like no other writer during her career" ("Recognizing" xi). In 2016, twenty-nine years after Laurence's death, Parks Canada designated her as "a person of national historical significance" (Laychuk). Academics have acknowledged various aspects of her life and work, and have discussed her writing about Africa and Canada. Notably, Andreea Topor-Constantin traces various articles and works of criticism that have drawn connections between Laurence's writing about Africa and her writing about Canada – by scholars such as Clara Thomas, Craig Tapping, and Karen MacFarlane (xii–xiii). Yet many people among the public are unaware of her commitment to the politics of decolonization, nation building, and multiculturalism, since public discourse and media on the author has centred on the Manawaka cycle, her five books about Canada. *Margaret Laurence Writes Africa and Canada* addresses the importance of Laurence's contribution to Canadian literature in the context of decolonization and nation building in 1950s Somalia and Ghana, and 1960s and 1970s Canada. It does so by acknowledging nuances in her writing and politics and contextualizing them within Canadian government policies and histories that were contemporary to her time. As such, this book offers a new approach to Laurence studies and shows how she was influenced by historical circumstances and contributed to the geographical and literary communities of which she was a part.

Laurence maintained a lifelong friendship and correspondence with Nigerian writers Chinua Achebe and Wole Soyinka; she lived in and wrote about Somalia and Ghana during the process of decolonization in the 1950s – and her experience affected her vision of Canada; she was involved in a committee on the creation of the new Canadian constitution; and she dedicated time and writing in her later life to Canadian policies toward sustainable energy resources. This book addresses all of these aspects of Laurence's life and work, which remain important and have become even more urgent today. It examines not only her writing about Africa and Canada, but also her unpublished business and personal correspondence, and it does so in the context of the place and politics within which the work was written. As such, this book argues that Laurence reimagined Africa and Canada and influenced changing ideologies of the Canadian nation itself.

Writing about Africa

Laurence and her husband, Jack, lived in the British Somaliland Protectorate (later to become Somalia) from 1950 to 1952, and in the Gold Coast (later to become Ghana) from 1952 to 1957. It was her husband's work as an engineer that brought Laurence to Africa: Jack was hired by the British government to construct reservoirs, or *ballehs*, in Somaliland, and to build the new port of Tema in the Gold Coast. Ironically, while Jack worked for the British colonial government, Laurence began to write books about Africa that clearly expressed her beliefs against colonialism. She published five books about Africa: *A Tree for Poverty* (1954), the first collection of Somali poems and stories to be translated into English, translated and interpreted by Laurence; *This Side Jordan* (1960), a novel set in Ghana; *The Prophet's Camel Bell* (1963), a memoir about her time in Africa; *The Tomorrow-Tamer* (1963), a collection of short stories about life in Ghana during decolonization; and *Long Drums and Cannons: Nigerian Dramatists and Novelists, 1952–1966* (1968), her only full-length work of criticism. These important books are testament to her commitment to language, culture, and literature in Somalia, Ghana, and Nigeria.

Laurence's politics in Africa involved resisting the cultural domination of African peoples and aligning herself in her writing with such Africans as Mensah, whom she discusses in "The Very Best Intentions" – an essay in her collection, *Heart of a Stranger* (1976) – and who was against imperialism in Ghana. Although she stood against the British, her writing indicates that she would not have wholeheartedly supported the ideologies of the new leader, Kwame Nkrumah. He became the main exponent of pan-Africanism in the 1950s and 1960s, when Laurence was living on the Gold Coast. The pan-Africanist movement that Nkrumah endorsed maintained that Africans can be unified and identified together rather than separately according to region or tribe. In *In My Father's House* (1992), Kwame Anthony Appiah criticizes the movement of pan-Africanism, emphasizing that the representation or idea of "Africa" is caught up in racist ideas. In Laurence's *This Side Jordan*, the English characters repeatedly define the African characters as if they are indistinguishable, as if they come from the same locale and have had the same history. Through such characters, whom she mocks, she critiques the racism implicit in the pan-Africanist idea that Africa is one. Therefore, one might argue that she was a forerunner to Appiah's post-colonial theory. While her writing does not align with Nkrumah's ideas, however, she did support his independence movement. She states in a letter to Adele Wiseman in 1952: "The country is well on its way to self-government, having a Prime Minister (Kwame Nkrumah, who seems a very intelligent and sincere young man ... the country has a good leader in him, I think)" (Lennox and Panofsky 77). Nkrumah eventually formed the Gold Coast Convention People's Party, became Ghana's first prime minister, and led the Gold Coast to independence in 1957. As Topor-Constantin notes, "The socio-political situation on the Gold Coast [and] the triumph of Nkrumah and the Convention People's Party ... were inspiring to [Laurence]" (54).

As Nora Foster Stovel points out in her introduction to the 2003 edition of *Heart of a Stranger*, Laurence "made her sympathy with Ghana's independence movement clear in her choice of the mammy-lorry slogans – 'The Day Will Come,' 'Authority Is Never Loved,' and 'Rise-Up, Ghana' – as epigraphs for *This Side Jordan*" (xvii). Much of *This Side Jordan* and *The Tomorrow-Tamer*, in fact, are about the Gold Coast's impending freedom from Britain. Laurence seemed optimistic about Ghana's freedom from Britain, but also wary of ongoing Western economic interest in and exploitation of Africa. Such wariness of imminent Western corruption is subtly invoked, for example, in Matthew's comment, in "The Drummer of All the World" (a story in *The Tomorrow-Tamer*), that "Independence is the new fetish, and political parties the new chieftains" (17). It is also invoked in "The Very Best Intentions," in Laurence's mention of Mensah's statement that he is pleased with independence "but would be even more pleased if [he] did not see quite such a large hotel being built by the government for visiting important personages" (*Heart* 28). That Laurence highlighted such comments in the voices of her characters demonstrates her keen awareness of neo-colonialism in Africa, and qualifies the independence movements she so avidly celebrated in her African work.

In her memoir, *The Prophet's Camel Bell* (1963), Laurence states, "my feeling about imperialism was very simple – I was against it" (25). In a letter written to C. J. Martin, the photographer for *The Prophet's Camel Bell*, Laurence wrote that if the memoir "attempts to show anything, it is that communication between peoples of different cultures is not a simple matter and that goodwill is not enough," further asserting that people must be accepted "in terms of their own concepts, not one's own." As Stovel points out in her introduction to Laurence's *Long Drums and Cannons*, Laurence was aware of post-colonial issues "long before post-colonial studies became current" ("Talking" 1). Laurence read and admired Octave Mannoni's *Prospero and Caliban: The Psychology of Colonization* (1950). Mannoni was the first to suggest that the colonizer rather than the colonized was psychologically abnormal. In *Black Skin, White Masks* (1968), Frantz Fanon argues that it is not only individual colonizers who can be blamed for colonization, but Western culture and the colonial system itself. Fanon's work had not yet been written when Laurence was writing about Africa, and seminal works such as Edward Said's *Orientalism* would not be available until the 1970s. Nonetheless, Laurence's writing anticipated the intellect of such writers. Despite the lack of materials on the subject, she countered imperialism and wrote against existing narratives written by nineteenth-century British explorers such as Henry Morton Stanley, David Livingstone, and Richard Burton. In fact, in *The Prophet's Camel Bell*, as I show in chapter 1, Laurence directly mentions and rebuts the romanticized African images of Burton's *First Footsteps in East Africa* (1856).

Laurence's experiences in Africa contributed to her deep concern about the domination and exploitation of peoples there by direct colonialist intervention. She made this concern evident not only in her memoir set in Somalia, but also in her novel set in Ghana, *This Side Jordan*. In that work, she delineates and critiques the British-run government and the posting of European personnel in governmental positions. In the novel and in her short story "The Pure Diamond Man," she also shows how the British began to dominate Ghana culturally, appropriating their art and selling their artifacts as cheap commodities in local markets. In her short story entitled "Mask of Beaten Gold" (1963), which was published in *The Tamarack Review* and was not included in the *Tomorrow-Tamer* collection, she criticizes the placement of an Ashanti mask in a London museum. She provided Canadians with a new and acute understanding of relations between Africa and the West: she supported the independence movements in African countries, but she also examined and depicted the complexities of economic, cultural, and artistic domination. Moreover, she went beyond merely depicting the colonizer as the dominant and the colonized as the dominated. Her resistance to reading colonizer-colonized relations in this simplistic way is particularly clear in "The Pure Diamond Man," in which the local Ghanaian, Tetteh, tricks an English anthropologist by turning his own colonial values against him and making him appear the fool.

Clearly, Laurence was in tune with the complexities of colonizer–colonized relations and identities, and, relatedly, she was both influenced by and contested Western ideas of Africa. According to V. Y. Mudimbe and Kwame Anthony Appiah, conceptions of Africa as empty, as singular rather than diverse, as a pristine Garden of Eden, and as wild and untamed, have had a long history. Such conceptions were evident in movements such as pan-Africanism and Negritude and with the work of scholars such as Alexander Crummell, W. E. B. Du Bois, and Léopold Senghor. Crummell's and Du Bois's pan-Africanism invoked "race" as a basis for moral solidarity and drew upon the doctrine of "racialism": the idea that a race possesses inherited characteristics that are specific to that race. The doctrine of "racialism" was a Western concept based on rising scientific and Enlightenment theories and Darwinian methods of classification. Senghor's Negritude, which began in France rather than in Africa, sought not only to unify Africans but also to celebrate being African. Although Senghor revised his views on Negritude before his death in 2001, in the 1950s and 1960s, when Laurence was in Africa, Senghor assumed "the racial solidarity of the Negro" (Appiah 6). Interestingly, however, he also sought to free blackness from the pathological space given it in Christian discourse, as did Laurence. In her writing and with her African characters, she worked against the way they were typically devalued by the Christian West, even as she herself was a Christian and held some Western ideologies.

Despite her anti-colonial beliefs, Laurence did not always succeed in uprooting Western ideas of Africa. Her entanglement in Western values is testament to ongoing and entrenched imperial ideologies in the Western world. Post-colonial theorists such as Simon Gikandi, in *Maps of Englishness* (1996), and Edward Said, in *Orientalism* (1978), have recognized the continuation of imperialism in the twentieth century. These critics, among others, have argued that the term "post-colonial" is dangerous because it implies that imperialism has ended: the colonialism of the past both extends into the present and exists in varying, even quite different forms. Said distinguishes between the kind of colonialism that was prevalent during the nineteenth century, when countries like Britain and France lived in and occupied the colonies, and twentieth-century imperialism, which he suggests was less direct but equally insidious. *Margaret Laurence Writes Africa and Canada* addresses how Laurence wrote about the continuation of colonialism in Africa, and how that continuation occurred during the movement from subordination to independence.

Laurence's entanglement in Western values is clear in *The Prophet's Camel Bell*, even as she acknowledges her awareness of her own fraught subject position. Near the beginning of that memoir, she states that she and Jack travelled to Africa "to simplify, to return to the pioneer's uncomplicated struggle" (11). While playing into Western epistemes of Africa as untouched and "simp[le]," she nostalgically connects her presence in Africa to the history of Canadian settlement: in Africa, she desired to go back in time to be the Canadian pioneer who settled the land. In the *Heart of a Stranger* essay entitled "A Place to Stand On," Laurence writes about how she felt a need to leave the subject of Africa and begin writing about Canada. "I always knew that one day I would have to stop writing about Africa," she states, "and go back to my own people, my own place of belonging" (6). In that same essay, she traces her genealogical roots back to the Scots-Presbyterian pioneers in Manitoba, and says of them, "This is where my own roots began" (6).

This book delineates Laurence's connection to the "pioneer," a "place of belonging," and her own "roots," as these concepts manifest both in Laurence's writing about Africa and her writing about Canada. It is important to acknowledge, in particular, the way such concepts converge and become politicized on the notion of "land" or "landscape," a familiar trope in Canadian literature. W. H. New explains that the word *land* "often functions as a familiar synonym for *dirt* or *ground* or *loam*," but "also resonates with notions of ownership or social attachment (*territory, home, property, estate, plot, yard, grounds, region, nation, world*)" (*Land* 7). The notion of land as "ownership or social attachment" is particularly relevant to Laurence's writing. In her proclamation to "return to the pioneer's uncomplicated struggle," she aligns herself with the white settler, and she suggests that to occupy Africa is to go back in time and place, to an earlier epoch. In *The Prophet's Camel Bell*, she also repeatedly contests those same Western views. Throughout her writing about Africa and Canada, as this book will show, she describes her women characters in the same language that imperialists and pioneers used to describe the land. However, she works within such imperial language and values in order to undermine and critique them. In *This Side Jordan* and *The Tomorrow-Tamer*'s "The Drummer of All the World," for example, Laurence employs and critiques the trope of land as woman in the characters of Emerald and Afua respectively. To this effect, she both engages in and debunks the Western discourse that defines women and the colonized as *"territory, home, property, estate,… nation, world"* (New, *Land* 7).

Writing about Canada

Laurence wrote five books about the fictional Canadian prairie town of Manawaka, based on her hometown of Neepawa, Manitoba, and known as the Manawaka series. They include *The Stone Angel* (1964), a novel about an old woman, Hagar, arguably one of Canadian fiction's strongest characters; *A Jest of God* (1966) and *The Fire-Dwellers* (1969), considered sister novels; *A Bird in the House* (1970), her semi-autobiographical collection of short stories about protagonist Vanessa MacLeod; and *The Diviners* (1974), a bestselling novel about settler-descendant and Métis relations, published at the inception of Canadian multiculturalism. She also wrote three children's books, a collection of essays called *Heart of a Stranger* (1976), and, at the end of her life, a memoir entitled *Dance on the Earth* (1989). *Margaret Laurence Writes Africa and Canada* highlights the different contexts about which she wrote: the decolonization and ongoing development of Africa and the continuing oppression of Aboriginal peoples in Canada. Juxtaposing these two contexts shows that Laurence's subject position was troubled not only when she was away, but also when she was at home. In Africa, she was aligned with and against imperialists and British and African women. In Canada, her ancestral history included settler colonization. Yet by gender and by her own self-positioning, she aligned and sympathized with the oppressed. Away and at home, the imperial and patriarchal histories that Laurence resisted were also those of which she was a part.

If Laurence's politics in Africa involved resisting ongoing colonization of African peoples, then in the same way, her politics in Canada involved resisting the ongoing oppression of Aboriginal peoples. These politics are evident throughout the Manawaka cycle in her historicization of the Métis leader, Louis Riel, and in her narrativization of the fictional Métis family the Tonnerres. She therefore addressed how domination and subordination manifested themselves within as well as between nations.

The Métis, those with a history of mixed European and Aboriginal heritage, are one of three recognized Aboriginal groups in Canada: the other two are First Nations and Inuit peoples. In her writing, Laurence was interested in a specific historical group of Métis from Western Canada, those of the Red River area of Manitoba. The history of the Red River Métis reaches back to early Canadian history. In the 1700s, two fur-trading companies, the Hudson's Bay Company (HBC) and the North West Company (NWC), competed in the Canadian West for trade with the local Aboriginal people. While the men who worked for the HBC were English, the men who worked for the NWC were Scots and French Canadians based in Montreal. Thus the growing population of Métis in the Red River area came to include people of mixed Cree, Ojibwa, Saulteaux, French-Canadian, Scottish, and English descent. By 1810, the Métis in this area were well established; in 1821, the HBC and the NWC merged; and throughout the 1830s and beyond, the Métis were disparagingly characterized by their race, particularly by those such as the HBC Governor, George Simpson: they were victims of the rising doctrine of "racialism." There was growing unrest among them, since the federal government ignored their requests for land claims and instead worked toward Confederation (1867) and the building of the Canadian Pacific Railway (CPR). This unrest ultimately resulted in the Red River Rebellion and the North-West Rebellion led by leaders Louis Riel and Gabriel Dumont. Riel was hanged for treason and Dumont fled to the United States at the same time that the Canadian Pacific Railway was completed in 1885. The coinciding of Riel's hanging and the completion of the railway was particularly ironic: Riel was unable to gain national recognition for his people while the railway was said to have united Canada geographically and symbolically from East to West.

As Laurence noted in her introduction to her essay entitled "Man of Our People," she was troubled by the history of the colonization of the Métis in Western Canada (*Heart* 161). Originally published in *Canadian Forum* as a review of George Woodcock's book, *Gabriel Dumont: The Métis Chief and His Lost World* (1976), and later published in *Heart of a Stranger*, "Man of Our People" analyzes the colonial history of the Métis, focusing on Dumont and Riel during the North-West Rebellion of 1885. In the Red River Rebellion of 1869–1870, the Métis of the Red River area of Manitoba fought for self-determination and land rights against English-Canadian colonizers. Continuing discontent led to the North-West Rebellion of 1885. Because Dumont escaped to the United States and was not hanged, as Riel was, he did not receive the same historical representation that Riel did. Laurence argued that, consequently, Dumont's contribution to the Métis cause was underestimated.

Laurence's "Man of Our People" emphasizes the history of colonization within Canada and the continuation of the colonial project. Referring to Gabriel Dumont, she states, "Has the voice of Gabriel anything to tell us here and now, in a world totally different from his? I believe it has" (*Heart*

166). In a move that reflects what critics Anna Johnston and Alan Lawson call "the indigenization of the settler," Laurence states that settlers who "came to this country as oppressed or dispossessed peoples" must "hear native peoples' voices and ultimately become part of them" (166). However, unlike the "indigenization" of which Johnston and Lawson speak, her impetus was toward cross-cultural understanding and reciprocity rather than appropriation. Her publisher, Jack McClelland of McClelland and Stewart, wrote in a letter to her that he found her last Manawaka novel, *The Diviners*, to be her most ambitious one. It was ambitious, he said, because she attempted to bring together the history of white settlers and Métis people in Canada: "You have confronted yourself with the formidable problem of relating the two streams of heritage" (*Imagining* 185).

Laurence was not only concerned with the ways in which Aboriginal peoples were colonized by British settlers in Canada. She also believed that Canada should distinguish itself from Britain and the practice of British cultural traditions. She expressed her reservations about how the domination and subordination of peoples persisted in twentieth-century North America in an essay entitled "Ivory Tower or Grassroots? The Novelist as Socio-Political Being" (1978). Referring to the cultural domination of the United States over Canada, she asserted that Canada "had been under the colonial sway of Britain once and is now under the colonial sway of America" (24). Such a statement demonstrates her adherence to a kind of Canadian nationalism that gained traction in the 1960s and 1970s. This nationalism maintained that Canada should sever its ties from Britain and embrace its multicultural history and identity. Relatedly, in terms of cultural domination, she and others argued that Canadian rather than British history and literature should be at the forefront of school curricula throughout the country. In Laurence's time, the notion that Canada was culturally dominated by Britain and America was a concern. Her writing about Canada, with the Canadian small prairie town at its centre, directly addressed that concern and showed that cultures, histories, and literatures in Canada were as worthy as those of any other country.

If Laurence was interested in the creation and independence of Canadian cultural identities, then she clearly fostered those identities in her writing: she foregrounded Canada's diverse history and culture. As can be seen in her primarily Celtic-Canadian and Métis characters in her fiction, she drew attention to early Anglo-Scottish settlers' and Métis' shared sense of dispossession from their lands. Johnston and Lawson explain that early Anglo-Scottish settlers to Canada were often themselves dispossessed from their home countries. Because of this sense of dispossession, they argue, early settlers did not maintain a strong allegiance to their home countries, as those sent to rule in colonies of occupation often did (362). Laurence knew the history of Anglo-Scottish colonization of Aboriginal peoples in Canada, and yet she strove to bring heritages together by foregrounding the ways in which these groups were expelled from their homelands. Her point of view is epitomized in the Biblical quotation from which she takes the title of her book of essays, *Heart of a Stranger*: "Also thou shalt not oppress a stranger: for ye know the heart of a stranger, seeing ye were strangers in the land of Egypt" (Exod. 23:9).

Moreover, Laurence's concern with the colonization of Aboriginal peoples and her concern with Canada as distinct from Britain and America were intertwined with Canadian nationalism. This point is significant because Canadian nationalist sensibilities changed throughout her lifetime, from a focus on Canada's ties to Britain to a sense of Canada as diverse. Her desire to work against the oppression of Aboriginal peoples, to bring together the "two streams of heritage," was aligned with new nationalist ideas, since she imagined Canada as united in its diversity. Also nationalist in nature was her desire to distinguish Canada from Britain. In so doing, she showed her understanding of Canada as a country with its own identity rather than as part of its so-called motherland. Laurence was writing at the same time that critics and writers such as Northrop Frye and Margaret Atwood were taking up questions of Canadian national identity, in *The Bush Garden* (1971) and *Survival* (1972), respectively. Thus her own project of defining what Canada was and who Canadians were is not surprising. She acknowledged Canada's history as a colony of Britain but also paid heed to how settlers colonized Aboriginal peoples and how Aboriginal people and immigrants continued to be oppressed. She valued the break from Britain but also knew and resisted Canada's ongoing imperialist practices.

Laurence's nationalism resisted imperialist impulses at home and abroad. However, not all nationalist sensibilities are anti-imperialist. In fact, nationalism is often aligned with imperialism. As Eva Mackey explains, Canadian nationalism, or more specifically, what Mackey calls the Canadian "narrative of nationhood," is created and sustained through images of collaboration and cultural contact between white settlers and indigenous peoples. This "narrative of nationhood" denies Canada's history of cultural genocide and suggests that there was and is benevolence between white settlers as representatives of the state and Aboriginal peoples:

> Aboriginal people are necessary players in nationalist myths: they are the colourful recipients of benevolence, the necessary "others" who reflect back white Canada's self-image of tolerance. Pluralism and tolerance have a key place, and an institutionalized place, in the cultural politics of national identity in Canada. (Mackey 3)

Laurence exposed such nationalist myths and actively resisted them in her writing. In *The Diviners*, Jules Tonnerre dresses in a fake Native costume to please his audience when he plays his guitar (287); later, he suggests that his brother drowned at the hands of the RCMP, and points out that such truth was not acknowledged (363). In these instances, Laurence at once shows how Jules portrays the Aboriginal person as a "colourful recipient of benevolence" (Mackey 3) and exposes that portrayal as a lie. She wanted to show the history and continuation of violence toward and colonization of Aboriginal peoples in Canada. While she hoped for a nation that would work toward cross-cultural understanding, she did not deny Aboriginal histories, and she was not silent about Anglo Canadians' "complicity in the displacement and destruction of Native peoples" (Brydon and Tiffin 23). She sought to expose and bring awareness to such violent and ongoing Canadian histories.

Throughout the 1970s, as Donna Bennett has explained, the view that Canada must affirm its own national identity was being challenged by the idea that Canada was a diverse mosaic that should not and could not establish a singular and monolithic identity (170). To a large extent, Laurence's viewpoint reflected this shift: Laurence was a Canadian nationalist who desired an independent Canadian identity apart from Britain, and she also valued immigrant and Aboriginal cultures. In *The Margin Speaks* (1997), Gunilla Florby suggests that Canadians are severed from their collective histories for two reasons: first, because the history of Canada does not adequately take into account the history of Aboriginal peoples; and second, because as Diana Brydon and Helen Tiffin point out, within settler-invader narratives there are silences "around [settlers'] own complicity in the displacement and destruction of Native peoples" (23). Florby argues that the separation from one's collective history creates what Robert Kroetsch calls "the genealogical quest of Canadian writing" (65). Certainly, Laurence's Manawaka cycle, "where myths of family origins represent the archetypal Western Canadian experience" (Kroetsch 22), is an example of such a genealogical quest. Laurence's writing about Canada is part of the national history and politics within which it is embedded. Her work was driven by the desire to emphasize the history of settler–Aboriginal relations.

Laurence's writing demonstrates the notion that nationalism in Canada need not obliterate difference. Rather, the construction and maintenance of the notion of difference sustains the very idea of Canada as a nation. Laurence's writing of difference is clear in her representation of immigrant characters such as the Ukranian Canadian Nick Kazlik in *A Jest of God* and Sandra Wong, the Chinese Canadian girl in *The Stone Angel*. Her belief that Canada must separate itself from British cultural traditions predicts

Donna Palmateer Pennee's argument, in "Looking Elsewhere for Answers to the Postcolonial Question" (2003), that Canada represents itself through a rhetoric of progression, growth, and maturity in its international relations policy. On this view, Canada is no longer a colonial dependency, as it once was; rather, it is a diverse and mature nation capable of independence within its own borders and aid beyond them.

The idea that Canada has progressed from colony to multicultural country in its own right plays into an ideology that might posit Western countries in opposition to a supposedly underdeveloped Africa. Just as movements regarding ideas of Africa, such as pan-Africanism and Negritude, are embedded within imperialist ideology even as they seek to resist it, so this kind of Canadian nationalism is also embedded within imperialist ideology. While Laurence believes in the decolonization of African countries, she, like others, cannot completely extricate herself from Western ideologies. She recognizes her complicity with imperialism in Africa when she states in *The Prophet's Camel Bell* that she was against imperialism but ultimately realized that, "I, too, had been of that company" (251).

Letters and Politics

When Laurence was writing her final and arguably most influential book, *The Diviners*, in the early 1970s, Prime Minister Lester Pearson had recently struck the Royal Commission on the Status of Women in Canada (1967), and women's groups had created the National Action Committee on the Status of Women (NAC) (1972) "to pressure government to bring the laws into conformity with the royal commission's recommendations" (Hamilton 55). Laurence was influenced by such events, as is evident in her participation in organizations such as the Canadian Abortion Rights Action League (CARAL), women's crisis centres, and The Women's Cultural Centre in Lakefield, Ontario. She was as interested in resisting the oppression of women in Canada as she was in resisting the oppression of Africans and Aboriginal people. In this book, I argue that Laurence's political work influenced women's rights in Canada and the perception and enactment of women's roles and places in the nation.

While she was politically involved with women's rights in the 1970s, her interest in the status of women in the nation began much earlier. As Wendy Roy explains, Laurence's writing about Africa could not have been influenced by the second wave of feminism. Betty Friedan's *The Feminine Mystique* was not published until 1963, the same year as Laurence's African memoir (Roy, "Anti-Imperialism" 34). While the first English translation of Simone de Beauvoir's *The Second Sex* was published in 1953, studies such as Kate Millett's *Sexual Politics* and Germaine Greer's *The Female Eunuch* were not published until 1969 and 1970 respectively. Interestingly, however, Laurence was profoundly influenced by an earlier generation of women – and, importantly, Western Canadian women. As Anne White explains, "On 18 October 1929, five Alberta women [Henrietta Muir Edwards, Nellie McClung, Louise McKinney, Emily Murphy, and Irene Parlby] were successful in achieving an historic ruling from the highest court in the British Empire regarding the legal status of white women in Canada" (216). These feminists are well known as the quintessential first-wave feminists in Canada, who changed the legal status of women. In "Books That Mattered to Me," Laurence cites them as influential to her: "Only in my young adulthood did I realize how far-reaching was the victory of such women as Nellie McClung and Emily Murphy, to have women recognized as persons. They won in 1929" (241). Issues pertinent to women in the North American context – issues such as equal opportunity for women to work outside of the home – are evident in Laurence's Canadian fiction. The character of Stacey in *The Fire-Dwellers*, for example, feels trapped within the confines of her body and her home, wishing to escape that which is deemed a woman's place. Likewise, the character of Morag in *The Diviners* plays the role of housewife for Brooke Skelton, but ultimately leaves Brooke, since she no longer wishes to maintain that role. In various ways, Laurence's writing addresses women's rights and works toward the freedom of expression and identity.

Laurence's works of literature reveal her anti-imperialist, nationalist, and feminist beliefs, and so too do her letters and documents related to her political beliefs. Her literature and letters show that she was immersed in the nationalist turn from a focus on British cultural tradition to a search for Canada's own identity. After World War II, Harold Troper explains, English Canada's image of itself as exemplifying British values began to change, and Canada began to search for and define its national identity. While, in a sense, Canada had been searching for and creating its national identity since Confederation in 1867, this impetus intensified after 1945. One can find evidence of this search, Troper notes, throughout the post-war decades – "the formal introduction of Canadian citizenship in 1947, the Massey Commission (a federal royal commission into the state of the arts, letters, and science in Canada which gave rise to the Canada Council), [and] the campaign to place Canadian studies in school curricula" (1001). In Laurence's writing, the nationalist turn of which Troper speaks and which came to its height in the 1960s and 1970s is evident in *The Diviners*, published in 1974. The protagonist of that novel, Morag Gunn, separates from the British character Brooke Skelton – allegorically, a separation of Canada from Britain. Morag negotiates tensions in gender and nation to create and understand her own identity.

In Laurence's letters and politics, this nationalist turn is evident in her attempt to help shape the new Canadian constitution. In 1982, Prime Minister Pierre Trudeau was working to establish a new Canadian constitution to replace the British North America Act (BNA Act), in place since 1867, under which constitutional decisions were made through Britain. Laurence was one of a group of writers and academics from English-speaking Canada who formed the Committee for a New Constitution prior to the constitution's patriation. She included some of the committee's documents in her unpublished papers held at York University. According to journalist Harry Bruce, who published an article in the *Montreal Gazette* titled "Doing Something! A Working Plan to Save Canada" (4 June 1977), the committee proposed that the Parliament of Canada and the National Assembly of Quebec should invent a "constitutional commission" that would "include equal representation from Quebec and English-speaking Canada, and it would hear all Canadians who want[ed] to help design a constitution that work[ed] in [that] time." Through this committee, Laurence attempted to shape Canada's future and tie it to the interests of the English, French, and Aboriginal peoples of Canada.

One of the most important recommendations made by Laurence and the other committee members was that there must be equal representation in the assembly of the commission between English, French, and Aboriginal peoples. "While regional balance should be assured as well," a committee press release states, "it is a serious evasion not to recognize the historic and contemporary reality of these three groups" (Committee 2). There was dissent particularly in Quebec with regard to the new constitution, leading to the Meech Lake Accord and its failure;[1] thus it is unlikely that the Trudeau government followed the recommendations of the committee to assemble a commission consisting of representatives from all three groups of people. Still, the importance of Laurence's involvement in the Canadian constitution – and thus her attempt to shape the Canadian nation itself – is generally underestimated by Laurence scholars. Laurence's vision of Canada as a coming together of difference, epitomized in the relationships between her Anglo-Scottish and Métis characters, was not only manifested in her literature. It was also prominent in the political work in which she engaged, and in the effect it may have impressed on government and the public perception and creation of Canada.

Implicitly, Laurence's writing works against the Indian Act of 1876 and its many subsequent amendments. Canadian expansionism in the 1800s was seen as fairer than American expansionism, and the Canadian way, embodied in the representation of the Royal Canadian Mounted Police (RCMP), was seen as peaceful and non-violent (Mackey 35; Day 118). This so-called non-violent method of assimilating Aboriginal peoples in Canada was institutionalized in the Indian Act of 1876. However, as Sugars and Moss point out, the Act "in fact deprived Aboriginal peoples in Canada of their basic human rights and in many instances was used to implement racist policies" (318). In 1969 – just a few years before Laurence published *The Diviners* – a government White Paper on Indian policy proposed to abolish the idea of Indian status. This move created resistance from Aboriginal groups who "saw it as a governmental means of reneging on their treaty promises" (Sugars and Moss 321). With the historical tales told by Jules Tonnerre and his father Lazarus in *The Diviners*, Laurence resisted the idea that the Canadian way of expansionism was more peaceful than the American one. With her literature and letters, she also resisted the state's push for Aboriginal peoples to assimilate into Anglo- and French-Canadian culture, and she opposed the persistent and ongoing denial of Aboriginal peoples in Canada.

After she completed the Manawaka cycle, Laurence dedicated herself to political causes: the contemporary women's movement, the anti-nuclear movement, the fight against war. *Margaret Laurence Writes Africa and Canada* addresses this phase of Laurence's career. I highlight Laurence's engagement in the pursuit and implementation of alternative energy sources. In our contemporary world of environmental disasters, depleting natural resources, and climate change, this cause is of more concern today than it was during Laurence's time, and so Laurence's dedication to it shows her acuity. Laurence supported the Public Petroleum Association of Canada (PPAC), Energy Probe, and the Council for Nuclear Awareness – associations that opposed nuclear energy plants and the proliferation of nuclear weapons. In fact, letters from the PPAC abound in the Margaret Laurence Papers at York University: they begin in 1976 and continue well into the 1980s. Laurence's correspondence with Imperial Oil, and her refusal to write a script for a television series they were to sponsor, demonstrates Laurence's passion for her political pursuits (Davis, "Margaret" 61). Laurence wrote letters to friends and other writers, but also to celebrities such as Gordon Lightfoot and Anne Murray, asking them to support sustainable energy resources.

Laurence condemned multinational corporations such as Imperial Oil partly because they were impinging on Aboriginal rights and exploiting their land. Her belief in collaborations between white settler-descendants and Aboriginal peoples was evident in her political work. When addressing such problems, Laurence sometimes appealed to her identity as a woman and a mother. In a statement against the nuclear arms race, for instance, Laurence wrote, "As Dr. Helen Caldicott has said, 'There are no capitalist babies. There are no communist babies. They are babies.' They are indeed, and we, who bear the world's children, will not stand by and see them slaughtered. We must all say NO TO WAR" (Statement). In such instances, Laurence drew upon and mobilized her gender identity in order to advance her ethical aims.

Laurence's advocacy for sustainable resources and her stance against war were intimately intertwined with her belief in Canadian nationalism, particularly her belief that Canada must not be dominated by American values. In a newspaper article entitled "Call for Halt to Missile Parts Manufacture, Author Urges," included in Laurence's archives at York, columnist John Munch reported Laurence's statement that "Canadians should pressure the federal government to ban test flights of the U.S. cruise missile in Canada and to halt production of parts for the missile here." In a panel statement for a conference called "Operation Dismantle," also included in Laurence's archives, Laurence stated that "social services are being cut drastically in America, and may soon be cut in our own country," while "550 billion dollars are spent world-wide on armaments including nuclear arms, and the sum is increasing." Her notion that Canada must separate itself from British cultural traditions, as exemplified in *The Diviners*, for example, took a new form here, in her political documents. Canada, she suggested, must also distinguish itself from America: economically, by refusing to provide oil and resources that destroy Aboriginal and Canadian land; and militarily, by maintaining a peacekeeping role beyond its own borders.

In the essay "Open Letter to the Mother of Joe Bass," included in the *Heart of a Stranger* collection, Laurence discusses two newspaper photographs: the first of an African-American boy who was shot by the police for stealing a six-pack of beer; the second, as Stovel describes in her introduction to that book, "of a North Vietnamese woman trying to wipe napalm from the face of her child" (xxvvi). In her discussion of the first photograph, she criticizes the American police for shooting Joe Bass and suggests that a shooting for such a small crime was an act of racism by the American state. In a letter to Ian Cameron dated 12 May 1970, she referred to this photograph and newspaper article, and described her sympathy, as a mother: "I think of a newspaper pic of the 12yr old negro boy shot by accident, it was said, on the streets of Chicago, the year David was 12.... [W]hose son, I asked myself; it seemed like mine." In her discussion of the second photograph, she speaks from the perspective of a mother and is sympathetic toward the Vietnamese mother who tended to her wounded child.

She called for an end to such acts of violence and racism by the United States. Ironically (since it is about American events), the essay exemplifies her Canadian nationalist stance. The essay was originally written for a collection of essays by Canadians about America, and it implicitly suggests that Canadians must take a stand, as peacekeepers, in relation to America's dominant and violent practices. Canada, she believed, must create itself anew and apart from Britain and the U.S.A.

Laurence clearly articulated how she felt at one with the place from which she came. In "A Place to Stand On," for example, an essay in *Heart of a Stranger*, she states that "Writing, for [her], has to be set firmly in some soil, some place, some outer and inner territory" (9); and in "Where the World Began," also in *Heart of a Stranger*, she asserts that the prairie landscape "formed [her]" (174). She insisted that one must remember and return to one's history. Just as Matthew, in *The Tomorrow-Tamer* story "The Drummer of All the World," nostalgically desires a return to the old Africa and his lost childhood, so Laurence, in her letters, essays, and fiction, returns to the pioneer life of a small town and her childhood experiences there. Matthew's old Africa is "The giant heartbeat of the night drums. The flame tree whose beauty is suddenly splendid" (19), as Laurence's Canadian prairie includes the northern lights that "[flare] across the sky ... like the scrawled signature of God" (170). She exposed the various complexities of small-town Canadian prairie life. As she puts it in "Where the World Began," "The town of my childhood could be called ... agonizingly repressive or cruel at times, and the land in which it grew could be called harsh.... But never merely flat or uninteresting. Never dull" (170). Moreover, her statement that her writing and the writing of many others "involved an attempt to understand one's background and one's past, sometimes a more distant past which one has not personally experienced" (*Heart* 6) implies not only her own background in a prairie town but also that of her settler and pioneer ancestors. *Margaret Laurence Writes Africa and Canada* argues that Laurence's venture abroad and her return home generated her understanding of the Canadian settler's divided subject position. This subject is not quite a member of the ancestral, imperial culture, yet also not truly "native" to one's nation, one's home.

✶ ✶ ✶ ✶ ✶

At the heart of *Margaret Laurence Writes Africa and Canada*, then, is an interrogation of what it means to posit the Canadian settler as essentially a divided subject, what Cynthia Sugars and Gerry Turcotte call "the in-between nature of Canadian identity" (xxi). This divided and complex subject is prominent in all of Laurence's writing: from her African work, to her Canadian work, to her personal and political correspondences. By foregrounding this subject position in order to complicate the idea of the Canadian settler in the modern and contemporary world, this book probes the spaces within and among Canadian subjectivities. This interrogation of how the settler is imagined in her work is important, especially as we move from an emphasis on nationalism, in her time, to contemporary "transnationalism" – "the ways in which national entities are criss-crossed by the global order" (Dobson xiii). Brenda Beckman-Long states that "Laurence's claim of a Scottish identity generates ... productive contradictions – that is, multiple identities – which were crucial to her literary development" ("Nationalism" 160). It is precisely these "productive contradictions" or "multiple identities" that enable the move from a fixed, monolithic national "We" to a complex, shifting sense of "Self" and "Nation." To consider how Laurence positioned herself in both Africa and Canada is to consider how she understood tensions within and among nations. My analysis of her work shows that she was deeply embedded within and influenced by the literary values and institutional constructs of her time. My analysis also shows that she was a part of Canada's nationalism, and that she was already beginning to be influenced by global forces.

Canadian literature has attempted to delineate the "we" that makes up the nation: from the establishment of the Massey Commission in 1951, to a movement toward loosening immigration policies in the 1960s, to the inception of state-implemented multiculturalism in the 1970s and 1980s, to the emphasis on post-colonialism in the 1990s and transnationalism in the 2000s. Despite the fact that Canada has historically practised British cultural traditions, however, the notion of a singular or monolithic Canadian identity, arguably, has not been on the agenda, at least since Canada's centennial year, 1967. Canadian literature, though, continues to interrogate Canadian subjectivities, increasingly in response to transnational and global forces. In *Imagined Communities* (1982), Benedict Anderson posits that the nation is necessarily "imagined as a *community*, because, regardless of the actual inequality and exploitation that may prevail in each, the nation is always conceived as a deep, horizontal comradeship" (7). Moreover, he argues that nations are imagined in relation to a real and created history: they "loom out of an immemorial past" (11). Laurence imagined the Canadian nation by interrogating relations between settlers and Aboriginal peoples. She did so by confronting a history out of which, as well as against which, the nation came into being. The concept of "nation" in this book is informed by Anderson's work and also by a variety of scholars on Canadian and multicultural literature and culture – Richard Day, Eva Mackey, Donna

Bennett, and others – who have studied nationhood in the modern and contemporary Canadian context.

The subject of *Margaret Laurence Writes Africa and Canada* might be read in Charles Pachter's portrayal of Laurence on the cover of this book. In this painting, Laurence sits in her own kitchen next to her shadow. There are two Margaret Laurences here: the so-called real Laurence, and the shadow that is her reflection and representation; Laurence herself, and the author who has become a Canadian literary icon – though both are part of a mediated, artistic representation of the author. The setting is domestic. Teacups and a plate are with her on the kitchen table, a space where, like many women writers of her generation, Laurence did much of her writing. The pairing of Laurence and her shadow uncannily insinuates the sameness and difference Laurence considers in her and her women characters' encounters with colonials and Africans in Africa. Laurence is both inside and outside her "Self" and her "home"; she is both a part of and apart from Africa and Canada, both of which she has inhabited; and she is both enmeshed within and separate from Britain or the so-called motherland, the Anglo-Scottish identity she embraces, and the history of Aboriginal peoples in Canada.

Part One

WRITING ABOUT AFRICA

One

Cultural Conflicts in
The Prophet's Camel Bell
and *This Side Jordan*

In her memoir about Africa, *The Prophet's Camel Bell,* Laurence identifies with and dissociates herself from both English colonialists and Somali women. In her novel about Africa, *This Side Jordan*, she negotiates Western notions of Africa. Her women characters are caught within Western configurations of both women and Africa, even as she actively works against such configurations. She was influenced by Anglo-Canadian feminism, particularly the early feminism of Nellie McClung, Emily Murphy, and the rest of the Famous Five; and yet, such feminists advocated eugenics, a movement intertwined with cultural superiority, racism, and the desire to perpetuate whiteness and British values in Canada. She would not have supported eugenics in Canada and actively resisted racism. The entrenchment of racism in the history of Anglo-Canadian feminism haunted Laurence in Africa. This entrenchment emerges as she and the characters she depicts in her work interact with and seek to aid Africans in Africa. Just as she could not fully escape the history of Western configurations of women and Africans, so she could not entirely escape the entrenchment of racism in Anglo-Canadian feminism. Often in these texts her values collide: to align herself with feminism was simultaneously to align herself with colonialism, which she did not wish to do; likewise, to occupy the position of a feminist in Africa was sometimes to assert oneself as culturally superior, which she resisted. The moments where Laurence's feminist and anti-colonialist ideologies conflict are some of the most moving and troubling instances in her writing on and about Africa.

In light of work by such theorists as Anna Johnston and Alan Lawson, it is not surprising that Anglo-Canadian feminism was caught up in value systems that would advocate for the perpetuation of white settler-descendants. Feminism contributed to the attempt to make Canada "home" for white settlers and their successors. Since early Anglo-Canadian feminism was influenced by its British counterpart, it also follows that this feminist ideology could be embedded in racist beliefs. As Antoinette Burton explains, "the languages of imperialism – articulating as they did the parameters of cultural superiority, political trusteeship, and sheer Englishness – [were] among the most readily available to women involved in various aspects of the British women's movement from the Victorian period onward" (2). Fighting for equality in education and suffrage, white women in Canada often pitted themselves against non-white immigrants and Aboriginal people, promising white men like-minded votes. Laurence was unwittingly affected by this historical embedding of racism within feminism. That history, in part, affected her actions in Africa.

The Memoir on Africa: *The Prophet's Camel Bell*

The Prophet's Camel Bell, published in 1963, addresses the author's experiences in Somaliland in 1951 and 1952, before the country gained independence from Britain. Laurence describes her position as the wife of an engineer hired to construct *ballehs*, large structures that collect water during the rains for the long dry periods in Somaliland's Haud desert. The first chapter of the memoir, titled, ironically, "Innocent Voyage," pokes fun at her own tourist-like position in Somaliland. "There you go," she asserts, "rejoicing, as so you should, for anything might happen and you are carrying with you your notebook and camera so you may catch vast and elusive life in a word and a snapshot" (9). She mocks herself as "innocent" and acknowledges that she and the place in which she resides cannot be reduced to or fully understood in language or image. More specifically, she implies that the memoir we are about to read and the photos she includes within it cannot adequately capture her experience. The second chapter, entitled "Footsteps," plays upon Richard Burton's *First Footsteps in East Africa* (1856) and challenges Burton's narrative. That she mocks her own stance shows that she is aware of her travel memoir's connection to Burton's work as a successor to it. She works within the genre of the travel narrative to counter the conquest of and claims to Africa as Burton depicts them.

On the one hand, as the wife of a Canadian engineer in Somaliland, Laurence was quite explicitly involved in construction and development in Africa: she therefore occupied the position of white colonial woman, a memsahib.[2] On the other hand, as a woman from Canada, a settler-colony that those in Laurence's time might have described as having been culturally colonized by Britain itself, she did not regard herself as a memsahib. In the memoir, she defines herself as apart from European women in Africa by rejecting English women's roles and English customs in the colonies. When Jack hires a servant, and when that servant calls Laurence "memsahib," she immediately rejects that title and states that it has "connotations of white man's burden, paternalism, everything [she] did not believe in" (23). Interestingly, however, she seems to enjoy the role of memsahib at certain moments in the memoir: when a Somali man says to her that "never in his entire long life had he known such a fine memsahib," she admits that she is flattered (40). Although she was not English but Canadian, she was still a white colonial woman; although she did not believe in British imperialism, she still fulfilled the role of memsahib to her servants and other Somalis. As Topor-Constantin puts it, "Margaret Laurence did not know either the taboos of her new home, or the appropriate rules of conduct" (83). Laurence already occupied an ambivalent position that reiterated Canada's position in relation to Britain: she was intertwined with colonial women's roles, but she also sought to break free of them.

In an attempt to separate herself from the English, Laurence explicitly details how her husband's and her own customs are different from those of the English: when their servant Mohamed brings them tea, she must explain that, unlike the English, she and Jack do not take tea in the morning (30). However, while in this instance she makes a point of distinguishing herself from the English in terms of customs, at other moments in the memoir she does not. When she returns from her venture to the Somali town, for example, she refers to the convention that discourages "European women" from travelling to the town without a white, male consort. In this instance, Laurence uses and understands the phrase "European women" as inclusive of herself (34). By explaining to Mohamed that she and Jack do not take tea in the morning, Laurence foregrounds the differences between her own Canadian customs and those of the English; yet by using the phrase "European women" to refer not only to such women but also to herself, she obscures the differences between English and Canadian women. She not only manifests her ambivalent position through such contradictory instances, but she also explicitly states and explains this position. Speaking of her husband's and her own stance as those who were part of colonial life and yet who desired to separate themselves from it, she states, "It was not easy for us to become accustomed to colonial life, and it was not easy for Mohamed to get used to our departures from it" (31).

Laurence clearly situated her and her husband's difference from the English in their status as *Canadians*. Even though the Laurences employed Somalis to cook and serve them, they did so with reluctance. When speaking of their relationship with their servant, Laurence states that "[to Mohamed] we were neither *Ingrese* [English] nor *Italiano*. We came from another and unknown tribe. 'Canadian peoples different,' he would say" (31). She also situates her "Canadian" status as distinct from English colonials in her discussion with the Baron, an acquaintance of hers who was "a major in the Somaliland Scouts" (228). When the Baron overhears a memsahib calling him "common," he confuses Laurence with the memsahib he overhears. He looks at Laurence and calls her a "bloody colonial." "I told him," Laurence asserts, "that there was only one thing worse than calling a Canadian an American, and that was to call one a colonial" (229–30). Laurence learned that simply being a white married woman in Africa constructed her as a colonial. She rejected such labels and located her difference from them in her national identity as a Canadian.

Laurence further separated herself from the English by indicating that she did not believe in English missions in Africa. As she explains, missionary work was banned in Somalia because the Somalis were strong Muslims and waged a war against missionary work. She supported the ban since she "could never believe in anyone's right to foist his religious views upon others" (235). However, she did not find the disjunctions between her own culture and religion and those of the Somalis easily reconcilable. When her servant Hersi states his belief that events occur solely at the doing of Allah, Laurence marks the difficulty in understanding his view (59). The disjunctions in culture and religion between herself and the Somali people, she suggests, trouble the relationships between them. As she said in a letter dated 8 June 1962 to her American publishing agent, Willis Kingsley Wing, she and Jack discovered the "complexities inherent in relationships with people of a totally different culture" during their time in Somaliland.

While clearly about Laurence's personal experiences in Somaliland, the memoir also articulates an emerging Canadian national imaginary. As I explain in the introduction to this book, from the 1950s onward, Canadian settlers began to create an identity separate from that of their British historical counterparts, evident in the Massey Report (1951). The report inaugurated incentives for Canadian artists and writers to create Canadian culture and protect it from the supposedly corrupt forces of Britain and America. This desire to create or identify a distinct Canadian national

imaginary was also prevalent in thematic approaches to Canadian literature, popular in the 1970s. In *Survival*, for instance, Atwood suggested that
the will to survive, in and against the wilderness and other people, was a
prominent theme that distinguished Canada's national literature. Similarly,
in *The Bush Garden*, Frye argued that Canadian literature was marked by
what he called the "garrison mentality" – a carry-over from the garrison,
in which forts separated themselves from the outside world. Frye believed
that Canadian literature depicted an ongoing desire for Canadians to separate themselves from outside forces such as Britain and America. Laurence's
repeated attempts to identify herself as a Canadian in *The Prophet's Camel
Bell* indicate the extent to which Anglo Canadians at this time felt they must
separate from Britain and America. Her insistence on her difference from
the British (and her inability, at times, to articulate that difference) is an
example of some Anglo Canadians' wish to distinguish themselves from the
so-called motherland.

Laurence's attitude toward Britain was complicated by her belief that
Canada was itself culturally colonized by the British. She applied this view
to her position as an Anglo-Canadian woman in Somaliland. That many
of the early Manawaka settlers in her fiction immigrated to Canada as a
result of the Highland clearances of northern Scotland in the 1800s suggests
that she perceived Canada as a country occupied in part by dispossessed
settlers and their descendants. That the identities of her primarily Celtic-
Canadian and Métis characters in her Canadian fiction are based on their
shared sense of dispossession rather than their allegiance to Britain exemplifies her belief in both early Canadian settlers and Aboriginal peoples as
disinherited. As such, she saw herself as different from the British, and she
rejected an identity in Africa that was aligned with the British memsahib
and colonialist.

At the same time that Laurence rejected an English identity in Africa,
she mockingly suggested for herself a quintessentially Canadian persona –
that of the pioneer. As Johnston and Lawson point out, early settlers desired
to be indigenous to the country they settled, creating a "native" identity
for themselves idealized in figures such as the Mountie, the pioneer, and
the woodsman. In her memoir, Laurence re-enacts this move when she
describes herself as a Canadian woodswoman and ironically associates herself with the American pioneer Daniel Boone. Boone was a folk hero whose
exploits were related in John Filson's *The Adventures of Colonel Daniel
Boone* (1794). The travel narrative describes how Boone led settlers through
the wilderness of the Cumberland Gap, and how he fought the Shawnee
Indians, including Chief Blackfish. In *The Prophet's Camel Bell*, Laurence
explains that, typically, white wives at that time did not go with their

husbands to Africa. Laurence was allowed to join Jack in Africa because
of Jack's description of her to the colonial authorities: "Jack explained carefully that his wife, being a hardy Canadian girl, was quite accustomed to life
in a tent.... The Colonial Office was convinced by the striking description
Jack gave of me as an accomplished woodswoman, a kind of female Daniel
Boone" (11).

If we read the comparison of Laurence with Daniel Boone without irony,
then it suggests her alignment with British imperialists in Africa: just as the
British negotiated and conquered the wilderness and peoples of Africa, the
comparison implies, so too North American pioneers negotiated and conquered the wilderness and peoples of North America. The comparison also
dissociates Laurence from white women and aligns her with white men: just
as men negotiate and conquer the wilderness, the argument goes, so too
can Laurence. Finally, Jack's comparison draws upon a preconceived conception of North American and African landscapes as wild and untamed.
Unlike the British, Jack suggests, Canadian girls are "hardy" because they
must negotiate the wilderness of Canada. Jack enabled his wife to travel to
Africa with him because his description of her connoted a masculine Canadian who could survive "in the face of 'hostile elements and/or natives'"
(Atwood, *Survival* 32).

Laurence, however, recognized the absurdity of her construction as a
Canadian woodswoman: "in fact, I had never camped in my life" (*Prophet's*
11). She at once creates and undercuts the representation of herself as an
adventurer. She also states that one of the reasons she and Jack travelled to
Africa to pave roads "where none had been before" may have been because
they had a desire "to simplify, to return to the pioneer's uncomplicated
struggle" (11). She expresses a sense of nostalgia and longing for that romanticized and even fabricated life of the Canadian pioneer. In other words, she
recognizes her dissociation from that "hardy" life and yet to a certain extent
seems to desire to return to it. She wishes to experience life before Western
development, even as she and Jack clearly participated in that very development. By simultaneously creating and undermining a Canadian pioneer
persona in her memoir, Laurence implies that Canadian national identity is
indeed imagined. It is through this dynamic and unstable negotiation of a
national imaginary that she reconceptualizes Canada in her writing about
both Africa and Canada.

In *The Prophet's Camel Bell*, Laurence often seems to be aligned
with that which is masculine and imperial. Jack's description of her as "a
female Daniel Boone" implies that she is like man who progresses forward
through time, occupying and conquering space in his adventures. Her own
description of her reasons for travelling to Africa might also align her with

masculinity – the pioneer-man who discovers and develops new lands. Interestingly, her association with masculinity allocated her a certain kind of freedom and privilege in Africa. After all, it was her so-called hardiness that enabled her to travel there. That Laurence was permitted to travel to Africa is noteworthy in light of Ann Laura Stoler's assertion that the dominant domestic arrangement of the colonies in the early twentieth century consisted of a colonized woman living with a European man. According to Stoler, because of the economic benefits of this arrangement (the fact that colonized women provided free domestic service, for example), colonial governments encouraged concubinage by "restricting the emigration of European women to the colonies and by refusing employment to married male European recruits" (348–49). Although some European women accompanied their husbands to the colonies during the time Laurence was in Africa, Laurence's account of Jack's description of her suggests that her status as a Canadian allowed her to defy certain restrictions placed on European women. In particular, it permitted her to travel to Africa with her husband when many European women could not.

Despite her alignment with the masculine, however, Laurence still experienced gender oppression while in Africa. For example, her position as a woman in a British colony restricted the social spaces she could occupy. This fact is highlighted by Laurence's account of her unaccompanied trip to the Somali town and market, where she quickly learns that such behaviour is socially and culturally unacceptable (*Prophet's* 34). Her presence there represents not only a gender transgression but also a racial one, and her transgression of racial boundaries makes her realize that she is neither separate from the "Christian conquerors" the Somalis resent, nor "immune" from the Somalis' "bitterness" against them (34). In the memoir her social mobility is further impeded when she associates with the governor's wife. She exclaims that although she feels an affiliation with her, social etiquette requires that she not develop a friendship. When she discovers that she and the governor's wife share an interest in translating Somali poems and folk tales, she thinks about inviting her over to continue the discussion. "I recalled in time," Laurence explains, "that this was not possible. One does not ask the Governor's wife to drop over for a beer. This kind of formality, which prevents people from talking with one another, seemed idiotic to me then, and it still does" (257).

Laurence again experiences gender restrictions when she unknowingly commits the faux pas of inviting African men into her house. When three Somali elders visit the Laurence home to question Jack about the construction of the *ballehs*, Laurence invites them in, even though Jack is not home. The men, Laurence notes, were "exceedingly polite ... but made no attempt to ask questions or discuss the matter" (40). After the men leave, Laurence's interpreter and servant, Mohamed, informs her that "a woman alone in the house must never invite men in.... To do so was a terrible breach of etiquette. Further, the elders could certainly not discuss any serious matter with a woman" (41). As a white woman and the wife of the engineer who manages the construction of the *ballehs*, Laurence occupied a superior position in relation to the Somali elders; but as a young woman and a foreigner in Somaliland, she occupied an inferior position in relation to them. Her subject position was troubled by existing gender hierarchies in Somaliland.

During the elder's second visit to the Laurence home – when Jack is at home – Laurence occupies the position of a silent bystander and listener as Jack converses with the Somali men. She effectively depicts both sides of the conversation. She is able to do so because she occupies neither Jack's position as a white male nor the Somalis' position as the ones whose land Jack develops. On the one hand, she speaks through Jack's voice while distancing herself from his perspective: "How to deal with these three maddening old men?" (42). On the other hand, she imagines the Somalis' line of thought without having to position herself in opposition to it. When the elders ask Jack if the English will build large towns for themselves beside the *ballehs*, Jack suggests that the idea is absurd, and says that the English would not live "permanently in the desert areas of the Haud for no reason at all" (42). Presenting the Somalis' side of the situation, however, Laurence indicates to the reader, "They [the elders] looked at him blankly. They could imagine it [the building of the towns] quite well. It would be no more insane than anything else the English did" (43). In this instance, she stands apart from Jack's position as a Westerner. Her perspective momentarily exempts her from power and frees her to present a perspective outside of her subject position as a white woman in Africa. This instance is important because it shows how her gendered position contributed to her sympathy for the Somali elders. It is also deeply problematic, because that position also prevented her from voicing that sympathy.

In these instances Laurence's social mobility was impeded both because of her race and because of her gender. If she were either a European man or an African woman, then she could travel with ease to the Somali town and market; if she were a white man, then she could invite the governor or another white man over for a beer; and if she were either a European or an African man, then she could invite the Somali elders into her home. One might argue that her gendered position limited her social mobility and restricted her actions, while her racial position posited her as one with the conqueror, he who limits and restricts. Yet it is not simply so. Positions of race and gender work together in such instances to restrict and impede one's social mobility. That a white woman was not to go to the local Somali town and market, and that she was not to invite African men into her home, suggests a fear of miscegenation. The prevention of a white woman from mingling with Africans in the marketplace is interesting in light of Cheryl Johnson-Odim's suggestion that markets were "urban areas where the colonized and the colonizers (both women and men) intermingled regularly and were drawn into one another's world views" (81). According to the logic of imperialism, the "mingling" of a solitary white woman in the marketplace could result in "degeneration" – the racist idea that whites could, under certain circumstances, "degenerate" into savagery (Young 46–47). According to this logic, for a white woman to take in "another's world [view]" (Johnson-Odim 81) could be to threaten, challenge, or even undo the imperial order.

Because of Laurence's complex subject position with regard to gender and race, and because of the disjunctions in culture between Laurence and the African people, her interactions with Somali women are some of the most intriguing moments in *The Prophet's Camel Bell*. Laurence's act of obscuring the cultural and historical differences between colonized Africans and Canadian women facilitated her identification with the Somali women she met. Nevertheless, her identifications with Somali women were never straightforward but rather fraught with complexity. As Barbara Pell explains, Laurence "felt isolated from both the conventional 'memsahib' community and the native women in *purdah*" (38). Early in the memoir, some Somali women ask Laurence if she has any medicine to ease their menstrual pain, which is particularly bad, she believes, due to the practice of clitoridectomy. She is uneasy and confesses that she does "not know what to say to these women" (75). Her assertion that "women had always lived with pain" indicates an identification with the Somali women; yet her qualification of that assertion – "Why should it ever be any different?" (76) – demonstrates an unwillingness or inability to help them and thus a dissociation from them. Furthermore, she expresses a sense of frustration and futility at being unable to help the women, exemplifying a concern and sympathy for them: "What should I do? Give them a couple of five-grain aspirin? ... The lunatic audacity of shoving a mild pill at their total situation was more than I could stomach" (76). Yet her act of ultimately turning away from the women – epitomized in her statement, "I have nothing to give you. Nothing" (76) – again emphasizes her cultural distance and dissociation from them. Interestingly, in the memoir she neither explores the cultural motivations for the practice of clitoridectomy nor explains what she means by "[the Somali women's] total situation" (76). What is clear is that she felt distraught at her powerlessness and, at the same time, she was also compelled to help. She found herself both aligned with and haunted by Western feminism and its entrenchment in cultural superiority – an imperial duty, as Antoinette Burton and Ann Laura Stoler explain, to "uplift" the colonized woman. She was frustrated because she could not quite attain a position outside of the imperial order, a position that would have allowed her, as a fellow human being, to reach across cultural and racial boundaries to aid the Somali women.

By the time the women came to Laurence for help, she had already, if inadvertently, established herself as a kind of medicine woman in the community. Before she narrates her encounter with the women, she relates an incident with an Illaloe, a Somali police officer who came to her for help with his earache. In response, she "ceremoniously" mixes together Dettol and water to swab his ear, and she is then stunned to hear that his earache is, in fact, cured (72–73). On the one hand, like Daniel Boone, who not only captured the American Indian but also adopted a position as a representative of that culture, here she seems to perform a Somali ritual as she makes her medicinal brew. On the other hand, however, her concoction might have worked in part because the officer believed in the power of Western medicine, which he perceived her to enact. She could have been understood as a medicine woman or a Western doctor. As such, in this instance she occupies a space between two subject positions. Seen in this light, her "five-grain aspirin" (76) might have been more effective than she thought. She may have overestimated the futility of her work and had more power than she knew.

Laurence's meeting with the eight-year-old prostitute who lived in the nearby *jes* – a "tea-shop-cum-brothel" (156) – was as troubling for her as her earlier encounter with the Somali women. The rhetoric she used to describe her interactions with the child prostitute, Asha, is remarkably similar to the rhetoric she used to describe her interactions with the Somali women who ask her for medicine. Just as she did not know how to respond to those Somali women, so she also did not know what to say to Asha: "We did not talk much, Asha and I, for I did not know what to say to her" (157). Her description of Asha's "unkept" appearance, and her observation that such an appearance was "an unusual sight here, where children were normally well cared for," indicates a sympathy and concern for the child (157). Her admission that she never asked much about Asha's life, and her explanation of that inaction – "My knowledge of Somali was too limited, and who would I get to translate?" (157) – suggests a dissociation from the Somali girl. As she sympathized with and yet dissociated herself from the Somali women who ask her for medicine, she sympathized with and yet turned away from Asha. She felt she had no other choice. Furthermore, she expressed the same frustration and futility in her inability to help Asha as she did in her inability to help the Somali women: the question she asked herself about her meetings with the Somali women – "What should I do?" (76) – is echoed in her statement regarding her interaction with Asha: "I did not know what to do" (156). Likewise, as she reluctantly turned away from the Somali women with her statement, "I have nothing to give you. Nothing" (76), she also ultimately turned away from Asha: "So, whether out of wisdom or cowardice, I did nothing" (158).

Laurence's meetings with Asha haunted her more so than her interactions with the Somali women who asked her for medicine. In the memoir she explains that in the evenings the men from Jack's camp who worked on the *ballehs* used the services of the prostitutes of the *jes*, where Asha resides (156); she also states that Jack decided to supply water for the *jes*, since it provided men from the camp with "amenities of one kind and another" (157). The use of the *jes* by members of their camp and Jack's decision to supply water to it suggest her unwilling complicity with the livelihood of the *jes* and Asha's situation. Importantly, she found that she could not ignore that complicity (157). On the one hand, her decision not to act on Asha's behalf might imply care for the Somali girl. Perhaps it was because she sympathized with her, in other words, that she could not "stomach" (76) getting involved in her situation. On the other hand, her awareness of her complicity with the livelihood of the *jes* and Asha's plight forced her to recognize that she was at one with the imperialists. Her identification with Asha was crosscut with her realization that she was complicit with her exploitation. Thus it was at this moment that Laurence came to realize the complexity of her own subject position. As she herself says later in the memoir, "This was something of an irony to me, to have started out in righteous disapproval of the empire-builders, and to have been forced at last to recognize that I, too, had been of that company" (251).

Laurence's position as a Western woman and her affiliation with the enterprise of constructing the *ballehs* debilitated her relationship with Asha. She was caught within a colonial and patriarchal system that perpetuated not only the exploitation of Africans, but also that of women and children. Because of this system, the "amenities" that the *jes* supplied to Jack's employees could be accepted and encouraged as an aspect of colonial life in Somaliland. If Laurence were to tell Jack's workers not to go to the *jes*, or if she were to tell Jack not to supply water to the *jes*, then Asha herself would suffer for lack of food and water. There was, then, no single or simple action she could have taken to oust Asha from her situation as child prostitute and yet keep her from poverty, possibly even death. As a fellow human being, she wanted to help Asha, but she was disturbed to find that her position as a Westerner prevented her from doing so in an easily identifiable way. Thus Laurence's decision not to act on Asha's behalf was not a decision that simply aligned her with empire. On the one hand, her sympathy with Asha's plight shows her humanity, her desire to cross that boundary that divides "Them" from "Us" (*Heart* 166); on the other hand, her inaction as a bystander and witness to Asha's plight is disturbing. It exposes the extent to which she was implicated within the system and people that perpetuated Asha's and others' exploitation.

Laurence's apparently stable subject position as an Anglo Canadian in Africa broke down at moments of interaction with Somali women. Her feminist impetus that would help the Somali women by giving them medicine and that would aid Asha was ironically impeded by her anti-imperialist motivation not to meddle in the Somalis' affairs. Just as she had to confront the history of her Scottish-Canadian ancestors as those who were dispossessed from their own land but were also colonizers themselves, so too she had to confront the history of Western feminism as part of imperial progress. As Antoinette Burton explains, historically, empire "shaped the lives and identities of those who participated in the women's movement, making it a constituent part of modern British feminist identities" (4). Laurence's role in Africa was caught within this history of British feminism, which influenced the Anglo-Canadian feminism of those such as Emily Murphy and Nellie McClung. Clearly this feminism was not at one with anti-imperialist and anti-racist beliefs and practices.

Historical interconnections between feminism and imperialism haunted Laurence's encounters with Asha. In what Mary Louise Pratt calls "the contact zone" – that place on the imperial frontier where cultural ideologies clash – she was debilitated at such moments of confrontation. Laurence came to realize that Western feminism, since it relies on Western ideology, did not enable her to engage easily in cross-cultural interaction and understanding. She began to realize that her own gender oppression was not the same as that of the Somali women she met. Laurence came to know, as bell hooks puts it, that "the idea of 'common oppression' [between women of different cultures] was a false and corrupt platform disguising and mystifying the true nature of women's varied and complex social reality" (43–44). Ultimately, Laurence became uncomfortable with her own position as a sympathetic woman and as an outsider as she came to realize that she was nevertheless aligned with empire. To put it in Helen Buss's words, Laurence could not "maintain her subject position as respectful learner, good researcher, comic westerner having her biases deconstructed by patient mentors." Often in the memoir, Laurence was "bereft of her strategies" (Buss 40).

The Novel on Africa: *This Side Jordan*

Whereas *The Prophet's Camel Bell* is about Laurence's life in British Somaliland in 1951 and 1952, *This Side Jordan* is a work of fiction that takes as its subject the end of British colonial rule in the Gold Coast, where Laurence lived from 1952 to 1957. Laurence's characters include both Africans and British colonials, and she addresses how those characters handle drastic changes to government rule, changes such as the introduction of "Africanization" – the policy by which British employees of the colonial government were replaced by African ones. In a CBC radio interview presented by Bill McNeil and Maria Barrett on 19 December 1960, Laurence said that she was in Ghana during "tremendous social upheaval," and that it was "one of the most interesting times that one could have been in such a country." She further explained that the novel is primarily concerned with the African schoolteacher Nathaniel Amegbe, a character who "desperately wants to belong to the new Africa," even though "his family constantly tries to drag him back, into the old ways, into the tribal life." As she put it in the CBC interview, crossing over the symbolic Jordan River into the promised land – undergoing vast social and political change – is done with great effort and difficulty, "not just on the part of governments, but on the part of every individual within that country" (McNeil and Barrett).

This Side Jordan takes up the lives of the married British characters, Johnnie and Miranda Kestoe, and the married Ghanaian characters, Nathaniel and Aya Amegbe. Johnnie works for the British colonial government in Ghana, whereas Nathaniel is an under-qualified teacher in a colonial school for local boys. By the end of the novel, because of Africanization, Johnnie must leave his post and he and Miranda must return to England, while Nathaniel struggles to find his place in the new Ghana. The novel begins with Johnnie dancing the highlife with an African woman, Charity, and depicts both the sexual tension between them and Charity's husband's jealousy of it. Johnnie, we find, is both attracted to and repulsed by women: he desires the African woman, Charity, and later, the African prostitute, Emerald (1, 231); and, yet, he asks his pregnant wife, Miranda, to turn her back to him so that he will not have to see her pregnant belly (57). Miranda, much like Laurence herself, is a white liberal who seeks to value African culture and distinguishes herself from colonials who denigrate Africa, such as the British Helen and Bedford (119). Nathaniel is torn between village life – the life of his ancestors – and the new Africa, which includes "progress," development, and Westernization. Through all of these characters, Laurence explored Ghana's transition from colony of Britain to independent nation that continues to be developed and exploited by the

West. Essentially, she criticized the imperial project, negotiating the conflicts between British colonials and local Ghanaians during a time of simultaneous decolonization and development.

In *This Side Jordan*, Laurence employed Western ideas of Africa even as she attempted to remain outside of them. Much of her novel about Africa discusses the struggle between the old and the new; the traditional, African ways and the modern, Western ones; a supposedly "underdeveloped" Africa struggling against a so-called civilized and developed West. One of the ways in which she juxtaposed the traditional ways and the modern ones was through configurations of rural and city life. W. H. New argues that cities in her writing "are variously signs of power, signs of social alternatives ... and embodiments of energy and imperfections, aspiration and decay" ("Margaret" 60). I would also argue that in her writing about Africa, Laurence most often associated the city with progress, the future, and the West. By contrast, she configured the rural, often ironically, as the site of the traditional and the atavistic – that which is anterior in time and place.

Jane Leney states that, in *This Side Jordan*, "an opposition between city and country is clearly established" and that "the dilemma for Nathaniel is to decide between remaining in the city as a schoolteacher or returning to his bush village to work for a chief" (70). The British school at which Nathaniel teaches seems to be a physical manifestation of the very dilemma of which Leney speaks. The school is located in the city, is named "Futura Academy," and is painted with the slogan "The Future Is Yours!" suggesting that it embodies progress. Yet it educates rural rather than city boys, and its regressive physical appearance starkly contrasts with its name: "it sagged, buckled, rotted and decayed a little more each year" (16). Simultaneously an embodiment of the city and the rural, the progressive and the regressive, the school highlights Nathaniel's twofold position as one who lives a new life in the city and yet struggles with the memory of life in the past and in the country with his people. The school is also an ironic statement on the promise of empire. It is at once the mark of future progress and the failure of that progress. As British, the school is representative of empire. Tellingly, however, it does not embody positive economic progression, but exemplifies empire's inevitable violence toward local Ghanaian culture.

Nathaniel states late in the novel that the city "isn't my home, this city of new ways, this tomorrow. You know where I belong. The village – back there, far back" (227). Through Nathaniel's statement, Laurence depicts the Western oppositional paradigm about which the African theorist V. Y. Mudimbe wrote – between the progressive city and the regressive rural African community, between the modern and the traditional. For Nathaniel, a return to his rural community would also be a return to the domestic, a coming back to his family, his uncle Adjei, and his ancestors: the colonial space of the African landscape is here also configured as a domesticated space. Laurence therefore works within the Western trope that depicts the colonized as the domesticated, for as Anne McClintock explains of British imperialism, "as domestic space became racialized, colonial space became domesticated" (36). Just as Laurence implicitly, if ironically, associates the rural African with that which occupies the space of the African landscape and anterior time, so she associates the rural African with the domestic and the familial. According to the imperial order, the city is "progressive" and the rural is "regressive," while, paradoxically, the rural is also that which is domesticated, tamed, familial. The colonized, in this framework, like women, are confined to their proper place. McClintock has suggested that "history is ... figured as *familial*, while the family as an institution is seen as beyond history" (39). That "the family as an institution is seen as beyond history" is evident in *This Side Jordan* in the discussion between Nathaniel and his uncle about coming home to his family in the countryside – "back there, far back" (227). That "history is ... figured as *familial*," in other words, "naturalized as an evolving family" (39), is evident at the end of the novel when the African characters Nathaniel and his wife Aya, as well as the English characters Johnnie and his wife Miranda, have children, thus continuing the presence of both the Ghanaians and the English in Africa.

To posit the city as progressive, Westernized, and modern, and the rural as traditional, even backward, is to reinforce the two categories which – as Karin Barber points out – "have dominated the study of African cultures" (1). Barber explains that Westernized African art is assumed to have grown out of the traditional, "as if the traditional gives birth to, and is automatically superseded by, the modern, Westernized, elite forms" (1). The traditional is thus "frozen into place as an origin or influence, which is co-opted to authenticate the modern by providing it with roots" (Barber 1). According to Barber, what is problematic about the binary of the traditional and the modern is that it obscures much of the art produced in Africa. Such cultural production cannot be put into categories such as "traditional or elite, oral or literate, indigenous or Western" because it "straddles and dissolves these contradictions" (Barber 2). Relatedly, in *This Side Jordan*, the city does not only represent Western progress in opposition to rural Africa, but it is also a place where Ghanaians contest that very opposition. While the construction of the city under colonialism was an act of violence by the colonizer toward the colonized, colonized subjects spoke back to empire and played out contradictions between traditional and modern within the very space of the city. Thus to understand the rural and the city as a binary opposite is to misunderstand both. Rather, they overlap and intertwine, continually creating dynamic cultures and identities.

Right from the beginning of the novel, Laurence shows how the city "straddles and dissolves" (Barber 2) the contradictions between Western and African traditions. When Johnnie dances the highlife with the African woman, Charity, for example, the narrator describes the nightclub where they dance as inclusive of "the wealthy and the struggling, the owners of chauffeur-driven Jaguars and the riders of bicycles" (2). Laurence thus invokes the presence of people who vary in class and wealth. The narrator also explains that "into the brash contemporary patterns of this Africa's fabric were woven symbols old as the sun-king" (2). Within the city of Accra where the nightclub resides, the narrator further indicates, one can hear the "old rhythms ... amid the taxi horns" (2). Even as Laurence works within the Western framework that describes the city as progressive and Western, the rural as backward and African, she simultaneously demonstrates how that binary opposition cannot be maintained. *This Side Jordan* shows how colonized subjects, as part of the very city of people who have colonized them, contest, negotiate, and rework Western values.

In the novel, the maternal, the familial, and the domestic are all associated with the African landscape. The Jordan River that Nathaniel must symbolically cross is a "womb" (247), the land of his ancestors a "forest" (248). The configuration of the rural African landscape as domestic space raises questions about gender and how it might be configured in the novel. Does the colonial understanding of the rural African landscape as domestic, familial space imply that such space is also gendered? If so, how is that understanding of the African landscape manifested in Laurence's novel about Africa? What might it imply about her subject position in relation to Western discourses about Africa? By creating a character such as Nathaniel, an African character who associates himself with the rural landscape, nature, and that which is anterior in time, Laurence works within an imperial ideology that conflates the African with the landscape he inhabits, the indigene with nature. By associating Nathaniel and his land with the domestic and the familial, she plays into a discourse that feminizes Africans and Africa, even if she might ultimately contest that paradigm.

Nathanial's home in the country is described as both feminine and maternal: with the statement, "the River would lap him [Nathaniel] around with its softness, the brown murky stillness of its womb," it is suggested that the river in the countryside is his original home, his mother's womb; and with his question, "How many times have I cut the cord that fed me?" Nathaniel implies that his original homeland is both a woman and a mother who provides him with nurturing (100). The rural Africa that the narrator and Nathaniel depict is a domestic space and also a feminine and maternal one. Thus an attempt to separate Nathaniel from the rural African landscape that is his home is also an attempt, in Stephanie Demetrakopoulos's words, "to fight his way clear of a devouring mother in the form of his people and the African mother/ river who call him back to his village" (45).

Demetrakopoulos suggests that, in *This Side Jordan*, "both male protagonists are driven away from and out of their pasts by fear of certain faces of the feminine" (45). This reading is particularly interesting when one considers that those "faces of the feminine" are also configured as faces of Africa. Alongside Nathaniel's negotiation of the rural African village, then, is Johnnie's negotiation of Africa and his representation of that continent as feminine: Nathaniel conceptualizes Africa as a feminine and maternal homeland just as Johnnie perceives Africa as distinctly feminine. Perhaps the most explicit example of such a perception of Africa occurs when Johnnie has sexual intercourse with the African prostitute, Emerald. His encounter with Emerald demonstrates Johnnie's view of her as the continent of Africa and himself as the colonialist: "She was a continent and he an invader, wanting both to possess and to destroy" (231). In addition, Johnnie's encounter with Emerald seems to demonstrate what Eva Mackey calls a "Western 'will to power.'" Citing Homi Bhabha, Mackey explains that "dominant power and political supremacy seek to '*obliterate*' difference" (4). Johnnie's understanding of Emerald in *This Side Jordan* is one that "destroy[s]" and therefore negates or obliterates the African woman's difference. In other words, rather than understanding Emerald as a person who might have complex and interesting similarities to and differences from himself, he views her as a lack, as Other to himself, as that which he is not.

Just as Western narratives depict the continent of Africa as empty, "passively awaiting the thrusting, male insemination of history, language and reason" (McClintock 30), so Johnnie describes the African woman he encounters as, "quite simply, a virgin" (231). Just as Western discourse depicts colonized land as vacant, so Emerald's face is "expressionless," and her body, "beautiful and young" as it is, is "blank" (231). And just as Western discourse posits the African land and the indigenous people that inhabit it as passive and backward, so Johnnie sees Emerald as bereft of agency. Johnnie's assertion that "she might as well have been drugged, lying there, or dead" (231) invokes the view that the African woman is bereft of agency; his indication that she does not speak the civilized language of English (230) suggests that he views her as primitive. As Wendy Roy asserts, "patriarchy merges with imperialist brutality" in this instance when Johnnie "sexually brutalizes [the] inexperienced prostitute" (*Maps* 50).[3]

With the encounter between Johnnie and Emerald, Laurence does not directly challenge the metaphorical linking of woman and the African continent, but instead works within that trope to show how woman and Africa cannot be known or possessed. Johnnie's expectations of the African prostitute, for example, are not met but rather continually undermined: when he expects her to speak English, he is surprised to discover that she does not ("Johnnie was startled, then he understood. She did not speak English" [230]); while he expects that she is an experienced prostitute, he soon finds that she is not ("It was then that he discovered the fantastic truth.... She was, quite simply, a virgin" [231]); and while he expects her body to be familiar to him as a woman's body, he again finds that it is not, since, after their sexual encounter, he sees that he has torn her clitoridectomy (233). Johnnie attempts to perceive Emerald through the confines of his own cultural frame of reference, but he finds that she does not fit that frame of reference. From one perspective, Johnnie's perception of woman and Africa as that which cannot be known or possessed works within Western narratives that would define both woman and the colonized as mysterious and exotic. From another perspective, however, it suggests that the Western discourses that define colonized people are not absolute.

It is noteworthy that Laurence chose to write this scene from Johnnie's perspective, through a third-person limited narrator. She decided to narrate the scene, that is, from the perspective of a male colonialist rather than through the eyes of an African woman. Furthermore, the novel as a whole features two *male* protagonists: Johnnie, an English colonial; and Nathanial, a Ghanaian. Later, in interviews and letters, Laurence would lament the fact that she did not have the courage to write from a woman's perspective, particularly with regard to the birth scenes that occur at the end of *This Side Jordan*. Her later work, though, would feature female protagonists and would be told from women's perspectives. Thus her decision to write about Canada, her own country, was also a decision to write about women.

In *This Side Jordan*, the "beating of the drums" to which the narrator refers throughout the novel might metaphorically suggest a rupture to Western ideology. The drums, which Laurence implicitly associates with that which is Africa, constantly sound "in the distance," and they are old and traditional: "These were the old drums" (56). They are also a force that Johnnie cannot ignore – "'Blasted drums,' Johnnie said irritably. 'They never stop'" (57) – and they represent the hope and the heart of Africans (247). While working within the trope that would define the Africans and the drums they play as ancient and timeless, Laurence uses that trope to suggest that the drums are ever consistent in their threat to disrupt what is Western and modern. With her depictions of Emerald and the drums of

Africa, then, she suggests that the colonized continually refuse the Western narratives that attempt to define them.

Johnnie's refusal to listen to the drums indicates his refusal to acknowledge what is African, and his refusal to acknowledge what is African is simultaneously a refusal to acknowledge the past and the feminine. Importantly, however, this refusal is Johnnie's, not Laurence's. Laurence constructs the character of Johnnie Kestoe in order to demonstrate how Western language conflates what is feminine with what is African. Thus her subject position as a white woman writing about Africa is not the same as the subject position of a white man writing about Africa. She is able to sympathize with African characters precisely because of the Western feminization of Africans and the African landscape in which they reside.

To emphasize, as Laurence does, Johnnie's unwitting association between what is African and what is feminine is to emphasize such an association in Western philosophy. Theorists such as V. Y. Mudimbe and Anne McClintock assert that African women have often been associated with the material, the earthly, the past, and the African landscape itself. The West has repeatedly constructed and thus established the idea that the masculine is spiritual and virile and the feminine is material. The material is precisely what the supposedly spiritual and virile masculine subject excludes in order to be.

The feminine forces that the character of Johnnie rejects might be thought of as the abject – that which falls away from bodies in order for them to enter a social and ordered world (Grosz 192). Feminist theorists such as Julia Kristeva and Elizabeth Grosz have associated the abject with feminine bodily fluids such as menstrual blood. McClintock emphasizes the idea that one must reject something to become a social body and the idea that what is rejected neither leaves nor stays put. Like the African drums that continue to disturb Johnnie in Laurence's novel about Africa, the abject, for McClintock, "haunts the edges of the subject's identity with the threat of disruption or even dissolution" (71).

What is particularly interesting about McClintock's discussion of the abject in relation to *This Side Jordan* is the way in which she extends the notion of the abject from that which an *individual* must purge in order to enter the social world to that which a *collective* must purge in order to enter the social world. She demonstrates how the abject relates to both individual and collective identities, and how it therefore stands on the threshold between "body" and "body politic" (72). Although she is not the first to do so, since Kristeva and others have also addressed the abject in relation to collectives, her reading is unique in that it addresses the abject as it applies to imperial history. Speaking of the history of imperialism, McClintock argues that "abject peoples are those whom industrial imperialism rejects but cannot do without: slaves, prostitutes, the colonized, domestic workers, the insane, the unemployed, and so on" (72). She not only speaks of abject peoples, but also of abject zones: "the Israeli Occupied Territories, prisons, battered women's shelters" (72). McClintock's insistence that the abject may be collective rather than just individual emphasizes the historical and material conditions of imperialism: she forces an acknowledgement of those groups imperialism elides. She also foregrounds the abject as both feminized and racialized. Her examples of abject peoples are primarily of women and the colonized.

In *This Side Jordan*, Johnnie's encounter with Emerald brings back the memory of his mother's death (Roy, "Anti-Imperialism" 52). The coming together of these two moments culminate as abjection. Laurence's description of Johnnie's encounter with Emerald is remarkably similar to her description of Johnnie's witnessing of his mother's death: Johnnie does not do anything for Emerald but cover her with a cloth, just as Johnnie's father does not do anything for Johnnie's mother – he does not call a priest or a doctor in time; Johnnie cannot understand what Emerald says because she only speaks Twi, just as Johnnie cannot recount to the priest what his mother said on her deathbed; and when Johnnie looks at Emerald after their sexual encounter, he sees "a clot of blood on a dirty quilt" (232), just as, when he discovers that his mother has died of an abortion, he feels that the fetus is nothing "more than a clot of blood on a dirty quilt" (59). Moreover, when Johnnie sees Emerald's blood and closes his eyes, he notes that "the sight was momentarily blotted out, but not the memory" (232); the "memory" to which he refers is not only the immediate memory of Emerald's blood but also the more distant memory of his mother's death. At this moment, Johnnie's confrontation with Emerald – that which represents Africa itself – is simultaneously a confrontation of his own personal past. At the same time, it is a confrontation of the feminine, the bodily, and the maternal. Johnnie confronts the abject when he confronts Emerald's bleeding and the memory of the blood. The memory of his mother's death, that is, does not stay put: it keeps coming back, haunting the boundaries of his masculine subject demarcation.

Throughout *This Side Jordan*, Johnnie repudiates the African as he repudiates the feminine and maternal. Facing Emerald, he is forced to acknowledge the African, his past, the feminine, and the maternal. In feminist and psychoanalytic terms, we might say that Johnnie finally faces what he has abjected. With this abjection, Johnnie asserts his identity as a European and masculine subject. By acknowledging that which he has abjected, Johnnie might qualify that absolute identity. Yet if he does acknowledge what he has repudiated, he does not acknowledge it completely. While he may make peace with his past by naming his child after his mother at the end of the novel, he still does not want to dwell on the significance of that name: "Reasons could be dragged up, no doubt … but he did not want to see them" (267). Hence, as Mary Rimmer points out, "Johnnie seems still caught in but unwilling to confront the uneasiness of his own past" (14).

* * * * *

In her essay "A Place to Stand On," Laurence discussed how much of her own writing was "an attempt to assimilate the past, partly to be freed from it, partly to try to understand [herself]" (*Heart* 14). She also maintained that writing "involves an attempt to understand one's background and one's past, sometimes even a more distant past which one has not personally experienced" (*Heart* 13). As the characters of Nathaniel and Johnnie in *This Side Jordan* negotiate their pasts, often configured in the novel as Africa itself, so Laurence herself negotiated her past and Africa in the writing of the novel. While Laurence perceived her own writing as that which confronted a personal history, she also saw it as that which confronted a collective, "more distant" history (*Heart* 13). In many ways, then, her writing about Africa, prior to her supposedly more mature writing about Canada, might have been a way to acknowledge and accept that personal and collective past. Likewise, her writing about an Africa that she mockingly viewed as traditional, timeless, and feminine, might have been a way to address and acknowledge her own qualified femininity. With such associations of Africa, Laurence played into long-standing Western representations of Africa that Mudimbe articulated; notions of Africa that Appiah delineated (such as the idea that Africa is a single, homogenous entity); and notions of Africa as "heathen, savage," what civilization is not. Laurence, then, wrote a memoir about Somaliland and a novel about Ghana that are both personal and public, individual and collective. In her work about Africa she sardonically confronted a self that was feminine at the same time that she conflated that self with the African places in which she lived.

In her memoir about Africa, Laurence's feminized gaze of imperial power was troubled by the existing gender hierarchy in Somaliland. In her novel about Africa, Laurence was able to portray the colonialist figure of Johnnie Kestoe as one who repudiates what is African and what is feminine, while simultaneously critiquing that imperial and patriarchal position. Contrary to many critics who have drawn attention to the prominent male characters in *This Side Jordan*, I argue that conceptions of the feminine are central to Laurence's writing about Africa. Despite the fact that *This Side Jordan* features two male protagonists, that is, I believe that the novel emphasizes and problematizes colonial and patriarchal conceptions of the feminine. As such, it is a feminist text. Yet equally important is Laurence's ambivalent subject position in the Africa she negotiated. My reading of *The Prophet's Camel Bell* shows that Laurence felt uneasy in both her stance as a white Westerner and in her attempts to sympathize and aid Somali people; my reading of *This Side Jordan* shows how Laurence problematized the colonizer Johnnie's relationship with both Africa and woman. Laurence's subject position was aligned with but not identical to both that of the white man and that of the African woman. She was at one with neither the "motherland" nor the indigene, a position that, according to Lawson and Johnston, epitomized white Canadian settlers and settler-descendants.

We might understand Laurence's divided and uneasy subject position in Africa, then, as a particularly Canadian one. When Laurence had just completed *The Stone Angel*, she wrote a letter to her friend Gordon Elliott, a professor at Simon Fraser University for whom she had once marked papers. To Elliott she stated, "I feel now that the African writing was not a kind of fluke, but was related to everything else, and the fact that I wrote for a while about Africa and now do not want to do so is not important" (letter dated 10 March 1963). Laurence suggested that her writing about Africa was a necessary part of her life pattern as a writer: she did not see her move from writing about Africa to writing about Canada as incongruous. This epiphany is remarkable when one considers that Laurence had not yet experienced the success that was to come with the publication of *The Stone Angel*. In a refrain that is later repeated by the writer-protagonist Morag Gunn in *The Diviners*, Laurence told Elliott about the personal importance of *The Stone Angel*, before it was published, and of her move from writing about Africa to writing about Canada: "I can't really explain how I feel about this novel – anyway, in some way it has restored my faith in myself and in the fact that my way of seeing is not so personal or private that it will not communicate something at least to some people" (10 March 1963). Words escaped her as she tried to articulate the profound influence that writing about Africa had on herself, on her writing of *The Stone Angel*, and on her work to come.

Two

Toward Cross-Cultural Understanding: Africa in *The Tomorrow-Tamer*

This chapter examines three of Laurence's short-stories about Africa, published in her short-story collection, *The Tomorrow-Tamer*, and shows how she worked toward cross-cultural understanding during a time of decolonization and increasing global development. I argue that she did not simply posit Western values against traditional African ones, but rather relayed a complex and dynamic relationship between them. The stories are set in the Gold Coast immediately prior to its constitution as the independent nation of Ghana in 1957, and they address that nation's struggle toward independence. Laurence depicted how African and Western traditions and cultures came together and how people came to dominate or be dominated by others. In many ways, the goals of social justice and human communication she advanced in these works were epitomized in a letter she wrote to the Nigerian novelist Chinua Achebe: "We have been aiming at some of the same things – the relationship with the ancestors and family; the necessity of continuing to try to communicate, however difficult this may be; the sense of social injustice, an outrage that has to be communicated in fiction through the dilemmas and tragedies of human individuals and not in any didactic way" (3 June 1984).

Critics have regarded *The Tomorrow-Tamer* as a unified collection, but the stories were originally published separately in such journals as

Queen's Quarterly and *The Tamarack Review*. Therefore, I've chosen to analyze three of the best stories in her collection. In interesting and nuanced ways, "The Pure Diamond Man," "The Drummer of All the World," and "The Rain Child" exemplify Laurence's work against social injustice and toward human communication, as she so aptly put it to Achebe. I consider these stories in order to show two important aspects of her work: how she demonstrates African resistance to continuing Western domination, and how she complicates relationships between characters of different cultures in order to portray fraught identities and subject positions.

The Pure Diamond Man

In "The Pure Diamond Man," as in many of the stories in *The Tomorrow-Tamer*, Laurence challenges Western notions of Africa and strives to present her readers with alternate representations of Africa. She reveals how understandings of Africa during decolonization were not essential but determined through a history of Western discourses on Africa that became dominant and understood as truth. V. Y. Mudimbe asserts that the West cannot speak of Africa outside of a Western epistemological framework and explains how Western discourse set up oppositional paradigms through which the West understood and continues to understand that continent. While the West represents "the rational," "progress," "civilization," and "advancement," Africa, in opposition to that West, comes to represent "the irrational," "the mysterious," that which is backward in time, that which is "savage." Interestingly, in his writing, Kwame Anthony Appiah further emphasizes Mudimbe's point: he suggests that even within Africa itself, discourses about that continent are entangled within Western ideologies. Any discussion of Africa, it would seem, has to some extent been influenced by an "idea" of Africa invented by the West. As Appiah puts it, the invention of Africa – the idea that Africa is a single entity – was largely an outgrowth of European racialism – the idea that a race possesses inherited characteristics that are specific to that race (Appiah 6).

The pan-Africanist movement, which sought to establish solidarity among Africans and which was lead by Kwame Nkrumah, was an influence on Laurence and her work. As I mention in the introduction to this book, Laurence supported Nkrumah politically but believed that Africans should identify by region or tribe. In "The Pure Diamond Man," through the African protagonist, Tetteh, and his interactions with the would-be English anthropologist, Philip Hardacre, she not only challenges Western representations of Africa but also presents the problem of holding and practising both African and Western values. In addition, she demonstrates how the colonized undermined the work and ideology of the colonizers – she shows how they spoke back to the empire that attempted to subscribe them.

"The Pure Diamond Man" begins with a conversation between two Ghanaian men: Tetteh and Daniel, (a "big newspaper man" [185]) in a local pub. Tetteh describes himself to Daniel as "Luck's very boy" (182) and relays to Daniel his story about how he duped an Englishman, Philip Hardacre, into believing in an African ceremony he faked and sold to him. Although the ceremony is interrupted and revealed to be fabricated by the local minister, the Reverend Timothy Quarshie, Tetteh remains lucky, since he ultimately finds a way to market a Ghanaian foot remedy to Westerners. The story of "The Pure Diamond Man" is the story that Tetteh relays to Daniel. Its title refers to Tetteh, who is a "diamond man" because he makes "cash" (185) by faking and selling African traditions. It also refers to Hardacre, who is a "diamond man" because he buys such traditions – both literally and ideologically – and because he has a family history of diamond mining in Ghana. Tetteh's act of duping Hardacre is an act of resistance against empire. It is an instance in which the colonized used hoax to take back the "diamonds" or "cash" that the colonizers continued to exploit in Africa. Laurence had a strong sense of how the colonized worked within Western and imperial ideologies in order to contest them, and she demonstrates this contestation with the example of Tetteh in this story.

Tetteh attempts to dupe Philip Hardacre into believing Tetteh's carefully staged act. Tetteh charges Hardacre a fee to witness a traditional African python ceremony, conducted by a fetish priest. The faked ceremony involves the sacrifice of a cockerel, some "drumming" and "magic sayings," and the calling of African pythons (195). In order to conduct the staged ceremony, Tetteh takes Hardacre to his home village, where he gets his father to play the role of fetish priest, his brother to play the role of the priest's helper.

According to Western anthropology in the 1950s, fetishes were objects, often woodcarvings, that were believed to have magical or spiritual powers – they were associated with animistic religious practices. Fetish priests, by this same anthropological account, were religious leaders who performed such practices. Starting in the seventeenth and eighteenth centuries, the Enlightenment mind "was felt to have transcended fetish worship and could look indulgently upon those still enchanted by the magical powers of 'sticks and stones'" (McClintock 227). However, "a decidedly fetishistic faith in the magical powers of the commodity underpinned much of the colonial civilizing mission" (McClintock 227). In other words, historically, colonizers denigrated African rituals as fetishistic, while denying that they engaged in fetishism themselves. Colonials, for example, misunderstanding African fetishes, both feared them and sought to destroy them; and, yet, those same colonials "were prone to fits of murderous temper" when Africans did not pay respect to their own fetishized objects – "flags, crowns, maps, clocks, guns, and soaps" (McClintock 230). In the Western mind, such colonial objects, like African fetishes, were thought to have great power: the flag and the crown, for example, stood for that which was much larger and more powerful than what they were in and of themselves. In "The Pure Diamond Man," Laurence both presents and undermines the Western notion of the African fetish and the fetish priest as those which must be feared and destroyed. She deconstructs and parodies the Western construction of the fetish as such.

Throughout the staged ceremony, Tetteh shows Africa and Africans as Hardacre would wish to see them – as they have been constructed, that is, by the West. When Hardacre questions Tetteh about the African ceremony he performs, Tetteh does not answer directly but emphasizes the mystery and leaves interpretation of the event to Hardacre: "'What's the significance of the leaves, Tetteh?' 'Magical medicine,' Tetteh said sternly. 'Do not touch please. Special for the gods of this house'" (193). Tetteh here plays into the preconceived notion that Africa is mysterious, a notion that is exemplified in such works as Henry Rider Haggard's *King Solomon's Mines* (1885), and Joseph Conrad's *Heart of Darkness* (1899). Further, in his performance for Hardacre, Tetteh invokes the Western notion of Africa as savage. For the sake of the performance, Tetteh dresses his brother Kwaame in a leopard skin. When Kwaame appears in front of Hardacre, he consolidates Hardacre's notion of the African as heathen by "[brandishing] his machete, newly-sharpened, within a few inches of Hardacre's face" (193). Thus with his fabricated performance, Tetteh confirms the Englishman's preconceived ideas about Africa, his belief that Africa is mysterious – "Your ancient culture had a weird magnificence about it" – and that African traditions are savage, exemplifying a "terrifying splendour" (187). Hardacre's use of the words "magnificence" and "splendour," moreover, bespeaks a kind of exoticism, an excess of Otherness that Tetteh ironically confirms. As John C. Eustace explains, "Hardacre's anthropological interest ultimately serves his neocolonial interest by allowing him to figure Africa as the site of invariable Otherness – an Otherness he can interpret, and hence control, with the help of scientific discourse" (22).

With the ceremony that Tetteh performs for Hardacre, Laurence not only invokes but ultimately undermines the idea that Africa is mysterious and savage. When Hardacre examines the fetish figures Tetteh uses for the ceremony, he says, "Intriguing – where did you get them, Tetteh?" and

Tetteh replies, "Secret place.... Perhaps later I will be telling you" (195). Yet when Tetteh's father, who has converted to Christianity, worries about having fetishes in his home, Tetteh informs him that fetishes are sold "like baskets of groundnuts in the city market" (195). Tetteh suggests to Hardacre that the fetish holds power and mystery, while revealing to his father that the fetishes do not hold such power: they are cheap and plentiful market commodities. The African fetishes and by extension Africa itself are clearly not mysterious and unknowable as Hardacre believes them to be. Laurence juxtaposes the official yet fabricated story that Tetteh relays with the one in which he speaks to his family in their own language.[4] While the story he gives Hardacre is full of mystery and tradition, the discussion with his family is more practical. Laurence exposes this fabrication and reveals new commodity fetishism in a burgeoning neo-colonial Africa.

Laurence further challenges Western representations of Africa by invoking and undermining the idea that Africa is primitive in relation to the so-called progressive or civilized West. Both Robert Young and Anne McClintock have analyzed the Western idea of Africa as primitive. Young explains how ideas about race in Victorian anthropology centered around two antithetical positions: the "progressivist," Enlightenment view and the "degenerationist" view. The "progressivist view" asserted "that men had gradually evolved from a savage state into a civilized one"; the "degenerationist view" derived from the Bible and asserted "that man had been originally created as white and civilized, but had in certain circumstances since degenerated into savagery" (46–47). While antithetical in theory, both positions posit Africans, as members of a supposedly inferior race, as savage in relation to Europeans, who are deemed civilized.

Tetteh sets out to consolidate Hardacre's view of Africa as mysterious and savage. In order to confirm this notion, Tetteh takes Hardacre to the village via an old road that is no longer in use. The old road plays into Hardacre's ideas about Africa as undeveloped, since it has "Fallen into the river. Grown over with vines and mangrove" (189–90). Laurence undermines the idea that Africa is undeveloped, that it is an "empty land" (McClintock 30), by contrasting that road with the new one. Far from primitive, the new road hosts lorries with "several dozen" passengers who wear "nylon shirts" and sit "amid the sacks of sugar and crates of yellow soap" (189). The road leads not to the bush but to a crowded marketplace. Furthermore, Tetteh constructs his own home as a primitive African hut for the English Hardacre, but in order to do so, he must remove objects that reveal worldly influence and Christian values – a "basin of Japanese manufacture," "three china saucers with the cups missing, embellished with Biblical scenes," and so on (191). The author reveals how African villages are not primitive but highly influenced by and embedded within colonial reminiscences and Western world values.

Laurence shows how Western and African traditions come to be inseparable in Ghanaian villages during the 1950s. In this way, she demonstrates Karin Barber's point that "there is a vast domain of cultural production which cannot be 'Western' in inspiration, because it straddles and dissolves these contradictions" (2). Tetteh's family members have converted to Christianity, but they still know African religions. Tetteh's father's concern over having the fetishes in their home suggests that he still has some respect for the religions of which they are a part. Tetteh's statement that fetishes are sold by the dozens in the local marketplace undermines the Western idea that the fetish is that which is mysterious and all-powerful. Yet it also suggests that African villages imported the system of capitalism, a system that profits from selling fetishes to tourists as symbols of traditional African religion.

An example of the importation of such capitalist ideologies is evident in Laurence's references to colonial products such as sugar and soap, which are brought into the village from the city in the lorry in which Tetteh travels (189). With the importation of soap, the British brought their products and their ideologies into rural Ghana. The manufacturers of Pears soap sought to "[brighten] the dark corners of the earth" ("Pears Soap Ad" quoted in McClintock 32) by "teaching the virtues of cleanliness" (McClintock 32). That company's ads in the late nineteenth century purported that this domestic commodity, soap, "purifie[d] and preserve[d] the white male body from contamination in the threshold zone of empire" (McClintock 32). Laurence's brief mention of the importation of "yellow soap" (189) into a Ghanaian village, then, is a subtle indication that the Ghanaians have adopted the British notion that one must clean, purify, and lighten the skin. She suggests that the nation is certainly not free from British colonialism, even though it is approaching independence from Britain. Local Ghanaians negotiate traditional values with British ones as items like sugar and soap continue to infiltrate rural Africa along with the Western values they bring with them.

Particularly interesting is the commodification of African fetish objects in "The Pure Diamond Man." Tetteh's description of the woodcarving fetishes he uses in the faked ceremony as cheap commodities (195) suggests a rejection of the Western notion that the fetishes are mysterious and powerful. By defining them as commodities, Tetteh plays into and subtly mocks the Western fetishization of the commodity itself. Although colonizers did not recognize it as such, the commodity, as McClintock points out, was certainly a fetishized object for the colonialist and Westerner (228–30).

Thus Tetteh's presentation of the woodcarvings as mysterious fetishes to the English Hardacre and Tetteh's subsequent comment to his father that the carvings are actually cheap commodities are enactments of an elaborate resistance to Hardacre and the empire he represents.

Tetteh's act of hoodwinking Hardacre into believing in the efficacy of the fetishes undermines the self-acclaimed superiority of Hardacre and the colonizers for which he stands. Tetteh shows that Hardacre believes in the superiority of his own position, while he simultaneously exposes the falsity of that belief and thus the tenuousness of that position. To re-situate the woodcarvings of the fake ceremony as a Western commodity fetish, rather than an African fetish, is to turn the Enlightenment notion that the West has "transcended fetish worship" on its head. Tetteh suggests that it is not the Africans who are "still enchanted by the magical powers of 'sticks and stones'" (McClintock 227), but rather the colonizers themselves. Although not understood by the colonizers as such, Tetteh uses "mimicry, appropriation, and re-evaluation" (McClintock 229) to demonstrate the absurdity of Hardacre's colonialist position.

Laurence's emphasis on the "yellow soap" that is brought into rural Ghana in the story, then, shows not only how Western ideology infiltrated rural Ghana, bringing so-called "lightness" to "darkest Africa." It also shows how soap functioned as a commodity fetish for the colonizer. Colonizers – through advertisements like those in the Pears Soap campaign – believed that soap literally and metaphorically cleaned and lightened the black body. Laurence therefore reveals that racism was implicit within the colonial enterprise, and she suggests that the colonizers fetishized that "yellow soap" (189): they attributed to it what they perceived as extraordinary, even magical, powers. Her emphasis on bringing soap to rural Ghana again turns the notion that colonizers have "transcended fetish worship" on its head (McClintock 227). Laurence, through Tetteh, implies that the colonizers unknowingly engaged in fetish worship while they pompously deemed themselves superior to it.

Moreover, the Reverend Timothy Quarshie's intrusion into Tetteh's staged ceremony ironically furthers Tetteh's strategic act of denying the oppressor the true knowledge of things and fooling Hardacre into believing in his assumed position of superiority. In the middle of the ceremony, "a voice like a judgment roared outside the hut.... Kwaame stood paralyzed, listening to the deep and god-like voice" (197). The Reverend then enters the hut, sees the ceremony, and reveals to Hardacre that Tetteh's family is Christian. In response, Tetteh's father admits to Hardacre and the Reverend that the ceremony is staged. After the Reverend interrupts and exposes the fabrication of the ceremony, he offers to bring Hardacre to the village's true fetish priest, Bonsu, on the condition that he donate a bell for the village church. The exposure of the fake ceremony does not set straight Hardacre's preconceived notions of Africa, but reinforces them. Hardacre, according to the Western ideals to which he subscribes, must go even deeper into the heart of Africa in order to find the mystery at its centre. Although it is the Reverend, not Tetteh, who gains the "cash" (ironically in the form of a church bell) from Hardacre in this instance, Tetteh still succeeds in tricking Hardacre into believing in his own Western ideals, ultimately playing into and yet mocking the idea that Africa is mysterious at its core.

The story continually points to the cross-cultural fertilization that occurs between the British and the Africans. As we have seen, Tetteh must remove all of his family's worldly goods from their hut in order to stage a traditional ceremony, and the Reverend Timothy Quarshie uses the local fetish priest's foot remedy. Interestingly, Tetteh also easily reconciles his country's desire to be free of the West with Western products and the system of capitalism that produces them. On his hat he wears button pins, one that proclaims the cry of his country," Freedom and Justice," and another that advertises "Amaryllis Light Ale" (184). In this instance, Laurence demonstrates how an African cry for freedom and a Western capitalist advertisement coexist in the most unlikely of places – button pins on a local Ghanaian's hat. Through figures such as Tetteh, she shows how Western and African goods and ideologies uncannily exist alongside one another.

In light of the story's emphasis on cross-cultural fertilization in Ghana, and in light of the fact that fetishes are discussed at Tetteh's staged python ceremony, it is worth noting that the fetish itself is not solely a traditional African phenomenon that occurred before contact with Europe. Laurence works against the idea that African traditions are absolutely separate from Western ones in this story, exemplifying how the two are, in 1950s Ghana, intimately intertwined. McClintock's explanation of the fetish as that which came into being at the point of contact between African and European cultures during early colonization supports Laurence's view. Tracing the history of the fetish, McClintock explains that, during the 1880s, "the discourse on fetishism moved from anthropology and the study of religion ... into psychoanalysis" (189). In Laurence's story, the fetish is associated with anthropology, since the would-be anthropologist Hardacre desires knowledge of it, and with religion, since it is posited as opposite to Christianity when the Reverend enters the ceremony where fetishes are present.

More importantly, perhaps, during colonialism the fetish embodied a contradiction in the value systems between Christians and Africans (McClintock 186). It became the symbolic ground or problem object "on which the riddle of value could be negotiated and contested" (187). This is clearly the case in "The Pure Diamond Man." Both that which holds powers Tetteh has forgotten (197) and that which is sold "like baskets of ground-nuts in the city market" (195), the fetish at once holds religious and monetary value. It resides on an uneasy borderline between deity and market commodity. While Laurence does not directly refer to the psychoanalytic association of the fetish in the story, Freud's theories on the fetish would have been relatively well known in the 1950s and 1960s, when Laurence was writing "The Pure Diamond Man." One might read this story, in fact, as a challenge to Freud's notion of the fetish, since Laurence draws attention to its anthropological and colonial history, a history Freud elides by positing the fetish as a delusion[5] and displacing it from the realm of colonization to the realm of the bourgeois European family in the nineteenth century.

Through the figure of Hardacre, Laurence critiques the notably Western discipline of anthropology. As Fiona Sparrow has pointed out in her study of Laurence's writing about Africa, before Laurence travelled to Africa, she thoroughly researched anthropological texts such as B. W. Andrzejewski's and R. S. Rattray's studies of Somali and Ashanti cultures. But what Sparrow does not discuss is how Laurence critiques anthropology through fictional characters such as the would-be-anthropologist Philip Hardacre. In *Subject to Colonialism* (2001), Gaurev Desai explains that James R. Hooker's 1963 essay, "The Anthropologist's Frontier: The Last Phase of African Exploitation" was one of the very first to argue that anthropologists came to Africa after World War I as "the handmaidens of colonial governments" (63). Subsequently, Desai asserts, scholars such as Jacques Maquet in "Objectivity in Anthropology" (1964) also began to assert how the discipline of anthropology was not neutral but caught up in the values practised by colonialists. "The Pure Diamond Man," as we have seen, demonstrates how Hardacre, by way of Tetteh's hoax on him, can only see Africa as it has been constructed for him by the West. Ultimately, then, Laurence, who published this story the same year Hooker published his essay, cleverly anticipated both Hooker's and Maquet's studies. To view the anthropologist's relationship with Africans as one of true understanding, she suggests, is to misconstrue that relationship.

It is noteworthy that Laurence challenged anthropology in other works. In her short story entitled "Mask of Beaten Gold," for instance – an African story that was not published in *The Tomorrow-Tamer* collection – the boy-protagonist's father makes the following statement when his son comments on a photograph of the death mask of King Kofi Kakari, a photograph he views in a book of anthropology: "It's made of beaten gold. Unfortunately, it's in London now. Pinched after one of the Ashanti wars" (12). In this instance, Laurence clearly commented on the economic exploitation of

Africa as well as the problem of English anthropologists "pinching" such items for their own gain.

Laurence sets up and undermines Western constructions of Africa in this story, and she debunks the idea that African traditions are absolutely separate from Western practices during the 1950s. Moreover, she shows how African traditions and Western ones come together, as is evident in the Reverend's adaptation of the fetish priest's cure for corns. Significant to this coming together of African and Western ways is the fact that the story is framed by another: Tetteh sits in a bar in the city and tells Daniel, a "big newspaper man" (185), of his attempt to dupe Hardacre. "The Pure Diamond Man" opens with a direct contrast between scientific Western ways, held by Daniel, and supposedly superstitious Ghanaian ways, held by Tetteh: "'One year ago, when I was young,' said Tetteh, 'I was always thinking I am Luck's very boy.' Daniel smiled. 'Scientifically, you realize, a consistently lucky person is an impossibility'" (182). Daniel here ridicules Tetteh, but it is Tetteh who ultimately comes out on top by adapting to Western capitalism. He will market Bonsu's foot cure, mocking and yet profiting from the Western notion that African remedies have mysterious and magical properties. He will have luck and success by putting a market value on an African fetish, appropriating an African remedy and subjugating it to the capitalist system.

We have, then, "a fairly strong decolonizing gesture in Tetteh, who … seems to challenge Western discourses by demonstrating how they mediate Africa to serve their own interests" (Eustace 24). Tetteh exposes Western notions of Africa through his trick-playing on Hardacre, and he also makes the coming together of Western and African ways work to his own benefit by marketing Bonsu's foot remedy. Yet Tetteh's triumph, I would argue, is not absolute. The subtle mentioning of Daniel as a "big newspaper man" is important, for he is the one to whom Tetteh relates his story. Daniel parallels the Western reader, one who holds scientific values and might be skeptical about Tetteh's luck. As a "big newspaper man," Daniel also reports such stories to the outside world. He is highly influenced by scientific values and Western ways, so his report of Tetteh's story will most likely be biased and influenced by Western ideology. Laurence frames "The Pure Diamond Man" within the story of Daniel and Tetteh, a story which makes one wonder if the final word – the word that is communicated to so many through the newspaper – will not be one laden with Western bias. At the same time, however, the audience to which Tetteh tells his story, Daniel, and, by extension, African and Western readers themselves, might be likened to the English Hardacre, around whom Tetteh's story revolves. Thus, with the framing of one story within another, Laurence leaves us wondering whether we, like

Hardacre, are duped by Tetteh's tale. Tetteh's strategic act of hoodwinking Hardacre and the framing of that story within another draws attention to the inefficacy of Western representations. Through the character of Tetteh, Laurence ultimately challenges the West's assumption that Africans are less intelligent than Westerners and shows how they act to resist empire.

The Drummer of All the World

"The Drummer of All the World" is a story about Matthew, an English boy who is the son of a missionary in Ghana. Matthew's father is determined to convert local Ghanaians to Christianity and therefore attempts to dominate through ideology. Matthew's mother also supports the missionary cause, "thumping the decayed hand-organ in the little mud church, chalking up the week's attendance, so many black souls for Jesus" (2). Matthew himself, however, does not support his father's imperialist and missionary endeavours. Instead, he makes friends with the African boy Kwabena, listens to the African drummers until he "know[s] the drummer was hypnotized with the sound" (7), and becomes immersed in the Ghanaian culture in which he resides. Matthew narrates the story from the point of view of a man who looks back upon his childhood. He grows up in Ghana, moves to England in his teens, returns for a visit when he is seventeen, and again returns to work for the government ten years later. When Matthew tells his story, Ghana is undergoing "Africanization" (the policy by which British employees of the colonial government were replaced by African ones), and so Matthew is about to leave his government post and return to England. As we discover through Matthew's story, each time he returns to Africa, he realizes how Africa has changed and at once mourns for the old Africa and for his lost childhood. What he comes to realize, ultimately, is what Laurence realized when she lived in Africa, that despite her "disapproval of the empire-builders … [she], too, had been of that company" (*Prophet's* 251).

Christopher Fyfe states that "drawing on the mythology of Africa as (in Hegel's words) 'the land of childhood,' whites could, without compunction, treat Africans as children" (21–22). Such is the case with Matthew's father in "The Drummer of All the World," who says to his wife, "Remember, they're like children, these people" (5). Matthew's father works to dominate the Africans through violence and proselytizing for his Christian ideology. His violence manifests when he "beat[s] six boys [in his mission school] in a single afternoon," and his domination through both violence and ideology occurs when he breaks the idols in the fetish huts (4). He also critiques the Catholics in the village for teaching Latin by rote, but he himself makes his missionary boys play hymns "until their mouths were sore" (4). Matthew's father appears much like a nineteenth-century colonial administrator whom Fyfe describes as "a father figure (from the mother country) among his 'children' [who] sees his career as a career of service to them" (22). For Matthew's father, that "service" is laden with violence. As in "The Pure Diamond Man," however, Laurence makes it clear that Western domination is not necessarily the final word. In a kind of mockery of the power of the written word and English discourse, "a green fur of mould grew over everything, *especially over my father's precious books*, irritating him to the point of desperation" (1, my emphasis). The missionary's word does not stand up to the forces of Africa: the mould that is living Africa quite literally overtakes that word. In such instances, Laurence exposes a breakdown in the attempted domination of Africa by imperialists and missionaries such as Matthew's father.

More interesting than Laurence's direct critique of imperialism through Matthew's father is her implicit critique of it through both Matthew and his African friend Kwabena. When Matthew returns to Africa at the age of twenty-seven, he finds himself in a tense conversation about politics with Kwabena. Matthew expresses to Kwabena his disdain for the new Africa: "Independence is the new fetish, and political parties the new chieftains. I'm not sure that much is gained" (17). On the one hand, with this comment, Matthew makes an insightful point regarding decolonizing Ghana: while Britain has officially pulled out, Western imperialism continues in various guises and forms. On the other hand, by indicating his dislike for Western influence on Africa – "independence" rather than "fetishes," "political parties" rather than "chieftains" – he implies that Africa should remain unchanged, ahistorical, static, in a position of "Other" to the progressive West. As Renato Rosaldo puts it, "In this ideologically constructed world of ongoing progressive change, putatively static savage societies become a stable reference point for defining (the felicitous progress of) civilized identity" (108).

Reading Matthew's statement as one that posits Africa as primitive, Kwabena naturally takes offence: "'So – ' Kwabena said thoughtfully. 'You would like us to remain forever living in thatch huts, pounding our drums and telling pretty stories about big spiders'" (17). As his reaction reveals, Kwabena has rejected his heritage and embraced Western ideals. As a child he wanted to be a fetish priest, but now he wants to be a Western-style doctor (15). Yet the tone of his statement of reaction suggests that he acknowledges the idea that to remain in the old world is to remain in it as it is constructed by the West. It is the West, Kwabena implies, that has created an image of Africans as "forever living in thatch huts," "pounding drums," and "telling pretty stories about big spiders" (17). This tense political conversation between them is also informed by racial and class differences,

differences of which Matthew becomes increasingly aware. As Gabrielle Collu puts it, "[Matthew's] life, his experience, his expectations, his opportunities are different from those of Africans in Africa because of the colour of his skin and the privileges that are associated with it" (23). It is only later in life that Matthew thinks about the fact that Kwabena was the son of their cook and his wife and that Kwabena "shared [his] mother with [Matthew] in exchange for [his] cast-off khaki shorts" (16).

Matthew and Kwabena's conversation reveals an impasse from which there seems to be no exit. Matthew's view is caught within the notion that Africans are primitive, static, ahistorical, whereas Kwabena's view tends to reject his own history and culture in favour of Western ways. Such an impasse is one that has been discussed among African philosophers. Simon Gikandi has written about the postmodernist philosopher Mbembe and the modernist philosophers Hountondji and Gyekye. While these philosophers differ on what Gikandi calls "the African crisis" – a crisis of representing and understanding decolonizing Africa – they all believe that "there is an urgent need to rethink how African worlds have been represented and interpreted" ("Reason" 155). Rather than accommodate Western practice, Mbembe would occupy a position of Otherness, that which is Other to reason, the rational, the civilized. Yet he also resists Western practice by refusing to replicate Otherness as it has been determined by the West. Like Trinh T. Minh-Ha, he would argue that "Otherness becomes empowering critical difference when it is not given, but re-created" (Minh-Ha 418). Hountondji and Gyekye, on the other hand, argue that "the African crisis arises from the failure of rational organization and self-reflection to take root in African thought and practices" (Gikandi, "Reason" 156). They suggest that African philosophy must appeal to reason, must dislocate itself from the position of Otherness that the West and reason gives it.

Matthew's and Kwabena's opposing views reflect the philosophers Gikandi discusses in his writing. Matthew, like Mbembe, seems to be opposed to accommodating Western reason; Kwabena, like Hountondji and Gyekye, embraces reason and Western values in order to oust Africans from the position of Otherness given to them in Western discourse. Matthew's position, in particular, however, is somewhat problematic. He laments Western influence on Africa, but when he hears that Kwabena wants to be a doctor, he also states that he "wanted to tell [Kwabena] that [he] knew how far he had travelled from the palm hut. But ... did not dare" ("Drummer" 15). Matthew paradoxically desires Africa to be free of British ways while still believing that to embrace those British ways – to become a doctor rather than a "ju-ju man" (15) – is to show "how far" one has come. He does not dare to say as much to Kwabena, perhaps because he is somewhat aware of his own problematic assumption that the West is more advanced than Africa.

Kwabena's subject position is one that is formed by the violent colonial discourse of which Mbembe speaks. That Kwabena adopts Western views that value "civilization" over "savagery," "progress" over "tradition," suggests that he is caught up in Western values, values upheld by those English colonizers whom he believes should leave Africa (11). Thus the violence of colonialism, Laurence implies, is not only a violence of physical suffering, but also a violence of language and ideology. Western epistemological values become so dominant and consecrated as truth that there is, seemingly, no way out; and yet, the violent result of the colonial enterprise often slips outside the reason of empire. Clearly, Africa and Africans are not reducible to the colonial discourse that seemingly subscribes them. As is demonstrated in the figure of Tetteh in "The Pure Diamond Man," for example, colonized subjects speak back to the empire through those colonial values within which they reside. As is demonstrated in the figure of Kwabena in "The Drummer of All the World," there is a "suffering" that Matthew, but not Kwabena, will never know. Kwabena's subject position is formed by – but ultimately exceeds and is not reducible to – the colonial discourses that inscribe him.

At moments, Laurence quite explicitly aligns Matthew with imperialist values even as he claims to be anti-imperialist and rejects his father's values outright. In one instance, Matthew explains how he went into the village with Kwabena, where they saw the body of a dead child:

> I was shown a girl child who had died of malaria, the belly bloated, the limbs twisted with fever. And what interested me most was that they had left her gold earrings on. Avariciously, I longed to steal those thin bright circles before they were wasted in the earth. (7)

Matthew turns his back on the suffering he sees – "the belly bloated, the limbs twisted with fever" – in favour of focusing on the possible fortune in the girl's jewellery. Just as British imperialists exploited diamonds and gold in Africa, so Matthew wishes to exploit the "gold earrings" that would be, in the language of an imperialist, "wasted in the earth" (7). In another instance, Matthew directs Kwabena away from the African girl, Afua, so that he may have her for himself. He says that doing so was "something totally strange to me" (10), implying that he performs this subtle yet covetous act almost against his will. As I mention in chapter 1, according to Ann Laura Stoler, colonial governments encouraged European men to take colonized women as concubines (348–49). Matthew's act of making sure Kwabena does not see Afua so that Matthew may have her to himself re-enacts this history. Just as the British imperialists sought to take Africa from the

Africans, so Matthew seeks to take the African woman away from a local Ghanaian man.

Matthew mourns the passing of traditional African culture, implying that he does not believe in the value of British influence on Africa. He also experiences the loss of traditional African culture as a personal loss. This mourning of the loss of African traditions to Western ways is not surprising, for Matthew is both inside and outside of the cultures and traditions he grieves. Matthew speaks Twi by the age of six better than he does English (2). He knows where all the fetish huts in the village are and listens to the spider stories that Kwabena tells him (5, 8). He learns African legends from Kwabena's mother, Yaa, and knows them as well as Biblical ones. "Listen, little one," Yaa says to Matthew when he is a child, "shall I tell you what the thunder is? In the beginning, when Odamankoma created all things – " (3). He is so immersed in Ghanaian culture, in fact, that he "call[s] God by the name of Nyame in [his] silent prayers" (10). What Matthew ultimately comes to realize, however, is that he also occupies a position that is outside of Ghanaian tradition and culture. By his very circumstance of being there as the son of a missionary from Britain, he is not at one with the place in which he resides. With his difference in race and class, and with, as Gabrielle Collu notes, the privileges that come with his white skin, he is outside of Africa. Because he is exempt from the suffering of Africa and Africans ("Drummer" 1, 10), he is not within the culture he laments. Thus Matthew occupies an uneasy subject position in Africa. While Ghana is his home and part of his very being, it is, he finally understands, that which is not his by right, that which belongs to another.

It is noteworthy that Matthew enacts what contemporary anthropologist Renato Rosaldo has called "imperialist nostalgia." Rosaldo defines the concept in the following way:

> [Imperialist nostalgia is] a particular kind of nostalgia, often found under imperialism, where people mourn the passing of what they themselves have transformed. Imperialist nostalgia thus revolves around a paradox: a person kills somebody and then mourns his or her victim. In more attenuated form, someone deliberately alters a form of life and then regrets that things have not remained as they were prior to his or her intervention. (108)

What is particularly intriguing about Rosaldo's notion of imperialist nostalgia is that Rosaldo directly connects it to innocent memories, such as those of one's childhood:

> Doesn't everyone feel nostalgic about their childhood memories? Aren't these memories genuinely innocent? Indeed, much of imperialist nostalgia's force resides in its association with (indeed, its disguise as) more

genuinely innocent, tender recollections of what is at once an earlier epoch and a previous phase of life. (108)

Speaking of his childhood days with Kwabena, Matthew, in "The Drummer of All the World," laments his loss of the land of Africa itself: "Ours [were] the thin-prowed fishing boats.... Ours the groves of slender palms.... Ours was the village, too" (9). He follows this lament with a connection of *his* Africa to *his* childhood. "This was my Africa," Matthew asserts, "in the days of my childhood, before I knew how little I knew" (9). Matthew, then, certainly experiences and exemplifies imperialist nostalgia, for his longing for Africa past is simultaneously a mourning for his childhood innocence. Matthew himself does not "deliberately alter ... form[s] of life" (Rosaldo 108) in Africa, but he does, as we have seen, unwittingly occupy the position of an imperialist and exemplify imperialist practices while mourning the loss of his home.

In *Writing Grief*, Christian Riegel argues that Laurence's writing can be "placed within the larger tradition of writing that explores the figures of death and mourning" (4). He maintains that each of the protagonists in the Manawaka series "finds herself in a state of liminality – an in-between state that demarcates a change in human development – and can only move through it by actively mourning" (6). I would argue that Matthew in "The Drummer of All the World" also goes through this "change in human development" through the process of mourning. Matthew's mourning is both similar to and different from the mourning of the characters in the Manawaka series. Matthew and many of Laurence's characters (such as Vanessa MacLeod in *A Bird in the House*) mourn the lost innocence of childhood. Those in the Manawaka series mourn for lost loved ones; however, Matthew mourns for the Western construction of the lost innocence of Africa, the old world as he thought he knew it. The "change in human development" comes as Matthew realizes that his Africa was an illusion: "life had allowed us [Kwabena and himself] this time of *illusion*, and ... the time was now past" (16, my emphasis).

Matthew describes the Africa he knew in his childhood as both frightening and comforting, qualities that are also often associated with one's childhood: the fright and excitement of new discoveries, the comfort of a mother's arms. He describes Africa as frightening when he asserts that every movement of insects in Africa "seemed to me the footsteps of *asamanfo*, the spirits of the dead" (2). He further states that "at night the wooden shutters would slam against the house like untuned drums, and the wind would frighten me with its insane laughter" (2). In both instances, Matthew describes Africa as haunted by those of the past, alive with "the spirits of the dead" and their "insane laughter" (2). Yet, somewhat paradoxically,

Matthew also describes Africa as comforting when he suggests that the drums are a living presence whose rhythm is a comfort (7) and when he reminisces about the casuarina tree at which he and Kwabena used to meet. "It was there that the wind spoke to us," he says, "whispering through the feather fans of the branches like the warning voices of the ancestors themselves" (7). Whether describing Africa as frightening or comforting, Matthew invokes the notion of the ancestors' presence, suggesting that what he mourns is a connection with the past. It is the past of Africa and the past of his childhood that are gone. But significantly, it is also his lost innocence that he mourns, for he now knows, as he before did not, that Africa is not his. "I think You [God] might have smiled a little at my seriousness," Matthew states, "smiled as Kwaku did, with mild mockery, at *the boy who thought Africa was his*" (10, my emphasis).

If Matthew misunderstands Africa as available for his taking, then he also misconstrues it as specifically feminine, playing into the ideology that understands it as such. Notably, that is, Matthew describes African women in the story as Africa itself. He conflates not only the loss of the old Africa with the loss of his childhood, but also the African mother with Mother Africa. When Kwabena tells Matthew that his mother, Yaa, has died, Matthew experiences this loss as the loss of his own mother (16). With his statement "You know as well as I do ... that she was more mother to me than my own mother" (16) Matthew refers not only to Yaa but to Africa itself. Africa was more mother to him, that is, than the "motherland." Mineke Schipper states that "in myth, woman has been associated (by man?) with nature ... as the life-giving mother figure" (37). In "The Drummer of All the World," Laurence, through Matthew, represents the African women Yaa and Afua as such a mother figure. Yaa is clearly a mother figure to Matthew: she rocks him in her arms, comforts him with African creation stories, nurses him as a baby, and loves him as he loves her (3). Afua, as Matthew describes her, is also a mother figure: she has "maternal strength" (12), and, when Matthew returns to Africa as a man, he sees that "around her the children nuzzled like little goats" (14).

Whereas Yaa seems to represent the old Africa, Afua, late in the story, comes to represent what Africa has become after colonialism. Mudimbe and Appiah assert that Africa is represented by the West as one vast entity, and McClintock notes that Africa is perceived as ancient and timeless. In the same way, Yaa, as the old Africa, is described as such: "I don't suppose she was really old," Matthew asserts. "But she seemed ancient as stone to me then, with her shrewd seamed face and her enormous body" (2). Like the description of Yaa, the later description of Afua is also one that invokes Africa as timeless, ancient: "Her body is old from work and child-bearing...."

Her breasts are old, ponderous, hanging" (14). Afua, however, now greets Matthew as "master" (14), foregrounding a hierarchical relationship that was not evident between Matthew and Yaa. Just as Afua's breasts are "always full of milk" (14), always giving, so Africa, in the eyes of the imperialist, is "always full" of resources, bequeathing its diamonds and gold to its so-called "master."

Matthew realizes that his love for both Yaa and Africa is exploitative, and it is this realization that causes him to know that his life in Africa was lived through "illusion" (16). He comes to know that he unwittingly engaged in exploitation of Yaa when he and Kwabena converse about her (16). Just as Matthew loves Africa but is in instances aligned with those who exploit its resources, so he loves Yaa but exploits her, taking milk from a mother who is not his own. Likewise, Matthew realizes that his love for Afua, like his love for Yaa, is also exploitative. When Matthew makes love to Afua, he says, "Possessing her, I possessed all earth" (12). He associates her with nature and the land of Africa itself, associations that Schipper suggests are common in African and Western myths alike. But Matthew also construes his relationship to Afua, and thus Africa, as one of possession. Just as he possesses Afua when he makes love to her, so he possesses the land of Africa itself. As Matthew himself puts it, "We were conquerors in Africa, we Europeans" (18). Thus, through the character of Matthew, Laurence repeats the trope that construes Africa as woman. In so doing, she demonstrates how imperial and patriarchal forces come together. She shows how the British man's exploitation of the African woman is neither unlike nor unrelated to British economic exploitation of Africa.

Therefore, Laurence plays into the Western idea of Africa as African woman in order to demonstrate how both are exploited. She presents the African woman as material, as nature, the earth, Mother Africa, in order to show how she has been represented as that which is to be exploited. In light of her strategy, it is particularly noteworthy that she chose a male character to narrate "The Drummer of All the World." She could not have made parallels between Matthew's unwitting exploitations of Yaa and Afua and Britain's imperialist exploitations of Africa if she had chosen a female character. Her choice reflects the complex relationship that European gender roles played in decolonizing Africa. As I explain in my discussion of *The Prophet's Camel Bell*, Laurence's own position as a woman in Africa was not easily understood by her or by those with whom she associated. Moreover, as is the case in *This Side Jordan*, even though Laurence chose to narrate this story from the perspective of a male protagonist, conceptions of the feminine are still central to her work. In the African novel, the character of Johnnie is "driven away from and out of [his past] by fear of certain faces of the feminine" (Demetrakopoulos 45). In "The Drummer of All the World," the character of Matthew must leave Africa not because of a fear, but because of his love for and yet exploitation of that which is construed as feminine: his surrogate mother, Yaa; Mother Africa; and his love, Afua. Africa is the living mould that covers Matthew's father's books; it is Yaa, "ancient as stone" (3); and it is Afua, who "danc[es] with her shadow" (9). At the end of the story, invoking all these associations, Matthew leaves Africa by addressing his love for Africa itself: "Africa, old withered bones, mouldy splendour under a red umbrella, you will dance again, this time to a new song" (19).

The Rain Child

"The Rain Child" is a moving story about being an outsider. The narrator, Violet Nedden, is a British schoolteacher who has worked in an African girls' school for twenty-two years and is approaching retirement and return to a "home" that is not truly home, the "motherland"; Ruth Quansah is an African student of Nedden's who has lived in England and struggles to fit in with the other African girls; and Ruth's father, Dr. Quansah, is a man who is at home neither in England nor in Africa. While critics have focused on Laurence's sympathetic depiction of these characters who are outsiders in their communities, few of them have examined the way the author works against imperialism and toward cross-cultural understanding. In addition, critics have not read Violet Nedden as a character whose divided subject position reflects and parallels that of the early Canadian settler who was at home neither in the "motherland" nor in the new colony. Admittedly, the story's subject is decidedly un-Canadian: a British protagonist teaches in 1950s Ghana. Read in a broader context, however, the story depicts the loneliness of characters who are displaced, willingly or unwillingly. These feelings of loneliness and displacement are ones that are shared by the characters in "The Rain Child" and Laurence herself, as an Anglo-Scots Canadian settler-descendant. As Karen E. MacFarlane puts it, "The notion of 'home' is ... one way of articulating Canada's complex, unsettled relation to the oppositional terms upon which postcoloniality has historically been dependent" (223).

In "The Rain Child," Laurence contrasts Violet Nedden with Hilda Povey, the Eburaso Girls' School's headmistress. While Povey feels "acutely uncomfortable with African parents, all of whom in her eyes [are] equally unenlightened" (106), Nedden does not. Nedden's opposition to the idea that Africans are unenlightened, however, is checked when she distinguishes Africans by class. "The fact that one father might be an illiterate cocoa farmer, while the next would possibly be a barrister from the city,"

Nedden asserts, "– such distinctions made no earthly difference to Hilda Povey" (106). On the one hand, Nedden's conviction here reflects Laurence's own conviction that Africans must be understood as individuals. While in Somaliland, for example, Laurence wrote in a letter to writer and friend Adele Wiseman, "Both the Somalis and the Europeans here seem to be very much a collection of individuals.... Perhaps as one sees more of the world, one tends to think less in terms of generalizations and more in terms of individuals" (Lennox and Panofsky 66). On the other hand, however, Nedden's distinction between "an illiterate cocoa farmer" and "a barrister from the city" exposes her alignment with a culture that values the Western traditions of reading, writing, and becoming educated over traditional African ways, that is, her alignment with a culture that values the vocation of a "barrister" over that of a "cocoa farmer." Nedden cannot exempt herself from those values and practices that the English brought to Africa and that are part of her life's work.

Violet Nedden further distinguishes herself from the headmistress, Hilda Povey, when she states that she refuses to tend an English garden: "I will have no English flowers.... My garden burns magnificently with jungle lily and poinsettia" (112). At the same time, however, she still takes part in the English practice of gardening, and her African servant, Yindo, "gently uproots" her garden flowers "from the forest" to place them at her property (112). Nedden's perspective on Ruth's friendship with the English boy, David Mackie, is different from Povey's: Nedden is not worried, that is, about the impropriety of an interracial friendship. Rather, she takes issue with their friendship because David shows Ruth Africa as if Ruth were a tourist. That is, he shows her Africa "from the outside" (124). Frederick Cooper and Ann Laura Stoler assert that "private collection of 'primitive' art has long signaled the distinctions of a bourgeois home while museum collections continue to celebrate the preserving and ordering of the Others' cultural artifacts as part of the high culture of a European public sphere" (13). While David Mackie collects African animals, not African art or artifacts, his hobby nevertheless re-enacts the imperial impetus to possess that which is not his own. Violet Nedden stands against David teaching Ruth "to celebrate the preserving and ordering" of Others, to celebrate the English possession of Africa. Ruth is "drawn to David because he spoke in the ways she knew, and of things which made sense to her" (123). Those ways, as Violet Nedden is acutely aware, are both English and imperial.

What is particularly intriguing about the character of Violet Nedden, and what makes her so like Laurence herself in *The Prophet's Camel Bell*, is that she is aware of the ways in which she is caught up in her own cultural values, even as she works against them. In "The Rain Child," Nedden quite explicitly mocks her own English position. An authority figure in the classroom, she is still "uncertain" and awkward: "a lady of somewhat uncertain gait, clumping heavily into the classroom with her ebony cane" (106). She also points out the absurdity of her presence and position in rural Ghana and the absurdity of Africans dressing in English school uniforms and learning a language that they may not use: "They [the students] felt free to laugh, my forest children, reticent and stiff in unaccustomed dresses, as we began the alien speech" (106).

The most interesting instance in which Nedden mocks imperial rule, however, occurs when she describes her "rattan garden chair" as a "throne" and depicts her awkward yet comfortable position within it. Nedden illustrates herself in her garden chair as an English queen: "I still sat enthroned in it each afternoon, my ebony sceptre by my side" (112). Yet she explicitly mocks her position as such. Her ebony cane, which she describes as a "sceptre," both "reassure[s]" and "mock[s]" her (132), as if it is a symbol of an imperialism that is no longer powerful, a prize that has outlived its game. Aligning herself with those who have been colonized by the English, rather than with the English colonizers themselves, Nedden buys this "garden chair" from "Jillaram's Silk Palace," a "tatty little Indian shop" (112). She revels in the fact that it is "splendidly garish" and comments that "the red had since been subdued by sun and the gilt was flaking" (112), making fun of the glory and splendour that it unsuccessfully represents, and exemplifying how it has outlived its time. Like the system of colonialism itself, the red imperial throne that represents it is exposed as futile, passé, and obsolete. Even Nedden, as the queen that possesses that "decrepit scarlet throne," is old and decrepit herself, awaiting her retirement and her return "home," to "that island of grey rain where [she] must go as a stranger" (133). The "trivial game" (113) of which Nedden speaks is not only the game of playing queen in her "scarlet throne," but, also, she implies, the entire system of colonialism itself. Through the character of Violet Nedden, Laurence critiques outdated and ongoing English and imperial practices in Africa after colonialism has ended: the continuing presence of schoolteachers like Nedden, the English-style education of African girls in rural communities.

The African student Kwaale's meeting with Nedden as Nedden sits in her "scarlet throne" (113) recalls the history of English colonialists meeting with African leaders. In other words, Nedden's ancestors' chronicles of ousting African leaders or "queens" and replacing them with English ones is invoked in this moment between Nedden and Kwaale. In the same vein, the interactions between Ruth and Kwaale repeat the interactions between the colonizers and the African people. Critic Gabrielle Collu states that, in "The Drummer of All the World," Kwabena teaches Matthew an African perspective, reversing the white teacher as carrier of civilization trope and therefore "challeng[ing] the exploitative (colonial and postcolonial) tradition of representing the Other" (31). The same might be said of Kwaale, Ruth, and Nedden in "The Rain Child": Kwaale teaches Ruth Twi (126) and teaches Nedden the absurdity of learning Wordsworth's poem "Daffodils" when she brings her a bouquet of wild orchids (107).

Laurence demonstrates the need for cross-cultural communication, and the presence of miscommunication, in the encounter between Kwaale and Ruth at the Odwira festival. At this festival, Nedden hears "a low shout of a young man near [Kwaale]" (127). He shouts to Kwaale, "Fire a gun at me," and following tradition, Kwaale bares herself (127). For Kwaale, as Nedden puts it, it is simply something "permitted at festival time" (128), whereas, for Ruth, who observes the incident, it represents "an extraordinary transgression of English propriety" (New, "The Other" 113). Paradoxically, the ritual is both severed from history and intimately tied to it. Kwaale and Ruth understand the ritual in the context of the present moment, but Nedden understands it as part of the past, noting that the custom "used to be 'Shoot an arrow,' for Mother Nyame created the sun with fire" (128). The incident is also implicitly historical because it invokes moments of cultural misunderstanding between Europeans and Africans during early colonialism. Furthermore, Ruth's perception of Kwaale's behavior as improper repeats the European construction of African women as overly sexualized. As Sander Gilman explains, "In the nineteenth century, the black female was widely perceived as possessing ... a 'primitive' sexual appetite" (45). Through Ruth's response to Kwaale's act ("I understand what she is.... She's nothing but a –" [128]) Laurence demonstrates how such Western and imperial perceptions of African women were maintained and continued, even by African women or girls who were influenced by English traditions themselves.

Just as Laurence does not know what to say to the child prostitute, Asha, in *The Prophet's Camel Bell*, so Nedden in this scene does not know how to remedy this conflict between Kwaale and Ruth. "I should have spoken then," she notes, "tried to explain one to the other" (128). Nedden understands how the past in the "fire a gun" custom is deeply embedded in the present, but, significantly, she also stands paralyzed between the two cultures. Aware of both Ruth's Western imperialist belief that Africans are improper and Kwaale's ritual that celebrates woman as the "source of life" (128), Nedden still cannot act on her principles to resolve the situation. She is, as Laurence herself is in *The Prophet's Camel Bell*, "bereft of strategies" (Buss 40).

As Wendy Roy suggests, Laurence's interactions with Asha are reimagined in "The Rain Child" and manifested in Violet Nedden's relationship with Ayesha ("Anti-Imperialism" 45). Unlike Asha, who remained a child prostitute and served men who worked on Jack's *ballehs*, Ayesha, in "The Rain Child," is rescued from her fate as a child prostitute and brought to the village where Violet Nedden, Ruth, and Kwaale reside. Just as Matthew's descriptions of Yaa and Afua in "The Drummer of All the World" are simultaneously descriptions of Africa, so Nedden's description of Ayesha might also be understood as a description of Africa. Men sought to possess the child prostitute, Ayesha, and, likewise, European men sought to possess Africa and exploit that continent's diamonds and gold. Thus Laurence's "The Rain Child" repeats the Western association of the black woman with Africa itself (as the earth, the body, the material), showing how both the black woman and Africa are exploited.

Just as the people of the village do not know where Ayesha's true home or birthplace is, so, too, one might argue, the West does not know, but seeks to understand, Africa's origins. In *Primate Visions*, Donna Haraway argues that embedded within Western imperial discourse is a desire for origins, a desire, that is, to find and know the beginnings of "man" (12). If, as Haraway asserts, the West locates "man's" origins in Africa as primates, then the West's desire to understand Africa is also a desire to understand the origins of the self. In the same way, Nedden's interactions with Ayesha can be understood as a desire to know the self. As in her other African works, then, Laurence's writing of Africa in "The Rain Child" is a writing of the Western self, an "attempt to understand one's background and one's past, sometimes even a more distant past which one has not personally experienced" (Laurence, *Heart* 13).

After Ruth witnesses Kwaale baring herself at the Odwira festival, she disappears, and Nedden is concerned about her whereabouts. Seeking consolation in Ayesha, Nedden "[does] something then that she had never before permitted [herself] to do" – she holds Ayesha, not to comfort the child, but to comfort herself (130). This moment recalls not only the moment when Nedden admits to Dr. Quansah that she came to Africa for herself, rather than for the Africans (121), but also the moment in "The Drummer of All the World" when Matthew surprises himself by turning Kwabena away from Afua (10). What is significant about all of these instances is that the characters of Violet and Matthew unwittingly engage in possessive acts. Nedden's use of Ayesha "for her own comfort" invokes men's exploitation of her as a child prostitute in the same way that Matthew's possession of Afua invokes the colonizers' exploitation of Africa itself. If Ayesha represents the continent and idea of Africa, then Nedden's act of embracing her for her own comfort is also an embracing of Africa. Problematically, however, that embracing for one's own comfort is a kind of exploitation. Similar to the imperialists that have gone before her, Nedden loves and exploits Africa in an attempt to know herself. Hence "The Rain Child" demonstrates how, in Edward Said's words, "European culture gained strength and identity by setting itself off against the Orient [read: Africa] as a sort of surrogate and even underground self" (3).

Gaurev Desai asserts that the question of African "rationality" during colonialism "was an attempt to put a scientific mask on popular racist (mis)conceptions of Africans in colonial times" (32). Violet Nedden differs from Hilda Povey in that she does not see all Africans as "equally unenlightened" (106) and recognizes the problem with giving the African girls an English education. However, Nedden relays not only the notion that both Kwaale and Ayesha are somewhat unintelligent, but also that it is acceptable for them to remain so. Of Kwaale she says that she "would [not] go on and take teacher training" but would marry, and Nedden believes "that would be the right thing to do" (112); of Ayesha she says that she had "begun to learn English" but "found it difficult," and so Nedden "[tries] not to press her beyond her present limits" (114). Thus Nedden's understanding of these girls as unintelligent might support Western discourse regarding the rationality of the African.

In addition, Nedden's depictions of Kwaale and Ayesha reflect the values of Western feminism. Written in 1962, "The Rain Child" exemplifies the Western feminist belief – put forth by such feminist writers as Simone de Beauvoir, Kate Millett, Gloria Steinem, and Germaine Greer – that women must be freed from domestic duties, gain economic independence, and have the choice to work outside the home. Nedden implies that working outside of the home (becoming a teacher, for example) is more worthy than marrying. Moreover, Nedden pities such African girls on account of the difficult lives she anticipates for them:

> But sometimes it saddened me to think of what life would probably be for [Kwaale], bearing too many children in too short a span of years, mourning the inevitable deaths of some of them, working bent double at the planting and hoeing until her slim straightness was warped. (112–13)

Such a statement demonstrates how Western feminist beliefs were sometimes aligned with imperialist ones. That Western women such as Violet Nedden were more likely to go on to teacher training than Africans such as Kwaale and Ayesha, and that Nedden, as English, values working outside of the home over "bearing too many children" and "planting and hoeing," problematically suggests that Western women were more progressive and advanced than Africans. The Western woman's movement toward liberation is here set against African women's supposed imprisonment. Given Nedden's depiction of the African girls' impending fate, it is not surprising that black African feminists or womanists struggled not only against representations of African women as Africa itself – as the earth, the body, the material – but also against Western women's imperial and patriarchal depictions of them. In her depictions of Kwaale and Ayesha, Violet Nedden does not work alongside African womanists who are "victimized on racial, sexual, and class grounds by white men" (Ogunyeme 67), but rather against them.

In some instances, "The Rain Child" works in the service of white feminism and against African womanism, while, in others, it works alongside African womanist values. African feminists such as Chikwenye Okonjo Ogunyeme strategically use the term "womanism" instead of "feminism." African "womanists," unlike Western feminists, Ogunyeme asserts, are as attentive to issues of race as they are to issues of gender. In "The Rain Child," when Ruth and Violet Nedden are at David Mackie's house, Nedden explains that "Mrs. Mackie complained about the inadequacies of local labour, and I sat fanning myself with a palm leaf and feeling grateful that fate had not made me one of Claire Mackie's employees" (122). Mackie's engagement in work outside the home suggests that she is a Western feminist who resists a role as a housewife, while her comment implies that her values are racist because her complaints about "the inadequacies of local labour" are quite clearly complaints against black workers. Thus Laurence, through Nedden, points to the hypocrisy of Western women such as Mackie who want liberation from domestic life while maintaining the oppression of Others. Laurence demonstrates the equality of African women in Ghanaian society when Violet Nedden discusses Kwaale's parents and their status in the community. Kwaale's father is a "village elder in Eburaso" who is "highly respected" but makes little money; Kwaale's mother, on the other hand, "with the cassava and peppers and medicinal herbs she [sells] in the market," is the one who supports the family (113). In "Actions Louder than Words: The Historical Task of Defining Feminist Consciousness in Colonial West Africa" (1998), Cheryl Johnson-Odim explains that market women in Nigeria before colonialism held some power in the community and were economically self-sufficient. Speaking of market women in Lagos, Nigeria, during colonial intervention, she states that "in the 1930s, the commissioner of the colony … suggested that the degree of power women exercised within certain markets should be 'nipped in the bud'" (84). Laurence's reference to Kwaale's mother as an economically self-sufficient market woman is a reminder that, in some ways, African women before colonialism had strong positions in society. It was only after colonialism, some African feminists or womanists have suggested, that they became victimized "on racial, sexual, and class grounds by white men" (Ogunyeme 67). Laurence's story suggests that some of the market woman's power and economic self-sufficiency remained, even after colonial intervention.

"The Rain Child" shows how Violet Nedden, a character who holds many of the same beliefs as Laurence herself, is against the English system of education for African girls, even though she is part of that very system. Laurence also creates a self-mocking Nedden who resists and yet resides in her imperial "throne" (112). Through Nedden's critique of Ruth and David's friendship, Laurence demonstrates how the West represents Africa "from the outside" (124). As in "The Pure Diamond Man," she critiques the anthropological impetus to collect cultural artifacts – or, in David Mackie's case, animals – from Africa, and exemplifies the imperial impetus to study and hence to know the Other. In some instances the story is aligned with Western feminism and imperialism, whereas in others it is aligned with African feminism and womanism and shows the equal economic status that market women such as Kwaale's mother have in Ghanaian society. Most importantly, perhaps, the story shows how Violet Nedden's attempt to understand Africa is an attempt to understand the self, a self who is both alienated from the "motherland" and at home in an Africa to which she is deeply attached. Nedden, perhaps like Laurence herself, must ultimately go back home "as a stranger" (133), "[bearing] the mark of Africa upon [herself]" (107) and always remembering how "the rain hovers" (105) and how "the air was like syrup, thick and heavily still, over-sweet with flowering vines" (105).

⋆ ⋆ ⋆ ⋆ ⋆

Margaret Laurence's *The Tomorrow-Tamer* portrays the difficulties in communication between those of European and African cultures and depicts various European and African characters as though they are not at home in the place where they reside. The stories interrogate how those who were influenced by European cultures and traditions were also embedded within Western representations of Africa, even as they might have worked against them. In "The Pure Diamond Man," Laurence not only challenged Western ideas of Africa and strove to present readers with alternate perspectives on that continent, she also drew attention to the problem of representation itself. Philip Hardacre searches for an authentic Africa, one that supposedly existed in pristine form before colonial contact; yet Laurence makes the point that there is no authentic Africa that can be known or understood outside of Western constructions of it. Tetteh succeeds in the new

Ghana by playing into Western capitalism; but Daniel, "a big newspaper man" (185) and one who is influenced by the West, will be the one who tells his story and thus represents Tetteh to the outside world. "The Pure Diamond Man" therefore exposes the kinds of miscommunications that can take place across cultures, the problems that mistaken and solidified assumptions can create. The story complicates the relationship between the dominant and the dominated in order to challenge preconceived Western notions of Africans (such as the African as an ignorant victim of colonization). In this way, Laurence advanced her cause of working toward human communication – "however difficult," as she said to Achebe, "this may be" (letter dated 3 June 1984). In "The Pure Diamond Man," Tetteh expresses his voice in a Ghanaian culture that increasingly intermingles and changes under the influence of the West.

"The Drummer of All the World" and "The Rain Child" both examine the idea of the divided subject. Both protagonists of those stories, Matthew and Violet Nedden, are Westerners who are torn between their love for Africa, what has become home, and their ties to the mother country. In MacFarlane's words, the "imperialist intervention has created a world of 'strangers' who exist *between* categories of definition, unable to occupy stable categories of race or identity because they are unable to find the 'real' place beyond the heterotopia to call 'home'" (229). This internal conflict is highlighted, in "The Drummer of All the World," by Matthew's simultaneous mourning for Africa's past and for his own lost childhood. Indeed, the "old" Africa and Matthew's child-self become one. Matthew is forced to realize that Africa is not his home, and this shatters his very sense of self. In "The Rain Child," Violet Nedden is aware of her own fraught position as a Westerner in Africa and mocks imperial rule as she resides in her garden "throne" (113). In some instances, Nedden is aligned with Western feminist values that set the so-called progressive European woman against the African, whereas in others she endorses African womanist notions and portrays African women as powerful. In both of these stories, the protagonists' attempts to understand the Africa in which they reside are also attempts to know the self. In this way, Laurence ultimately realizes in these stories what she says of her own experience in Africa, that "the last thing in the world that would occur to you is that the strangest glimpses you may have of any creature in distant lands will be those you catch of yourself" (*Prophet's* 10).

Part Two

WRITING ABOUT CANADA

Three

Community and the Canadian Nation in *The Stone Angel* and *A Bird in the House*

In the previous two chapters I discussed how Laurence exemplified a divided colonial subject in her writing about Africa. Characters in her writing about Africa feel ties to home – Britain and Canada – and they also feel ties to the African countries that their ancestors have colonized. Laurence's characters in her writing about Canada also portray a divided and complicated subject position. In this way, there is continuity in her movement between her African and her Canadian work that few critics have discussed. In her books about Canada, which are set in the fictional Canadian prairie town of Manawaka, all of the Anglo-Canadian protagonists, in one way or another, confront the history of their settler-invader ancestors. They feel conflicted between the culture of their ancestors and the multicultural nation in which they reside. The protagonists of the Manawaka series move back and forth between histories, both personal and national, and the present moment that emerges from those histories. In this regard, *The Stone Angel* and *A Bird in the House* are particularly important works: they exemplify a complicated and divided settler position more so than *The Fire-Dwellers* and *A Jest of God*. In *The Stone Angel*, protagonist Hagar Currie-Shipley is of Laurence's grandparent's generation, pioneers of the Canadian prairies. Hagar is an elderly woman who reflects upon her life. In *A Bird in the House*, by contrast, the protagonist Vanessa MacLeod is a young girl who strives to understand her heritage and looks forward to her life as an adult. Both protagonists struggle to determine their identities and to understand their nation.

The Stone Angel

The Stone Angel begins with a description of the central symbol of the novel, a gravestone statue that is the stone angel itself, and gestures toward previous generations of pioneers on the Canadian prairies. The novel ends with the words "And then – " (308), suggesting Hagar's death, but framing death as a transition, a movement from one state to another, from one generation to the next. Thus the novel's beginning and ending foreground history, ancestry, and the continual movement of time. As Hagar Currie-Shipley narrates her life, she moves back and forth between past and present. In "Time and the Narrative Voice," Laurence stated that time in all of her stories is not limited to the time of the character's life, but "represents everything acquired and passed on in a kind of memory-heritage from one generation to another" (155). She further indicated that, in her writing, she tried to depict a "longer past which has become legend, the past of a collective cultural memory" (155). Her decision to begin with *The Stone Angel*, the story of her grandparent's generation, suggests a confrontation of her own ancestral, national, and collective history, an attempt to bring together the present and the past.

The narrative technique and form of the novel mimic Hagar's divided subject position. As in *The Diviners*, which begins with the river that "flow[s] both ways" (11) and is narrated in a complex and non-linear way, *The Stone Angel* moves back and forth in time. Through her memory, Hagar's present is juxtaposed with her past. Like the symbol of the river, the symbol of the stone angel anticipates this movement. That the stone angel stands in memory of Hagar's mother, "who relinquished her feeble ghost as [Hagar] gained [her] stubborn one" (3), suggests generational change and the passing of time. Hagar's lament, "So much for sad Regina, now forgotten in Manawaka – as I, Hagar, am doubtless forgotten" (4), is a call to remember rather than to forget, to pay heed to the generations of ancestors and the women that came before. As critics have noted, the stone angel not only marks Hagar's mother's death but also "proclaims the dynasty" of Hagar's father (3). Jason Currie views Hagar as a possession he owns when he sends her to school, where she learns embroidery, to refine her. Upon her return he looks upon her "and nod[s] as though [she] were a thing and his" (43). Similarly, as the description of the stone angel suggests, Jason Currie clearly viewed his now deceased wife as that which he owned (3). The stone angel, blind as Hagar is stubborn, stands in the present but marks the past, just as Hagar resides in her elderly body while her memory inhabits her youth. Both Hagar and the stone angel rest uneasily on the boundary between life and death, as Hagar confronts a distinctly patriarchal and colonial ancestral history.

The in-between space that both the stone angel and Hagar herself inhabit might be understood in relation to McClintock's theoretical work on boundaries and margins. Citing Mary Douglas, McClintock states that "margins are dangerous. Societies are most vulnerable at their edges, along the tattered fringes of the known world" (24). Discussing Julia Kristeva's notion of abjection as that which one expels or rejects but from which one does not fully part, McClintock argues that certain members of society inhabit abject zones: "the slum, the ghetto, the garrett, the brothel" (72). In *The Stone Angel*, the cemetery functions as such an abject zone: it rests on the boundary between the living and the dead and resides between Hagar's past and present. The stone angel in the cemetery marks Hagar's mother's existence at the same time that it marks Hagar as motherless. We can view the cemetery in the novel as an abject zone because it exposes that which is rejected and repressed. For example, in the cemetery, Hagar secretly witnesses her father ending a private romance with Lottie Dreiser's mother, who bore Lottie out of wedlock (18). Jason Currie "never let on at all that he'd so much as exchanged a word with her" (19); he therefore rejects and represses a relationship of which he is ashamed. As Donna Palmateer Pennee puts it, "Jason's sexual hypocrisy was known to Hagar who witnessed, without thoroughly understanding, the end of his liaison with, and fear of contamination by, Lottie Drieser's mother in the town cemetery, where not all 'weeds,' it seems, were kept from encroaching on the borders of civility" ("Technologies" 15). McClintock argues that during colonialism, "bounds of empire could be secured and upheld only by proper domestic discipline and decorum" (47). Laurence exposes the lie that such decorum and discipline was upheld by Western Canadian settler colonials such as Jason Currie.

The cemetery in Manawaka also functions as an abject zone when Hagar's son, John Shipley, like Jacob in Genesis, wrestles with the stone angel. When Hagar is middle-aged, John drives her to the Manawaka cemetery, where they find that the stone angel has fallen. After John struggles to put the stone angel upright, they discover that "someone had painted the pouting marble mouth and the full cheeks with lipstick" (179). Amelia Del-Falco suggests that the fall of the stone angel parallels Hagar's own fall (85). This is true not only of Hagar's "fall" from life to death, but also of her fall in class, from a wealthy "Currie" to a working-class "Shipley." The stone angel not only literally falls over, but she also falls from grace – from the "costliest" (3) angel in the cemetery, and a representative of feminine purity, to a "wanton" creature (180). Later in the novel, when Hagar is at the cannery at Shadow Point – arguably at her lowest and most desperate – she seemingly plays dress-up and puts June bugs in her hair. Like the stone angel, she falls from grace: "my cotton housedress bedraggled, my face dirt-streaked, my hair slipped out of its neat bun and hanging down like strands of grey mending wool.... Then I recall the June bugs and could die with mortification" (220). With the fall of the angel, Laurence shows how Victorian and modern women were viewed as either angel or whore. With the incident between Lottie Dreiser's mother and Hagar's father, Laurence upsets the notion that settler colonials such as Jason Currie were proper and moral. With the stone angel, who symbolizes Hagar herself, Laurence suggests that women are not so-called angels in the house, but rather complex and multi-sided human beings.

Laurence represents the abject – improper moral conduct on the part of Jason Currie, and the angel as "wanton" (180) – in the abject zone of the cemetery: that which resides on "the fringes of the known world" (McClintock 24). It is particularly noteworthy, however, that she rejects the notion that the abject should be repudiated and repressed. Instead, she reassesses the repudiated and repressed as worthy and suggests that the hidden should be revealed. She foregrounds what McClintock has called "abject zones" in order to reverse the imperial order and turns colonial notions of such zones on their head. For example, in the encounter that Hagar witnesses between her father and Lottie Dreiser's mother, it is possible that Jason Currie cares for, even loves, Lottie's mother. He is impeded from expressing that love and engaging in a public relationship with her, however, because society condemns it. And of course, Jason Currie, as a settler colonial pioneer, is particularly invested in the Scots-Presbyterian settler society of which he is a part. In an interview with Michel Fabre, Laurence explained that she believed people in general have potential for great emotional communication between them, but that few people ever reach that potential (200). Hagar's witnessing of the end of the relationship between her father and Lottie Dreiser's mother is an example of the potential for but ultimate failure of such communication between two people. Another example in which Laurence foregrounds and reassesses the abject is evident in the author's description of the fallen stone angel. Hagar condemns the stone angel's "wanton" exposure (180). Read in the context of Hagar's relationships with her father and husband, however, that exposure might be celebrated. Because the stone angel, who represents Hagar herself, now exhibits a more dynamic and multi-sided woman, she challenges Jason Currie's belief that Hagar is "a thing and his" (43) and Bram Shipley's belief that Hagar does not experience sexual pleasure. In a feminist and anti-colonial gesture, Laurence reworks "abject zones" into dynamic sites that have revolutionary yet unfulfilled potential.

If the Manawaka cemetery is a boundary zone that exists between the living and the dead, the present and the past, then the nuisance grounds similarly reside on tenuous boundaries. There, Hagar uncomfortably confronts and denies herself. As young girls, at the nuisance grounds, Hagar Currie and Lottie Drieser witness some discarded eggs hatching in the hot July sun. Hagar's description of the chicks, "prisoned by the weight of broken shells all around them" (27), parallels Hagar's own life. Hagar leaves the "broken," patriarchal and "prisoned" homes of her father, Jason Currie, and her husband, Bram Shipley. Her present home is also "broken," since she is dismayed by Marvin and Doris's plan to send her away from home, to the seniors home, Silverthreads. In addition, she is presently prisoned in the elderly body that is her home. Just as the chicks are "prisoned" and "broken," so too is Hagar; and just as she rests on the boundary line between life and death, so too do the chicks that she sees. Moreover, Hagar cannot look at the chicks, "an affront to the eyes" (28), as she cannot look, in her metaphorical blindness, at her own life circumstances.

Later in life, Hagar is haunted by her witnessing of the chicks and Lottie's merciful killing of them, but Lottie has forgotten about the incident entirely (213). On the one hand, Lottie's act of forgetting this incident might suggest that it was more personal and troubling to Hagar than it was to Lottie. On the other hand, however, it might suggest that Lottie has repressed the incident, whereas Hagar has not. In the instance in which Lottie kills the chicks, Hagar views Lottie as strong and confident, in direct juxtaposition to her frail constitution (213). Critic Hildegard Kuester interprets Hagar's witnessing and Lottie's killing of the chicks as foreshadowing the death of Hagar's son and Lottie's daughter (27). When Hagar's son John and Lottie's daughter die in an accident, Lottie falls apart, whereas Hagar is shown to be strong, even as that perceived strength is actually a kind of numbness (243). Like the statue in the cemetery, Hagar has turned to stone.

For Hagar, the unpleasant memory of the chicks in the nuisance grounds will not rest or go away, and in this way that memory constitutes a haunting that is indicative of the text and Laurence's work as a whole. *The Stone Angel* and her other writing, that is, address the notion of the past erupting into the present because something in that past has not been resolved. This haunting begins with *The Stone Angel*, her first novel about Canada, and continues on to its culmination, as Laurence herself indicated, in *The Diviners*. In an interview, Laurence directly stated that she herself was "haunted" by the history of her ancestors, settler-invaders who oppressed Aboriginal peoples. Speaking of the Métis Tonnerre family in *The Diviners*, Laurence said, "I did not think of [the Tonnerre family] coming into all of my Canadian novels, but of course [they do]. Apparently I felt quite haunted" (Fabre 201).

Pointing to the work of Ken Gelder and Jane M. Jacobs, Cynthia Sugars and Gerry Turcotte explain that "the postcolonial nation is haunted by 'ghost stories' and that the reappearance of these suppressed 'stories' or histories produces an uncanny and haunted space in the narratives of nationhood" (viii). Sugars and Turcotte further explain that, in much modern and contemporary Canadian literature, "there is an aura of unresolved and unbroachable 'guilt,' as though the colonial/historical foundations of the nation have not been thoroughly assimilated" (ix). Canada has not sufficiently confronted itself and its troubling, sometimes racist, sometimes oppressive past. The nation has, rather, repressed and repudiated it, only to have it return as the "uncanny" in the figures of ghosts who continue to haunt until they are put to rest. *The Stone Angel* engages in this project of exposing the ways in which people and the nation have been and continue to be haunted by their pasts. It demonstrates the process of confrontation and renewal as Laurence's characters begin the process of coming to terms with individual and collective histories.

Hagar is haunted when her son Marvin and his wife, Doris, take her to visit the seniors home, Silverthreads, in the hope that they will be able to arrange for Hagar to live there. At the seniors home, Hagar is forced to confront herself, her own personal history. Like the cemetery, the home teeters on the boundaries between life and death, present and past, as the residents within it await their turn for death. She moves from inside the home to outside of it: to the garden, and then to a gazebo within the garden. As she moves to the very edges of Silverthreads – that which is already a boundary zone – she simultaneously moves toward her own personal history. She moves *outside* of the seniors home and *outside* of her own body at the same time that she moves *inside* of herself: her history and her spirit. At this moment, she paradoxically cannot see where she is going ("Darkness has come") and is "gifted with sight" (105). When she sees what might be interpreted as a ghost, she is lead from blindness to insight. The man or ghost who is "sitting there" (105) holds a "carved stick or a cane" (105), a symbol, perhaps, of one who guides the blind. The text echoes Shakespeare's *A Midsummer Night's Dream*, when Lysander, because of a magic love potion, mistakenly falls in love with Helena. Hagar recognizes, or, rather, misrecognizes, the ghost as her late husband, Bram: "I can see he's bearded. Oh – So familiar he is that I cannot move nor speak nor breathe. How has he come here, by what mystery?" (106). Hagar is soon called back into the seniors home and the home of her body, and she acknowledges that the person she sees in the gazebo is a man, not a ghost. But she has been haunted. She has glimpsed a different kind of existence and has been lead toward death. At this moment, she experiences an epiphany as present and past, body and spirit, life and death, are conflated into one.

Just as Hagar is haunted at Silverthreads, so too is she haunted at the cannery at Shadow Point. At Silverthreads she is haunted by the ghost of her past, a stranger who takes the form of her late husband, Bram Shipley; at Shadow Point she is also haunted by the ghost of her past, a stranger, Murray Lees, who takes the form of her late son, John Shipley. The ghost-ing that occurs at Shadow Point is even more significant than that which occurs at Silverthreads. Here, Hagar does not just glimpse the ghost of her past, but confronts it, accepts it, and arguably is reborn because of it. The cannery at Shadow Point is at the edge of the ocean at the North Shore of Vancouver, much like the nuisance grounds are at the edge of Manawaka. The cannery is and contains that which society has cast off – it is "a place of remnants and oddities" (215). At times, the cannery in which Hagar tempo-rarily takes refuge seems to be a ship. Describing the ocean she hears right outside the cannery, for instance, she exclaims, "the sea is only the sound of water slapping against the planking" (225). Like Odysseus, perhaps, she is on an epic sea journey. But interestingly, Laurence describes the cannery at Shadow Point not only as if it is a ship *on* the ocean, but as if it is a ship *beneath* the ocean. The description of the cannery as a "sea-chest of some old and giant sailor" (215), with "discarded fishing nets" and "oily hempen ropes" that "lie like tired serpents" (215), suggests a sunken, underwater ship. In a sense, as Hagar descends down the "two hundred earthen stairs" (185) to Shadow Point, she simultaneously moves back in time, back into a watery womb before she was born, a womb that is the ocean in which the ship rests. When she leaves Shadow Point and ascends the stairs – symboli-cally, Jacob's ladder to heaven in Genesis – she arrives "swaddled in blan-kets" (254), as if she is born anew.

At Silverthreads, Hagar first meets her ghost, the man she perceives to be Bram Shipley, in darkness; similarly, at the cannery at Shadow Point, when she first meets Murray Lees, they "face each other in the darkness" (220). Just before she begins to confess to Murray what troubles her soul the most, the death of her son John, Hagar, through the first-person narrative voice, muses, "I open my eyes and find there's no light in the room" (235). Yet Hagar is "gifted with sight" (105) at the moment she sees the ghost whom she recognizes as Bram Shipley, and she will gain insight through the ghost who is Murray Lees. Brenda Beckman-Long argues that *The Stone Angel* is a confessional novel, because of its "depth of characterization: the protagonist's presence and the reader's sense of privilege in being party to her story" ("*The Stone Angel* as Feminine Confessional Novel" 48). Certainly, the scene in which Hagar and Murray Lees converse in the cannery can be read as confessional – not only in the literary sense, as Beckman-Long argues, but also in the religious sense. Each confesses to the other in order to purge his or her soul. After Hagar tells the story of John's death, she is surprised to hear a voice – the voice of Murray Lees – say "Gee, that's too bad" (244). Her recount of the trauma that haunts her, the death of her son, John, has been spoken, mobilized, just as Hagar herself turns from stone to flesh and releases her tears: "I'm crying now, I think. I put a hand to my face, and find the skin slippery with my tears" (244). Hagar is freed not only because she voices her story, but also because her story is heard.

After she tells her story, Hagar momentarily mistakes Murray Lees for her son John and apologizes to him for not welcoming him to bring his girlfriend, Arlene, home (247). This apology is important. She feels that because she did not welcome them both into her home, she is responsible for John's death: he died in an accident with Arlene, away from home. In response to her apology, Murray plays the part of John, and responds, "It's okay.... I knew all the time you never meant it" (248). Unlike Murray Lees, who plays the part of another in order to appease Hagar, Hagar Currie, early in the novel, cannot bring herself to play the part of her deceased mother in order to ease her dying brother Dan's pain. Hagar's momentary experience of Murray Lees as the ghost of John Shipley allows her to heal the rift in her relationship with her deceased son. But her apology and Murray's acceptance of it occur not only in the context of conflated time – Murray is the ghost of John – but also in the context of conflated place. Hagar has reconstructed the cannery as her house: "an overturned box is my table, and another is my chair" (216). Just as Murray is John's ghost, so too the cannery is Hagar's house, remade. The cannery is a place that rests between uncertain boundaries since it teeters between past and present, here and there.

Sugars and Turcotte state that "being haunted is intimately connected to the activity of haunting, and ... possessing is always already a negotiation with dispossession" (xx). True to Sugars and Turcotte's statement, at Shadow Point, Hagar both *haunts* and *is haunted*. When she is alone at the cannery, she witnesses two children on the beach, playing house. Hagar is haunted by the children as her past erupts into her present and the children become her mirror. First, she witnesses her own childhood in their play, as her subject position is split between her present and her past. Second, she remembers John and Arlene "playing house" in her own home, and regrets not welcoming them there. Finally, she views her present moment in the mirror of the children, since she presently "plays house" at the cannery. She is haunted by her personal history as she watches the children at play. Yet she also engages in haunting herself. When she finally speaks and, offers the children some food, thus giving away her hidden presence, she scares them, and they run away: "Now they fancy they're Hansel and Gretel, rushing headlong through the woods, wondering how to avoid the oven" (189). Hagar is invaded by her past as she herself comes across as an intruder, a threat to others.

Importantly, Hagar's subject position of both haunting and being haunted mimics the settler-invader's position in Canadian history. Laurence plays with the notion of possession and dispossession, demonstrating, to put it in Sugars and Turcotte's words, "ways the colonial becomes postcolonial, and, by extension, how postcolonialism is itself 'haunted' by its grounding in a compromised history" (xx). Hagar's past haunts her and comes to bear upon her present. Similarly, in settler colonialism, the troubled national past of settler-invader–Native relations haunts and comes to bear upon the present. This unsettled national past has been evident in historical events within and beyond Laurence's time. These include the Oka Crisis of 1990, which resulted in violent confrontation between Mohawk protesters and the Quebec police force – backed up by RCMP and Canadian Forces personnel – over the construction of a golf course on a Native burial ground; Canada's endorsement, in 2010, of the United Nations Declaration on the Rights of Indigenous Peoples – a step toward healing the history of oppression of Aboriginal peoples, including the injustices that occurred at residential schools; and the establishment of the Truth and Reconciliation Commission in 2008, which enabled Aboriginal people to voice the injustices they suffered under the residential school system and to have their stories heard. These, of course, are just a few of many such examples. The history of the oppression of Aboriginal peoples by settler-invaders continues to manifest in the present as the nation begins to come to terms with the trauma of its history and works toward reconciliation and renewal.

In *The Stone Angel*, Hagar is haunted by her past and her grief regarding the death of her son; in Canadian history, as Anna Johnston and Alan Lawson explain, many Anglo-Scots settlers were themselves dispossessed from their own lands, and were haunted by that dispossession. In *The Stone Angel*, Hagar "haunts" the children she sees as she realizes that she is, in fact, an invader in the cannery, which is not her home, and an invader in the children's play area; in Canadian history, settlers and their descendants came to realize that they were the intruders upon the lands and rights of Aboriginal peoples. Thus Hagar occupies a split subject position, split between her present and her past, and that subject position parallels and reflects the history of settler-invaders' mentality. Settlers, themselves expelled from their homelands and haunted by their pasts there, came to realize that they were also invaders who "haunted" Others and "settled" a land that was neither historically nor rightfully their own. Just as post-colonialism, in Sugars and Turcotte's interpretation, is "[grounded] in a compromised history" (xx), so the subject positions of settlers and their descendants are also "grounded in a compromised history" (xx) – that is, in the lie that they and their people settled empty and unclaimed land.

The accident in which John Shipley dies occurs on the train tracks of a trestle bridge. Lazarus Tonnerre dares John to drive across the bridge, which he does, crashing into an unscheduled freight train (240). This tragic event and Lazarus's part in it is foreshadowed earlier in the novel, when Hagar sees John, a child, playing with the Tonnerre boys at the trestle bridge and "daring each other to walk across it" (128). Upon learning the cause of John's death, Hagar says that no one is to blame, but that is, to her mind, a lie. As discussed earlier, she believes the fault is her own, and suffers from feelings of guilt because of that belief. Yet her assertion that the accident is "no one's fault" (240), coupled with her question, "Where do causes start, how far back?" (240), might also suggest that John's death is Lazarus's or his own fault. After all, it is Lazarus who dares John to drive across the bridge and John who agrees to accept the dare. On this reading, "How far back?" takes on a different kind of meaning, one that is more national and cross-cultural in context. If, in the present moment, John's death is Lazarus's or his own fault, then Lazarus's unworthy act of daring him, and his own nonsensical acceptance of it, might be traced back and faulted to the history of conflict between settlers and Aboriginal peoples.

It is also significant that John's death is by train, and that it takes place at the railroad, since trains and railroads are recurring presences and symbols in Laurence's work. Speaking about the construction of the Canadian Pacific Railway in the late 1800s, Cynthia Sugars and Laura Moss state, "The railway became a symbol of [Prime Minister John A.] Macdonald's national dream, and a sign of the enormity of his vision for the new nation" (255). As Sugars and Moss further explain, "When the CPR was granted the contract in 1881, it was ... given 25 million acres of land – land that was already inhabited by Métis and Aboriginal peoples – which it then sold to settlers and immigrants as a way of recouping some of the costs of building the railway" (256). How ironic that Lazarus, a Métis, dares John, an Anglo-settler-descendant, to risk his life on the monument that was built to unify Canada at the expense of Aboriginal lives. The connection between the completion of the railroad and the defeat of the Métis people is clear:

the Métis leader Louis Riel was in jail when the CPR was completed, and he was executed two weeks later (Sugars and Moss 258). Although herself a nationalist, Laurence implicitly questions the very grounds upon which the nation was built. Canada came into being at the same time that it repressed and excluded Aboriginal peoples. Like Hagar and many of the other characters of Manawaka, the nation itself problematically represses what is Other to it in an attempt to create unity and identity.

The notion that John Shipley's death at the railroad tracks refers back to the history of the construction of the CPR and the oppression of Métis people invokes the idea of justice, or lack thereof. Justice, exchange, currency, and trade are all part of settler-Aboriginal history in Canada. In *The Stone Angel*, Hagar is able to leave her marriage to Bram Shipley because, unbeknownst to Bram, she has saved some money from selling eggs (126). In order to leave Bram, Hagar also sells her mother's "opal earrings, … sterling silver candelabra," and china dishes (136). Hildegard Kuester points out that Hagar sells her mother's inheritance at the same time that John trades away the Currie plaid pin, her father's inheritance (45). Thus Hagar is able to escape Bram Shipley only at the expense of "the material loss of both her maternal and her paternal heritage" (Kuester 45). One might say that Hagar has exchanged her lineage for her freedom. This exchange is particularly intriguing when thought of in relation to Anglo-settler history. Early Canadian settlers, that is, might have forfeited ties to their homeland in order to attain freedom in the new country.

While explaining that her mother died in childbirth, bearing her, Hagar says, "Father didn't hold it against me that [her mother's death] had happened so. I know, because he told me. Perhaps he thought it was a *fair exchange*, her life for mine" (59, my emphasis). In the instance in which Hagar sells her inheritance, she is the agent of the exchange; in the instance in which Jason Currie feels, at least in Hagar's mind, that he has exchanged his wife for his daughter, Hagar is the object of the exchange. The idea that she is an object, indeed, a commodity, is furthered in Jason Currie's perception of her when she returns from school: he looks at her as if he owns her (43). Already, the concept of exchange is mobilized in *The Stone Angel*. In a feminist gesture, Laurence shows how Hagar is forced to forfeit the material representation of her lineage and how she is problematically viewed by her father as an object of possession.

John exchanges the plaid pin – Hagar's father's heirloom and a symbol of her Scottish settler heritage – for Lazarus Tonnerre's knife (177); this trade is symbolic of the fur trade, the trade of goods between Aboriginal people and early explorers in Canada. John then trades the knife for cigarettes, and he explains to Hagar that "it wasn't much of a knife" (177), implying, perhaps, that it was not a fair trade. As we have seen, Hagar gives up her mother's inheritance in order to purchase freedom from her husband; here, she gives the pin to John in order to pass on her lineage, only to have him trade it away. In the first instance, Hagar parts with her past, represented by her mother's goods, in order to break free; in the second instance, she parts with her past, represented by the pin, in order to re-establish a lineal relationship with her son. The plaid pin has the motto "My Hope Is Constant in Thee" engraved upon it (*Diviners* 458), and the corresponding war cry is "Gainsay Who Dare" (*Stone Angel* 177; *Diviners* 458). The motto is significant because it implicitly refers to Hagar's hope in her son. The war cry is significant since John trades the pin and then accepts Lazarus's dare to drive across the bridge, leading to his own death. Perhaps because the pin is no longer in his possession, John does not pay heed to the war cry that directs him not to accept the dare. Without the pin's reminder, he becomes disconnected to his heritage and himself, and he does not have the tenacity to resist Lazarus's dare.

In *The Diviners*, Morag Gunn receives the Tonnerre knife as a gift from her adopted father, Christie Logan, the one who traded John Shipley a pack of cigarettes for it. Also in *The Diviners*, Jules Tonnerre receives the plaid pin from his father, Lazarus. Finally, Morag and Jules discover this fact and decide to trade back, so that Morag receives the Scottish pin, and Jules the Tonnerre knife. This moment represents not only reparation between Morag Gunn and Jules Tonnerre, but also the potential for reparation between Anglo-settler-descendants and Métis people. And this time, Morag and Jules acknowledge that the exchange is a "fair trade" (504). When Jules dies, he wills the knife to Pique, and upon receiving it, Pique asks Morag if she would give her the pin. Morag responds, "Not right now, Pique. It's some kind of talisman to me. You can have it, though, when I'm through with it.... When I'm gathered to my ancestors" (474). This conversation suggests, perhaps, that Pique accepts her Métis heritage while her Anglo-Scots one is not yet fully available to her. While neither complete nor conclusive, Laurence works toward cross-cultural understanding and against racism in these instances of trade, wills, and the passing of generations as she moves from the writing of *The Stone Angel* to the later writing of *The Diviners*.

A different understanding of exchange, that of one individual paying for the sins of another, is also evident in *The Stone Angel*. For example, at Shadow Point, Hagar encounters a seagull, which flies inside the room of the cannery. Hagar's statement, "*A bird in the house means a death in the house*," invokes Laurence's forthcoming collection of short stories and foreshadows Hagar's own death. Hagar "flings" a "wooden fish box" at the bird, intending to "shoo the creature away," but "horribly, the crate catches the gull, and it falls" (217). Two dogs come to pursue the bird and so enable Murray Lees to come into the cannery. By process of displacement, the gull is sacrificed for Hagar's sins: Hagar unwittingly injures the gull; the injured gull functions to distract the dogs from Murray Lees; and Murray – because the dogs are distracted – is able to come to the cannery where he receives the story of Hagar's supposed sins – her feelings of guilt, regret, and grief regarding the death of her son John. As Atwood puts it, "You owe a debt to the gods, so let something or someone else pay it for you" (*Payback* 66). Whereas Murray Lees enacts the role of the priest when Hagar confesses her feelings of guilt regarding her son's death, the gull plays the role of the sacrificial lamb who pays for and takes away Hagar's guilt.

We can see, then, how the notions of exchange, debt, and paying for one's sins or guilt are at play in *The Stone Angel*. But how, we may ask, are they relevant to Anglo-settler society, Canadian imperialism, and the divided subject that is so prominent in the settler mindset and in Laurence's writing about Africa and Canada? In order to answer that question, we might look at Hagar's relationship with Mr. Oatley, the man for whom she works as a housekeeper, after she leaves her husband, Bram Shipley. Pretty well ignored by Laurence critics, the relationship between Hagar Shipley and Mr. Oatley is of significance in *The Stone Angel*. McClintock states that, in the imperial order, "women who were ambiguously placed on the imperial divide (nurses, nannies, governesses, prostitutes, and servants) served as boundary markers and mediators" (48). Hagar occupies such a boundary position in settler-colonial Canada in her relationship as a housekeeper for Mr. Oatley. Mr. Oatley, retired when Hagar keeps house for him, worked in shipping and illegally smuggled Chinese wives into Canada. During this time, Chinese immigrants to Canada were charged a head tax that deterred men from bringing their wives to Canada. Laurence imagined and therefore drew attention to the possibility that there were people, such as Mr. Oatley in *The Stone Angel*, who profited from importing Chinese women. According to the *Canadian Encyclopedia*, in Canada in 1931, "out of a total Chinese population of 46, 519, only 3,648 were women" ("Chinese Canadians"). The character Hagar in *The Stone Angel* would have been born prior to the completion of the Canadian Pacific Railway in 1885. Between 1881 and 1884, 15,701 Chinese people entered Canada, many of them hired to construct the railway (Li 358). The Canadian nation-state implemented racist laws against the Chinese, including a head tax, which encouraged Chinese people to return to China after the completion of the Canadian Pacific Railway (358). After the Chinese Immigration Act was passed in 1923, most Chinese people were prevented from immigrating to Canada until after World War II (358).

In *The Stone Angel*, Mr. Oatley explains to Hagar how he "pack[ed] the females like tinned shrimp in the lower hold, and if the Immigration men scented the hoax, the false bottom was levered open, and the women plummeted" (158). Mr. Oatley assures Hagar, "They knew the chance they took when they began" (158). However, Hagar cannot help but feel complicit in his import of Chinese women. She perceives the money she receives from him for her wages as dishonest, and she feels responsible for the poor conditions the Chinese women suffered: "whatever he left me in his will, I earned it, I'll tell the world" (156). In this regard, Hagar's subject position in *The Stone Angel* is not unlike Laurence's in *The Prophet's Camel Bell*, where she feels complicit in the perpetuation of the child prostitute Asha's victimhood but also feels helpless to do anything about it. Furthermore, Laurence's failure to help Asha not only shows her knowledge that she is to a certain extent aligned with colonialism, but also demonstrates a critique of the colonial enterprise itself. In the same way, Hagar's sense that she is complicit in the Chinese women's plight because she receives wages from Mr. Oatley shows Laurence's critique of the system that enabled it: a Canadian government that imposed the head tax and engaged in state-implemented racism against existing and potential Chinese immigrants to Canada. Therefore, in her development of the business relationship between Hagar and Mr. Oatley, Laurence brings forth and asks us to question and consider notions of justice, currency exchange, fair pay, the colonialist role of the Canadian nation-state, and the treatment of immigrants.

Hagar returns in memory to her relationship with Mr. Oatley at the end of the novel, when she meets her roommate at the hospital, the seventeen-year-old Sandra Wong. Hagar muses:

> My absurd formality with this child is caused by my sudden certainty that she is the granddaughter of one of the small foot-bound women whom Mr. Oatley smuggled in, when Oriental wives were frowned upon, in the hazardous hold of his false-bottomed boats. Maybe I owe my house to her grandmother's passage money. There's a thought. (286)

Here, Hagar expresses the injustice that immigrant Chinese women suffered during early immigration to Canada. In addition, she feels that she is not exempt from causing, at least indirectly, this injustice: she served Mr. Oatley, who did not provide good conditions for the Chinese wives he illegally imported. .Hagar experiences a unique connection to Sandra Wong when she gets out of bed, barely able, to get Sandra a bedpan. After the nurse reprimands Hagar, Sandra and Hagar laugh together (302). Hagar has enacted a giving, selfless act. This moment need not be read as though it were a direct atonement for Hagar's perceived complicity in the suffering of early Chinese immigrant women. Yet, just as the final trade of the Currie plaid pin for the Tonnerre knife might be read as a reparative moment – one that reaches back through the generations and the historical relationship between Anglo-settlers and Métis people – so too can this moment be read as such. This instance of connection and understanding between Hagar Shipley and Sandra Wong works against the oppression and racism that Chinese immigrants and their descendants suffered. It imagines a coming together of Anglo and Chinese descendants in Canada during the early twentieth century.

Clearly influenced by the time and place in which she lived, Hagar is of two minds with regard to Sandra. On the one hand, Hagar's perception of Sandra might be read as essentializing: she views her as an "ethnic other" who is static and unchanging. Hagar describes Sandra wearing a traditional Chinese housecoat: "I felt the material – she held a sleeve out, so I could see how it felt. Pure silk, it is. The embroidery on it is red and gold, chrysanthemums and intricate temples" (302). On the other hand, however, Hagar's connection to and with Sandra is especially poignant, given that "throughout the latter half of the nineteenth and the early part of the twentieth century, the Chinese in Canada were viewed by the white population as aliens who could be utilized in menial jobs but were not to be trusted as equals" (Li 359). Hagar acts out of selflessness in risking herself to get the bedpan for Sandra, and they share a laugh; more broadly, Laurence works against the nation-state's racist laws and the problematic prevalent white perception of Chinese Canadians.

Perhaps the most moving part of *The Stone Angel* occurs when Hagar resides with other women in a non-private room in the hospital. This instance happens before she moves to a semi-private, where she rooms with Sandra Wong. It is a significant moment in the text in terms of the notion of exchange and the mobilization of a new multiculturalism. If boundaries and borders are tested in abject zones such as the Manawaka cemetery and the nuisance grounds in Laurence's books, then here, boundaries and borders are tested between the "Self"(one's identity, one's ego) and, to use Julia Kristeva's term, the "semiotic": a paradoxically pre-linguistic poetic language. Jason Currie, as we have seen, establishes his Self, his Anglo-pioneer identity, upon owning his land and women at the expense of Aboriginal peoples and a true and equal relationship of exchange between himself and Others. He establishes his "Self," that is, by repression and denial. By contrast, Hagar and the other women in the hospital submit themselves to communal exchange between and among them.

At night, the women call out and talk in their sleep unabashedly. While Hagar is initially horrified to find that she, too, is talking at night ("It can't be true. I have no recollection" [259]), such an uninhibited exposure allows her to connect with women such as Elva Jardine. Moreover, another patient, Mrs. Dobereiner, sings and speaks in German. Singing and speaking in a language which is not understood by others are both aspects of Kristeva's semiotic, which "produces in poetic language 'musical' but also nonsense effects" (1167). The cacophony of voices, the inadvertent speaking of private thoughts, and the singing and speaking in languages other than those known to Hagar – all these are disjointed and unsettling. Yet it is precisely this unsettling of one's established "Self" and "Identity," that which is created through denial and repression, that ultimately leads to liberation. The community of voices of which Hagar is a part is both feminine and multicultural. It is, as Kristeva puts it in "From One Identity to Another," a community which is "*heterogeneous*" (Kristeva's emphasis), revolutionary because it has the potential to "destroy ... accepted beliefs and significations" (1167).

The Stone Angel, then, is a brilliant invocation toward a revolutionary vision of Canada. The book foregrounds the movement between the present and the past, beginning with the symbol of the stone angel herself, and later in the text, demonstrating a community of multicultural and feminine voices in the Vancouver hospital where Hagar is staying. Laurence interrogates spaces such as the cemetery and the nuisance grounds, places where those who are no longer, and that which is unwanted, end up. She suggests that we unearth and face the past, rather than continue to repress and deny it. Therefore, the book resonates not only on an individual level in relation to the protagonist, Hagar Currie-Shipley, but also on the national level in relation to the history of Anglo-settler–Métis relations. Thus, with *The Stone Angel*, Laurence challenged the nation-state's vision of itself as a nation of two solitudes, English and French, and implicitly argued that Canada must be understood in terms of what Julia Kristeva has called "heterogeneity." This heterogeneity can be seen through Hagar's relationship to the Chinese-Canadian character Sandra Wong, and, to a lesser extent, through her relationship to another fellow patient in the hospital, the German Mrs. Dobereiner. The novel must be understood, then, in terms of its radical re-envisioning of the nation. Laurence's vision posited a dynamic and ever-changing multiculturalism and feminism at the centre of Canada's national imaginary.

A Bird in the House

The eight stories in Margaret Laurence's *A Bird in the House* begin when the protagonist of the stories, Vanessa MacLeod, is ten years old, and they trace ten years of her life. In her essay "Time and the Narrative Voice," Laurence stated of *A Bird in the House* that "the narrative voice had to speak as though from two points of view, simultaneously" (158) – Vanessa speaks as a child and as an adult looking back at her childhood. The stories are unified by Vanessa's continuing search for herself in relation to her community; and they are fragmented by the split narrative voice and their presentation out of precise chronological order. It is not surprising, then, that Laurence chose to write Vanessa's story in a short-story sequence, a genre that allowed her to go back and forth in time and alternate between adult and child narration. Vanessa's attempt to understand herself was also Laurence's attempt to write the nation. Vanessa, an emerging writer, writes and creates herself in relation to the Anglo-Scots and Irish pioneers that are her ancestors and in relation to the people that make up the small town of Manawaka. When Laurence was writing these stories in the 1960s, Canada was also constructing itself – its national imaginary – in relation to Others. Paradoxically, that is, Canada was being imagined and presented in the public domain as unified through fragmentation and diversity.

Laurence foregrounded Vanessa's love for writing and creation of narrative. Historically, nation building was achieved, in part, through storytelling. Canadian nation building relied on European tropes of progress and mapping the land to construct history, and so accepted notions of "Canadianness" are rooted in Eurocentric foundations. Stories of Canada's past employed Eurocentric settler empowerment and legitimization, and such stories became inculcated in the historical and literary consciousness of the nation. As Anna Johnston and Alan Lawson point out, Canadian settlers were often ostracized from and tied to their homelands; yet they also invaded Aboriginal land. The English-Canadian "settler," then, "uneasily occupied a place caught between two First Worlds, two origins of authority and authenticity" (370) – that of England, the "mother country," and that of the indigene. In *A Bird in the House*, Vanessa MacLeod negotiates this fraught and conflicted space between settlers of her own heritage and the indigene as she writes her personal and national identity. Through Vanessa, Laurence played into Canada's Eurocentric "grand narrative" that legitimized the settler. However, the Eurocentric settler narratives that Vanessa hears and creates never quite fit or match up to her lived experience, and so Laurence ultimately contested the legitimization of the settler story.

The stories that Vanessa hears about the heritage of her family reflect settler-descendant anxieties. Vanessa's paternal grandmother, Grandmother MacLeod, maintains that she is a "lady" and continually identifies with her Scottish heritage. Although she does not smoke, Grandmother MacLeod displays an ashtray that reads, in "gilt letters," "Queen Victoria Hotel, Manawaka" (*Bird* 23); she tells Vanessa that the Scottish clan of her ancestry "is a very ancient clan" (49); and she orders "linen tea-cloths" and "lace handkerchiefs" from "Robinson & Cleaver" (51–52). Grandmother MacLeod's alignment with her Scottish heritage, however, is continually undermined. Vanessa repeats to Aunt Edna what Grandmother MacLeod has told her, that her ancestors were "constables of the Castle of Kinlochaline" (52). "Castle, my foot," replies Aunt Edna. "She was born in Ontario, just like your Grandfather Connor, and her father was a horse doctor" (52). Likewise, Vanessa's Uncle Dan demonstrates his Irish ancestry by speaking with an Irish accent and singing Fenian songs, despite the fact that he is a Protestant. Yet his alignment with the Irish is ironized. When Vanessa asks if Uncle Dan was born in Ireland, for example, Aunt Edna replies, "Mercy no.... The closest he ever got to Ireland was the vaudeville shows at the old Roxy.... He was born in Ontario, just like Grandfather. The way Uncle Dan talks isn't Irish – it's stage Irish" (36). Influenced by both Grandmother MacLeod and Uncle Dan, Vanessa must position herself in relation to her relatives' simultaneous alignment with and dissociation from their ancestral roots. When told that Dan speaks "stage Irish," for example, she protests to her mother, "You always told me I was half Irish," and her mother replies, "Well, you are" (36). Vanessa negotiates and is caught between the motherlands of her ancestors and the homeland of Canada in which she currently resides. She vacillates between the two, trying to understand and categorize each in an attempt to discover and create her personal and national identity. In her memoir about Africa, *The Prophet's Camel Bell*, Laurence shows that she was uneasy about her position as a Canadian who was aligned with neither English colonialists nor local Somalis. In her stories "The Drummer of All the World" and "The Rain Child," set in Ghana, Laurence's English protagonists feel at home in neither Africa nor their "motherland," England. Laurence extended this motif in *A Bird in the House*, where Vanessa negotiates representations of her ancestral history in an attempt to understand her place in Canada.

Vanessa creates her personal and national identity not only by hearing her relatives' stories, but also by writing her own. In a way, she resists the stories and histories her relatives pass down to her. "The idea of inherited characteristics had always seemed odd to me," she exclaims (36). As a young girl, she makes a "clothespeg doll," which will be an "old-fashioned lady." Her frustration at her inability to make the doll, as Nora Foster Stovel has noted, demonstrates her struggle to define or "make" herself in relation to those "old-fashioned ladies," her women ancestors (*Divining* 227–28). Thus Vanessa employs an image of the pioneer woman to understand herself, yet her frustration and dissatisfaction with the doll show that she does not integrate that image fully with her own identity. Settler narratives frequently imagine the Canadian landscape as empty and frightening (Johnston and Lawson). So, too, do Vanessa's. She plans "in her head" a story about an infant who is baptized by Total Immersion and "swept away by the river ... towards the Deep Hole near the Wachakwa bend, where there were blood-suckers" (*Bird* 25). This story repeats settler narratives' construction of the land as empty – a "Deep Hole" – and frightening – "where there were blood-suckers" (25). Further, Vanessa's stories play into the settler impetus to "lay claim to the land" (Johnston and Lawson 264). Her story about pioneers, "The Pillars of the Nation," suggests through its title that settlers made up the foundation of Canada.

Grandmother MacLeod and Uncle Dan do not quite fit or match up to the homelands with which they associate themselves; likewise, Vanessa's clothes-peg doll of an old-fashioned lady does not quite fit Vanessa's own sense of her heritage. In a similar vein, Vanessa's stories, while informed by settler narratives, do not work: they are always challenged and contested. When Vanessa finds out that Grandfather Connor was a pioneer, for exam-ple, she abandons her story, "Pillars of a Nation," since Grandfather does not match up to the settler's romanticized and heroic persona. "If pioneers were like *that*, I thought, my pen would be better employed elsewhere" (*Bird* 68). To an extent, Vanessa perpetuates an imperialist narrative that legiti-mizes the European settling of the land: she accepts the privileged Euro-immigrant identity that she has inherited from her ancestors. And yet, that legitimization is constantly checked and qualified in *A Bird in the House*, through her inability to bring her own narratives to fruition.

Canada's history of European invasion and settlement of what was Aboriginal land is relatively recent. Thus, in Canada, it is a complicated matter to lay a claim to the land upon which one resides in order to define citizenship or nationhood: most citizens, or at least their ancestors, did not always reside on the land to which they intended to stake a claim. W. H. New points out that "land" in Canadian literature is not a "neutral refer-ent" but "resonates with notions of ownership or social attachment" (*Land* 5). Moreover, says New, "land" shifts from a "designation of locality" to a "designation of activity" when it is understood as a "*space* or *place* or *site*" of challenge to the accustomed borders of power" (*Land* 6). In *A Bird in the House*, the house of Vanessa's maternal grandfather, Grandfather Connor – which is known to the townspeople of Manawaka as "the old Connor place," and to the family as "the Brick House" – is a claim to the land on which it stands. It represents both an "icon of stability" and a "medium of change" (New, *Land* 6). The collection of short stories is filled with Vanessa's chang-ing perspectives on and in relationship to "the Brick House." The collection begins and ends with a description of this house, and the house is described as "part dwelling place and part massive-monument, ... the first of its kind" (*Bird* 11).

According to Johnston and Lawson, the settler cultivated the land and marked it as settled in order to tame the so-called threatening wilderness. Laurence's descriptions of "the Brick House" mark this settlement but also undermine its validity. While the house marks Timothy Connor's presence by its "monumental" status, it does not successfully "tame" its surroundings. It is "sparsely windowed as some crusader's embattled fortress in a *heathen wilderness*" (my emphasis), and its spruces were "taller than the house" (11). Interestingly, Laurence's description of the spruces' boughs employs images of both the untamed wilderness and the early settler, as if they are intertwined: the spruces' branches are "as rough and hornily knuckled as the hands of old farmers" (11). Settlers and the landscape they inhabit become one. In its final description at the end of the book, the Brick House has been overgrown: "The caragana hedge was unruly. No one had trimmed it properly that summer." Vanessa wants to tell its new owners to "trim their hedges" (191). As an adult, she returns to see the house under new ownership. Her statement that she "had not thought it would hurt [her] to see [the Brick House] in other hands, but it did," reveals her ambivalent relationship to the house and the settlement it represents. On the one hand, her desire to retain ownership of the house parallels the settler's desire to "lay claim to the land." On the other hand, she actively resists that desire: "But it was their house now, whoever they were, not ours, not mine" (191). The Eurocentric "grand narrative" of what it means to be "Canadian," as W. H. New explains, relies on "the image of settling the land – measuring, marking, and clearing it" (*Land* 87). Ironically, Vanessa lets go of that desire for order and demarcation in order to foster her own sense of identity. Just as she defines herself anew by cutting ties from her past – she can afford to go to university in Winnipeg because her mother has sold the MacLeod china and her grandfather's old bonds (*Bird* 187) – so too does she write herself anew by separating from the Connor home that was once her own.

That *A Bird in the House* posits Canadian settler-descendant identity in relation to the house or the home is also evident in Vanessa's relationship to the MacLeod house, the one in which Vanessa lives until her father dies. As a ten-year-old child, Vanessa waits in her home for her mother to return from the hospital, where her mother is undergoing a Caesarean section, a risky affair in 1930s Manitoba, when and where these stories take place. Vanessa describes the nooks and crannies of the house in relation to her relatives and previous occupants of the house:

> The unseen presences in these secret places I knew to be those of every person, young or old, who had ever belonged to the house and had died,

including Uncle Roderick who got killed on the Somme, and the baby
who would have been my sister if only she had managed to come to life.
(46)

In addition, she associates the portrait of the Duke of Wellington at the top
of the stairs metonymically with her Grandfather MacLeod, positing the
house as at once masculine and settler territory: "The stern man was actually the Duke of Wellington," she says, "but at the time I believed him to be
my grandfather MacLeod, still keeping an eye on things" (46). The "odd-
shaped nooks under the stairs, small and loosely nailed-up doors at the
back of the clothes closets, leading to dusty tunnels and forgotten recesses
in the heart of the house" (46) might represent, in feminist and psychoanalytic terms, the feminine, the unconscious, and the abject: Vanessa retreats
into her inner fears as she worries that her mother might die while giving birth. The portrait of the Duke that stands for Vanessa's grandfather
MacLeod, by contrast, represents the masculine, English colonial values of
so-called heroic conquest and settlement.

Johnston and Lawson remind us that the displacement of indigenous
peoples in Canada was "cultural and symbolic as well as physical" (363):

> Increasingly, the white settlers referred to themselves and their culture
> as indigenous; they cultivated native attributes and skills (the Mount-
> ies, cowboys, range-riders, gauchos, backwoodsmen), and in this way
> cemented their legitimacy, their own increasingly secure sense of moral,
> spiritual, and cultural belonging in the place they commonly (and reveal-
> ingly) described as "new." (363)

In *A Bird in the House*, Laurence mobilizes this trope of settler as indigene,
particularly through Vanessa's understanding of Grandfather Connor. Just
as settlers and nature are conflated in the description of the spruce trees'
branches as "hornily knuckled" (11), so Grandfather Connor becomes the
bear coat that he wears and that he earned and made. The skin had been
given to him as payment, "in the days when he was a blacksmith," and he
"had it cobbled into a coat by a local shoemaker" (62). When Grandfather
Connor wears the coat, Vanessa thinks of him as "The Great Bear," and says
that he "stalk[s] around the Brick House as though it were a cage" (63).
Vanessa associates Grandfather Connor with the Canadian landscape and
wilderness, with "Great Bear Lake" (64). If colonial discourse in settler-subject countries conflates Aboriginal peoples with the supposedly "vast" and
"empty" land that they inhabit, then one might argue that Vanessa engages
in that colonial discourse. She posits Connor as both Aboriginal and at one
with Canadian land. Grandfather Connor wears the local bear skin whose
origins are "only a hundred miles from Manawaka" (62), and he becomes
the lake and land with which it is affiliated. Great Bear Lake, it is worth

noting, is described as unsettled and untamed: "a deep vastness of black water, lying somewhere very far beyond our known prairies of tamed fields and barbed-wire fences, somewhere in the regions of jagged rock and eternal ice, where human voices would be drawn into a cold and shadowed stillness" (64). Finally, when Vanessa sees "the Bear Mask of the Haida Indians" in a museum (86), she is reminded of Grandfather Connor, and so directly associates him with the Haida Indians. The masculine settler-subject, it would seem, has been indigenized and legitimized by Vanessa in the figure of Grandfather Connor.

The last paragraph of "The Mask of the Bear," where Vanessa describes the Haida Indian mask, is quite distinct from the rest of the story. While the story takes place over a short period of time, the last paragraph occurs "many years later" (86). Vanessa describes the mask as "ugly and yet powerful," and sees a "lurking bewilderment" in it (86). She does not directly associate the mask with her grandfather Connor. Yet the reader is invited to make this connection because of the title of the story, and because Connor's character has a bear-like exterior but also a vulnerable, human side, as shown in the depiction of Connor weeping on Vanessa's shoulder (79). While preparing *A Bird in the House* for publication, Laurence's editor suggested that Laurence revise or remove this ending to "The Mask of the Bear." In response, Laurence wrote:

> I think this ending <u>must</u> stay, unless the title is not used – otherwise, the title Mask of the Bear does not mean anything. I also think that this ending <u>belongs</u>.... The ambiguity which is felt towards Grandfather by Vanessa <u>must</u>, I think, be apparent throughout (Clara Thomas Archives, box 2, file 8, page 2; Laurence's emphases)

Laurence's comment to her editor about the "ambiguity" Vanessa feels suggests that Vanessa dissociates and distances herself from her grandfather as a patriarch, a settler, and a pioneer but also associates with him as a vulnerable and sympathetic human being, an ancestor, and a Canadian. Laurence clearly depicts a sense of the settler-descendant split subject through Vanessa MacLeod, who is both at one with and apart from her ancestral and patriarchal past.

As well as increasingly referring to themselves as indigenous and creating representative figures such as the Mountie and the pioneer, white settlers "began to tell stories and devise images that emphasized the disappearance of Native peoples" (Johnston and Lawson 363). Thus the story of the "dying race" of indigenous peoples was written. Just as Laurence works within the trope that defines the settler as indigenous, so too does she work within the trope that describes the indigene or the Métis as "the dying race." Nowhere is this more prevalent, in the book, than in the canonized but hotly contested story, "The Loons." In this story, the disappearance of the loons from the lake at Vanessa's childhood cottage is symbolically linked with the disappearance of the Métis girl Piquette – the only person who can hear the loons' cries, a person who also subsequently dies (*Bird* 118–20). Furthermore, the disappearances of the loons and Piquette are associated with the changing landscape surrounding Vanessa's childhood cottage. The small pier that Vanessa's father built, for example, is replaced by a large one built by the government (119). Significantly, "Diamond Lake" is renamed "Lake Wapakata," "for it was felt that an Indian name would have a greater appeal to tourists" (119). Laurence, then, foregrounds not only the disappearance of Piquette and her people, but also the appropriation of Aboriginal land, language, and culture by white settlers. The Aboriginal name, notably for the tourists, marks the disappearance of the indigene but also the assumption of that part by white settlers. The lake's name marks the white settler's new and assumed role or place as indigene. Laurence foregrounds "land," to use New's terms, as "*territory, home, property*" (*Land* 5), which is a site of power that can be redefined, politicized, and overtaken.

Laurence draws attention not only to settlers' claims to land that was not rightfully their own, but also to settlers' wilful dispossession of Aboriginal people from that land. She recognizes, that is, how Aboriginal peoples were not perceived by settlers as rightful occupants of the land they had inhabited for centuries. Yet critic Janice Acoose draws attention to Laurence's statement, near the beginning of "The Loons," that the Métis family in Manawaka, the Tonnerres, "did not belong among the Cree of the Galloping Mountain reservation, further north," and that they also "did not belong among the Scots-Irish and Ukrainians of Manawaka" (108–9). Acoose argues that Laurence fails to recognize that the Métis "have their own space in Canada – which too many have died fighting to keep – just as the 'Indians' and the whites do" (222). In opposition to Acoose, I argue that in "The Loons," Laurence acknowledges the Métis right to the land and laments their dispossession from it. She demonstrates this sensibility with specific references to Métis history in the Red River area of Manitoba: her mention of the Battle of Batoche, a key battle in the North-West Rebellion, for example, and the hanging of the Métis leader, Louis Riel (108).

Acoose also criticizes Laurence for creating a Métis character, Piquette Tonnerre, who "is represented as a victim who is consistently victimized" (221). Tracy Ware makes a similar claim in "Race and Conflict in Garner's 'One-Two-Three Little Indians' and Laurence's 'The Loons.'" I argue, however, for a differentiation between Laurence's viewpoint and Vanessa's in "The Loons" and throughout *A Bird in the House*. Certainly, Laurence and Vanessa have a lot in common, as Nora Foster Stovel has noted in *Divining*

Margaret Laurence. But to conflate the author's viewpoint with the narrator's is to disregard the care Laurence has taken to construct narrative voice. Laurence herself explained the complexity of narrative voice in "Time and the Narrative Voice." Of the narrative perspective in "The Loons," Laurence said, "The tone of the narration had to change as Vanessa recalled herself at different ages, and this meant, for me, trying to feel my way into her mind at each age" (158). As a child and as a young adult, Vanessa attempts to understand herself partly in relation to Piquette, and this attempt results in Vanessa's view of Piquette as a victim. But this viewpoint is not necessarily Laurence's, and it is quite probable that Laurence's voice remains separate from Vanessa's, even at the end of the story. Vanessa, as a white settler-descendant, is dependent on a particular vision of Piquette and her people's history. While Vanessa may not fully realize the implications of that self-identification, Laurence certainly knew that the histories and fates of white settler-descendants and Métis were conflicted and fraught.

In "The Loons," there are three key moments when Vanessa perceives and attempts to understand Piquette. In the first instance, Vanessa is a young child who views Piquette as romanticized and idealized. In the second instance, she is a teenager who is "repelled and embarrassed" by her (114). In the final instance, she hears from her mother that Piquette has died in a house fire, and she associates her with the vanishing loons (117). One could argue, as Acoose and Ware do, that the story repeats racist settler and settler-invader notions of the Aboriginal person as the noble Indian, the whore, or the drunk, and a member of the dying race. However, each of the instances in which Vanessa perceives Piquette reveals a mismatch between what she has learned about so-called Indians and how she perceives and interacts with Piquette. For example, as a child, she mistakenly views her as a "daughter of the forest" (112), and she explains that her view is based on her knowledge "of Big Bear and Poundmaker, of Tecumseh, of the Iroquois who had eaten Father Brebeuf's heart," and on the poetry of Pauline Johnson (112). By drawing attention to how misinformed Vanessa is about Piquette despite the fact that she has read much about "Indians," Laurence criticizes the ways in which Aboriginal people were and are represented as noble Indians and savages in history books and literature.

When Vanessa, as a teenager, is "repelled and embarrassed" by Piquette, who wears a "skin-tight skirt" and "teeter[s] a little," but not because of "her once-tubercular leg" (116), Laurence, through Vanessa's eyes, might be said to repeat the racist stereotype of the Aboriginal person as whore or drunk. But that view is complicated by Laurence's references to the history of Métis oppression by English settlers at the beginning of the story (108), and by Piquette's statement to Vanessa that Vanessa's deceased father was "the only person in Manawaka that ever done anything good to [her]" (116). While Vanessa, like the white settlers before her, might identify herself against the victimized Piquette and her people, she also sees herself as a part of the reason for her plight: her ancestors oppressed Piquette's; and Vanessa herself, like most of the community of Manawaka, does not opt to do anything good for her. Finally, while Laurence repeats the trope of the dying Indian through Piquette's death, she simultaneously problematizes that trope. In a move that anticipates the work of Johnston and Lawson, Laurence describes and draws attention to how white settlers and settler-descendants problematically created indigenous identities for themselves in order to lay claim to the land on which they resided. In the story, they drive out the loons with development as they drive out the Aboriginal peoples with their violence, and they appropriate the landscape, which is conflated with the Aboriginal peoples, by giving the lake an Aboriginal name.

Vanessa's second encounter with Piquette recalls Laurence's meeting with the child prostitute, Asha, in Laurence's memoir about Africa, *The Prophet's Camel Bell*. In the memoir, Laurence comes to the realization that she is complicit with Asha's situation. The men from Laurence's husband's camps use the services of the prostitutes in the *jes*, while the camps supply the *jes* with water. In "The Loons," Vanessa comes to understand her complicity in Piquette's suffering through her tie to her ancestors and the community of Anglo-Scots settlers in Manawaka. "The Loons," though, is as much about grief and loss as it is about Vanessa's changing relationship with Piquette. Just as Matthew grieves for his lost childhood and his lost African home in Laurence's short story about Ghana, "The Drummer of All the World," so Vanessa grieves for her father and her cottage at Diamond Lake. Just as the settlers and the landscape in which they reside come together in Laurence's image of the Brick House's spruce branches, "knuckled as the hands of old farmers" (*Bird* 11), so Vanessa's grief for the loss of her father and the lake cottage become intertwined. She states that neither she nor her father "suspected that this would be the last time we would ever sit here together on the shore, listening [to the call of the loons]" (115). We might return, then, to Renato Rosaldo's concept of "imperialist nostalgia," where "people mourn the passing of what they themselves have transformed" (Rosaldo 108). While Vanessa acknowledges that she is at one with the history of white settlers who oppress and appropriate Aboriginal peoples and the lands upon which they reside, she simultaneously mourns for the loss of Diamond Lake, as it once was, for the loons, and for Piquette and the Métis people.

Thus Vanessa is undeniably, if reluctantly, connected to the history and presence of colonialism in Canada. According to critic Margaret Osachoff, the word "colony" comes from the Latin *colonia*, which invokes "farm, landed estate, settlement" (222). "For the colony in a hostile or newly conquered country," Osachoff asserts, "connection with the parent state is of utmost importance: the mother-country is the source of all standards, the home of culture and civilization" (222). We might understand this notion of "colony" in relation to Laurence's writing about Africa, in which central characters such as Matthew and Violet Nedden have a complicated relationship to England, their "motherland," an affection for it and yet a separation from it. We can also understand "colony" in relation to Laurence's writing about Canada, in which her settler-descendant characters negotiate their relationship with the "old country" against their identities within the community of Manawaka and the land on which they reside.

Moreover, Laurence makes connections between colonialism and war in *A Bird in the House*. Vanessa tries to understand her Canadian identity and heritage, as well as the so-called motherland, England, in relation to war. Laurence undermines the idea that Vanessa's Scottish and Irish ancestors were valiant heroes: Aunt Edna tells Vanessa that Grandmother MacLeod's people were not "constables of the Castle of Kinlochaline" and that Grandmother was simply born in Ontario (52), and Vanessa comes to the realization, in "The Loons," that her settler ancestors and herself – as members of the community of Manawaka – are responsible for Piquette Tonnerre's suffering. In a similar vein, Laurence undermines the idea that war is romantic and glorious, and she links that challenge to the notion of ancestry, since the people of Manawaka serve in the First and Second World Wars by virtue of Canada's ties to England, Ireland, and Scotland. Vanessa hears but cannot accept Canada's Eurocentric grand narrative on the value of war. The letter from Vanessa's father, Ewen, to Grandmother MacLeod states "how gallantly Rod had died" and was "almost formal" in its tone (52). Yet that notion is revealed as a fabrication when Ewen says to Vanessa's mother (Beth) "*I had to write something to her, but men don't really die like that, Beth. It wasn't that way at all*" (59). Thus, in *A Bird in the House*, colonialism and the idealization of war are asserted and undermined.

Travel away from Manawaka – and thus away from all that is depicted as stifling about small-town life – is also associated with war. Vanessa discovers her father's books, which include *Travels in Tibet*, *Seven-League Boots*, *Arabia Deserta*, and *National Geographic* magazine (56). At this discovery Vanessa suddenly realizes that her father had a longing to travel (56), a longing, perhaps, that he might have thought going to war could fulfill. War and travel are further romanticized when Vanessa discovers that her father had a French girlfriend when he was a young man at war (107). However, that romanticization is consistently challenged in the text: Vanessa refuses to go to the Remembrance Day parade in Manawaka because she is ashamed, not proud, of the soldiers, "plump or spindly caricatures of past warriors" (84); and she cries at the thought of her father witnessing his brother's death at war (86). Once again, popular romantic representations of war are undercut and shown to be fabricated.

Laurence's reference to *National Geographic* magazine when naming Ewen's books highlights the elevated status of travel and war. In *Reading National Geographic*, Catherine A. Lutz and Jane L. Collins argue that that the magazine has historically constructed peoples of the non-Western world as primitive and exotic by manipulating the photos and the perspectives from which they are taken, as well as the narratives that frame them. The book also examines how American politics determined the content of the magazine. For example, *National Geographic* stopped including Westerners in photographs of Vietnam during the Vietnam War because the public did not support the American presence there (206). Laurence's experience of living in and writing about Africa made her well aware of the construction of people and places as exotic. As she explains in *Heart of a Stranger*, the "Dance of the Ancestors [is] slicked-up, prettified, and performed forever in the same way" so that tourists are "provided with an embodiment of their own fantasies" (201). Laurence's references to *National Geographic* magazine and the other travel books that Ewen owns in *A Bird in the House* suggest a desire for freedom from the stifling small town of Manawaka – freedom to travel to faraway and supposedly romantic places. Vanessa sympathizes with this desire, even as she recognizes that it is a fantasy. She muses on her father's desire for this freedom "during the Second World War, when [she] is seventeen … and desperately anxious to get away from Manawaka and from [her] grandfather's house" (107). Her sympathy here is so strong, in fact, that she grieves for her father "as though he had died just now" (107). Much of Laurence's work suggests that place, and especially the prairie landscape, is a part of the author herself and the characters of her Manawaka fiction. She also, however, reveals the small town as a place of entrapment. Yet an escape from the small town to go to war, Laurence implies, is not an escape: for the individual, that departure means violence, even death. In addition, for the nation, to go to war is to serve Britain, so the escape represents a return to rather than a departure from the "motherland."

Of all the stories in *A Bird in the House*, the one that most overtly critiques how war can devastate an individual is "Horses of the Night," and it does so with the character of Chris, Vanessa's cousin, who is ultimately mentally destroyed by serving in World War II. Chris is both associated with and separated from the landscape in which he resides. Like Grandfather

Connor, who wears the bear coat and is aligned with "Great Bear Lake," Chris is of the North. For Vanessa, Chris's home is "part of the legendary winter country where no leaves grow and where the breath of seals and polar bears snuffled out steamily and turned to ice" (121). Yet both Chris's and Vanessa's descriptions of the lake near his home reveal a separation from it, even a fear of it. For Chris, "Millions of years ago, before there were any human beings at all, that lake was full of water monsters. All different kinds of dinosaurs" (127). For Vanessa, the lake "existed in some world in which man was not yet born. [She] looked at the grey reaches of it and felt threatened" (138). The lake represents Chris when he experiences a "mental breakdown" (142) after the war, what we would now call post-traumatic stress syndrome. Vanessa describes the lake as "distant, indestructible, totally indifferent" (138). Chris is "indestructible" in the letter he writes to Vanessa from overseas: "they could force his body to march and even to kill, but what they didn't know was that he'd fooled them. He didn't live inside it anymore" (143). Further, just as the lake is "distant" and "indifferent," so too is Chris, who is now "passive," "the animation gone from his face" (142). Thus his departure from Canada to serve in the war paradoxically marks a physical separation from the land and a mental connection back to it. However, that connection is not one of fondness, but rather draws upon the trope of the land as "savage, earthly wilderness" (New, *Land* 22). He is engulfed by the very land he fears. The lake symbolizes the deep chasm or abyss of mental illness into which he falls, like the horses in World War I who fall into the mud (141). At the end of the story, Vanessa describes Chris's troubled mind as "the land he [journeys] through" (144). She says that Chris, like the lake, is "inhabited by terrors, the old monster kings" (144).

War, as it is conceptualized in *A Bird in the House*, reflects Laurence's pacifist beliefs and anticipates her activism for nuclear disarmament in the 1980s, an important aspect of her work. Laurence addressed Canadian involvement in both world wars with the characters of Ewen and Rod (World War I) and Chris and Michael (World War II). She disagreed with Canada's alignment with Britain and Scotland during these wars, and in this way, she critiqued Canada's ongoing practice of British cultural traditions. She suggested that Canada continue to establish its own nation and culture apart from the "motherland." That Chris is associated so strongly with the Canadian prairie landscape shows the prominence of Canada as part of, and deeply affected by, war, even when those wars were not fought on Canadian soil. Both Ewen and Chris are traumatized by these battles: Ewen by the death of his brother, Rod, and Chris by witnessing and engaging in the killing of others. This suggests that Canada must rethink its role in such wars. Laurence challenged her readers to confront and take heed of the traumas and affects of Canadian soldiers at war.

In Robert Duncan's National Film Board of Canada production, *Margaret Laurence: First Lady of Manawaka*, produced in 1978, Laurence explained how war directly influenced her life. During the early 1940s, when Laurence was in high school, she had very few boys in her class: they were all away at war. In the film, Laurence said that she vividly recalled reading the *Winnipeg Free Press* when the casualty lists were released: she knew many of the names on those lists. In *A Bird in the House*, the characters of Chris, in "Horses of the Night," and Michael, in "Jericho's Brick Battlements" seem to be modelled in part after Laurence's boyfriend, Derek, whom she dated when she was in college. In 2004, Laurence's childhood friend, Helen Warkentin, donated the letters Laurence wrote to her in 1945 to the Clara Thomas Archives at York University. These are the earliest letters written by Laurence in the archives. In *A Bird in the House*, Vanessa says that during the Second World War, she "was seventeen and in love with an airman who did not love [her], and desperately anxious to get away from Manawaka and from [her] grandfather's house" (107). In a 1945 letter to Helen Warkentin dated "Monday," Laurence wrote, "You know Helen, I wish now that I'd married Derek before he left. I would be in England now and it would somehow be better." In *A Bird in the House*, Vanessa finds out from her mother that her cousin Chris has had a mental breakdown, due to his experience in the war (142). In a 1945 letter dated "Tuesday," Laurence told Helen that she had heard from Derek's friend Alan that Derek was still alive, "but has had some sort of mental breakdown." Clearly, Laurence incorporated autobiographical elements into *A Bird in the House* and wrote about her experience of war and her boyfriend Derek through the characters of Chris and Michael – Vanessa's soldier boyfriend in the final story in the collection, "Jericho's Brick Battlements," who, unbeknownst to Vanessa until the end of the story, is already married.

Critic Jamie Dopp argues that the small town in Canada "retains a powerful hold on our imaginations precisely because we associate it with a simpler, more innocent time, a time that involves a romanticized version of our own childhood, and we want to believe that we came from that place" (83). The town, then, can be a place of entrapment, that which one wants to leave, but also a place of nostalgia, a place to which one wants to return. Such is the case for Vanessa, who so frequently wants to escape the town and the Brick House, but who longs for Manawaka later in life, and who has difficulty seeing the house in someone else's hands: "But it was their house now, whoever they were, not ours, not mine" (191).

In *A Bird in the House*, Laurence split the narrative voice between Vanessa's childhood and her memories of that childhood; she wrote Vanessa's narrative as a collection of short stories rather than as a novel; and she presented those short stories out of chronological order. I argue that this structural presentation mirrors Canada's national imaginary as unified through fragmentation and diversity. Throughout the 1970s, there was a shift from perceiving Canada as a monolithic nation to perceiving it as a diverse mosaic that should not and could not establish a singular and monolithic identity (Bennett 170). *A Bird in the House*, first published in 1970, anticipated this shift. Vanessa seems to conceptualize white settlers as separate from the land that they inhabit: Timothy Connor brings spruce seeds to the Brick House, and Vanessa notes that these seeds are "not indigenous to that part of the prairies" (11). And yet, Vanessa also makes Timothy Connor indigenous by associating him with the land and with the Haida Indians. Laurence was uncomfortable with any sense of Canada as monolithic, as belonging to the white settlers who claimed it.

In "Time and the Narrative Voice," Laurence said of the narrative voice in *A Bird in the House* that "it is … an expression of the feeling which I strongly hold about time – that the past and the future are both always present, *present* in both senses of the word, always now and always here with us" (156). In her response to her editor about revisions to *A Bird in the House*, Laurence defended this movement back and forth in time through narration. For example, at the end of the title story, Vanessa discovers a letter and photograph of a French woman whom her father, Ewen, had dated during his time at war. In that moment, she feels "as though [her father] had died now" (107). In relation to this part of the story, Laurence wrote to her editor:

> I think this ending should remain, as it pinpoints what Ewen meant, those years before, when he spoke to Vanessa about being away from the town during the war. She did not know, then, what he meant, and now she sees it, years after his death. It <u>has</u> to be like this. In a way, she <u>does</u> grieve as though her father had just died now, because she is for the first time seeing him as an individual not as her father. And it's too late for her to let him know she understands. (William Ready Division of Archives, box 2, file 8, page 3; Laurence's emphases)

Likewise, in response to her editor's query about the structure of "Horses of the Night," Laurence explained: "I <u>do</u> feel strongly that to put this story into a different form, with the younger Vanessa in flashback, would simply be to ruin it. It takes the thread of <u>Chris</u> through all the ages at which Chris's dilemma impinged on Vanessa's life" (William Ready Division of Archives, box 2, file 8, page 4; Laurence's emphases). Moreover, in "Time and the Narrative Voice," Laurence stated that Vanessa's grandfather MacLeod "momentarily lives for his granddaughter" when Vanessa views his collection of Greek tragedies and realizes how lonely he must have been, having no one to discuss them with in a small prairie town (158). In this collection of short stories, then, the fragmented form and structure of the stories and the split narrative voice serve to make the past present. This past is not only Vanessa's individual past, but also her familial and ancestral past, as well as her national and communal past. In a story such as "The Loons," the history that Laurence brings to the present belongs to the Métis people. Vanessa is connected to – though not directly a part of – that history.

If Laurence addressed the notion of a split subject, of negotiating fraught settler-subject identities in *A Bird in the House*, then that notion is particularly prevalent at the end of the book. Vanessa is like her grandfather Connor, who "proclaimed himself in [her] veins" (191). The pioneer, configured as Connor himself, is the "knuckled" (11) farmer who is at one with "his" land. And yet, even as Laurence made Manawaka and the Brick House Vanessa's home, she still contested the legitimacy, the authenticity, of that home. Vanessa associates herself with neither the landscape nor the indigene, and instead maintains a sometimes frustrated, sometimes satisfactory distance from her settler and pioneer ancestors: "darn this old thing [the clothespeg doll]" (21); "the idea of inherited characteristics always seemed odd to me" (36). In the end, it is Vanessa's letting go of order and demarcation that leads to her recognition of identity: "I could not really comprehend these things, but I sensed their strangeness, their disarray" (61). In the final statement of the book, Vanessa says of the "old Connor place," the Brick House: "I looked at it only for a moment, and then I drove away" (191). Paradoxically, Vanessa lets go of a fixed home in order to "come home."

✶ ✶ ✶ ✶ ✶

Both *The Stone Angel* and *A Bird in the House* exemplify how Laurence reimagined Canada, not as a nation that practised only British and French cultural traditions, but, rather, as a nation that was and is heterogeneous, diverse in cultures and backgrounds. Both Hagar Currie-Shipley, in *The Stone Angel*, and Vanessa MacLeod, in *A Bird in the House*, are haunted by their ancestral histories in Canada, histories that involved a denial of the presence of Aboriginal peoples. In these works, Laurence exposed the lie that early Anglo-immigrants were settlers rather than invaders. She also exposed the lie that Canada's history is non-violent: she asks us to remember settler-invader violence toward Aboriginal peoples, and she asks us to remember Canada's involvement in World Wars I and II, the violence that Canadian people suffered there. In these two books, she foregrounded and valued the presence and importance of early immigrants, European and non-European, and their undeniable part in the creation and establishment of Canada itself. The subject positions of Hagar Currie-Shipley and Vanessa MacLeod are essentially divided between their ties to an ancestral past, rooted in Scotland and Ireland, and their varying and dynamic identifications with a new and emerging notion of a multicultural Canada and a Canada that was haunted by and just beginning to acknowledge Aboriginal histories. In the 1960s and 1970s, when Laurence wrote these books, immigration policies were changing in Canada, as the federal government loosened restrictions. While the implications of this historical moment on Laurence's Manawaka series are evident in *The Stone Angel* and *A Bird in the House*, they become even more prominent in *The Diviners*, as I discuss in the next chapter. I hope it is clear by now, though, that Laurence unearthed and unsettled troubling Canadian histories as she described and created changing ideologies of the Canadian nation itself.

Four

Narrating Nation in
The Diviners

The Diviners imagines a Canadian nation that is unified in its diversity, and one that seeks to make reparative gestures between, in Jack McClelland's words, "the two streams of heritage," that of the founding settlers and that of Aboriginal peoples (185). The novel "enacts the desire for a nation that ... reconciles white and Native peoples" (Fagan 251). It posits settlers and their descendants, if uncomfortably, as "at home" in Canada, in the land they choose as their own. As in her writing about Africa, with this novel, Laurence exemplified her stance as a Canadian nationalist. This kind of nationalism manifested in the 1970s and was espoused by her publisher, Jack McClelland, who promoted Canadian literature representative of the diverse regions and cultures of Canada. Laurence situated Canada apart from Britain and worked against the practice of British cultural traditions; yet she also believed that Canada should be a unified nation, held in part by reparation between white settlers and Aboriginal peoples. As I demonstrate in previous chapters, Laurence's writing about Africa and Canada explicitly shows an awareness of the author's and characters' alignment with British and North American values. *The Diviners* implicitly challenges Western values and stable settler subject positions through self-reflexivity and a continual questioning, reworking, and revising of those values.

Laurence was able to challenge Western values in part because she was influenced by the feminist sensibilities of her time when she was working on *The Diviners*. As Roberta Hamilton explains, from the late 1960s

onward, feminists in Canada critiqued the family as an institution, argu-
ing that marriage was "a property relationship in which women gave men
the rights to their bodies, their reproductive capacities, their sexuality, and
their labour" (64). Significantly, *The Diviners* was published in Canada in
1974. At that time, such feminist critiques of the family were familiar to the
Canadian public and to Laurence; the Royal Commission on the Status of
Women in Canada, established by Prime Minister Lester Pearson in 1967,
had recently tabled its landmark report (1970); and women's groups had
created the National Action Committee on the Status of Women (NAC)
(1972) (Hamilton 55). Laurence was involved with the feminist issues of the
time, which is evidenced not only in her Manawaka novels but also in her
participation in organizations such as the Canadian Abortion Rights Action
League (CARAL), women's crisis centres, and other women's groups, such
as the Women's Cultural Centre in Lakefield, Ontario. Her involvement
with these organizations, among others, is well documented in her papers
at the Clara Thomas Archives and Special Collections at York University.

The Diviners is the lengthiest novel in the Manawaka series. It is the
final novel of that series, and, arguably, along with *The Stone Angel*, it is the
most acclaimed of the five books: Laurence won the Governor General's
Award for the novel in 1974. The novel is essentially about the character of
Morag Gunn, and it is written from that character's perspective. It begins
with Morag, a middle-aged woman, looking at the river "that flowed both
ways" (11) outside of her home in rural Ontario and contemplating her life:
her own childhood experiences in a Canadian prairie town, and her present
relationship with her teenage daughter, Pique. The novel moves back and
forth between Morag's past and present, and it delineates that character's
search for herself and her ancestral roots. A large portion of the novel is
dedicated to her relationship with and marriage to her English professor,
Brooke Skelton, a relationship that she experienced in her 20s. Seeing no
way out of her role as literary wife and housewife, she leaves Brooke and
has a child, Pique, with her childhood friend, a Métis, Jules (Skinner) Tonnerre. Morag is ashamed of her roots as a girl from the small prairie town of
Manawaka, and she is ashamed of her status there as the adopted daughter
of the garbage collector, Christie Logan. Yet, despite her attempted connection with England and Scotland through her romantic relationships – first
with the English Brooke Skelton, and, later in her life, with the Scottish
Dan McRaith – Morag ultimately returns to Jules Tonnerre and comes to
the conclusion that the "land of her ancestors" is Canada, "Christie's real
country. Where [she] was born" (415). Morag comes back home, back to
her prairie roots and back to Canada.

When writing *The Diviners*, Laurence was influenced by her previous perceptions of Western imperialism in Africa, and by recent feminist movements in Canada. *The Diviners* clearly draws a parallel between European settlers and their descendants who appropriated land and resources from Aboriginal peoples, and men who appropriated women's "reproductive capacities, ... sexuality, and ... labour" (Hamilton 64). Paradoxically, with this book, Laurence critiqued patriarchy through the institution of the family and specifically through the marital relationship between the characters of Morag Gunn and Brooke Skelton. Yet she constructed the future of the Canadian nation in familial terms through the characters of Morag, her lover Jules, and their daughter Pique. Laurence was a feminist in that she resisted the notion of ownership of women by men; she was also a nationalist, since she imagined a nation that worked to bring Anglo-Scottish and Aboriginal descendants together in the very institution of the family that feminists marked as patriarchal. The Canadian family of Scottish-Métis descent that Laurence constructed, however, was not a traditional one in which the man was the head of the family and the woman domestic housewife. Rather, Morag and Jules maintain independence from one another. After Morag leaves Manawaka, she and Jules come together only four times: Morag stays with Jules when she leaves Brooke; she sees him twice when he visits her and Pique; and she visits him before he dies. Morag has difficulty describing to Pique her and Jules's non-traditional relationship: "I guess you could say love. I find words more difficult to define than I used to. I guess I felt – feel – that he was related to me in some way" (254). Through Jules, it is as if Morag feels a kind of kinship with the Métis nation. Laurence both employed and challenged the traditional notion of the family in order to critique the discourse and practice within which it was embedded.

Canada, Aboriginal Peoples, and Immigration

In order to understand Laurence's divided subjects, it is important to look at emerging multiculturalism in Canada and the related construction of Canada's national imaginary in the early 1970s, when Laurence was writing *The Diviners*. This examination is essential to a study of the novel because Laurence foregrounds the Scottish heritage of the main character of the novel, Morag Gunn, as she contemplated her own Scottish heritage in many of her autobiographical essays and letters. In *The Diviners*, Morag goes to Scotland in search of her personal and genealogical history, and she ultimately discovers that Canada, not Scotland, is her home: "It's a deep land here [in Scotland], all right," Morag says. "But it's not mine, except a long way back. I always thought it was the land of my ancestors, but it is not" (415). Looking at multiculturalism and nationalism in relation to *The Diviners* enables an understanding of how the novel might have played into and helped to shape a new and shifting sense of Canada's national imaginary.

The Diviners may be read not only in terms of Morag's search for her own personal identity, but also in terms of a search, allegorically, for Canada's national identity. As I mention in the introduction to this book, Laurence was writing at the same time that Northrop Frye and Margaret Atwood were taking up questions of Canada's national identity. Alongside mainstream English Canada and other writers in the 1970s, Laurence began to seek an identity for the Canadian nation apart from Britain and British values. One demonstration of Laurence's desire to sever Canada's cultural practices from Britain's is evidenced in her strong responses to the banning of *The Diviners* in some Ontario schools. Laurence quite adamantly fought for the study of Canadian curricula in the Canadian education system. She sought to replace British content with Canadian content in the school system. Regarding the banning of *The Diviners* from schools, Laurence explained in a letter to her friend and writer Adele Wiseman that if the school trustee James Telford won out, she would have to "make a personal statement." Implying that the implementation of Canadian literature in schools was at stake, she stated, "It goes far beyond the question of my book and [Alice Munro's]" (Lennox and Panofsky 351). Laurence's fight for a public voice occurred not only in her works of fiction, but also in her work within politics, humanities and the arts, and her local community.

A solid manifestation of Canada's vision of itself as distinct from Britain is evidenced in the establishment of the Canadian constitution in 1982, an initiative that had been spearheaded by Prime Minister Pierre Trudeau. As I mention in the introduction to this book, Laurence was one of a group of writers and academics from English-speaking Canada who formed the Committee for a New Constitution. Through this committee, Laurence engaged in a critique of constitutional proposals. In a press release dated 23 June 1978, the committee stated that it had "serious reservations about the Trudeau proposals" and suggested changes to them. Specifically, the committee was against the federal government's intention "to adopt a new constitution through an ordinary act of parliament and by consultation at federal-provincial conferences." Instead, it suggested that the new constitution "be drafted by a popularly elected constituent assembly and ratified by referendum" (Clara Thomas Archives, 1980-001/015 [32-1971]).

The committee made the following recommendation with regard to the constituents of the assembly:

> [The assembly] should be structured so as to recognize explicitly the existence of three charter groups in Canada: the English-speaking majority in

the whole country and the English-speaking minority in Quebec (including Canadians of other ethnic origins); the French-speaking majority in
Quebec and the French-speaking minority in the other provinces; and
the native peoples. While regional balance should be assured as well, it is
a serious evasion not to recognize the historic and contemporary reality
of these three groups. (Clara Thomas Archives, 1980-001/015 [32-1971])

That the committee insisted upon an assembly that was made up of the
two founding nations of Canada as well as First Nations reveals the privileged position of those groups – at least in the eyes of the committee – in
determining Canada's national imaginary. While the committee's statement
referred to "Canadians of other ethnic origins," it subordinated those Canadians to a group of English-speaking citizens and mentioned them only
in parenthesis. The three groups of people that the committee desired to
determine Canada's new constitution did not explicitly include newcomers
to the country.

While the "two streams of heritage," or, to use Hugh MacLennan's
phrase, the "two solitudes," were typically thought of in Canada as the English and the French, in *The Diviners*, those two streams were reconfigured
as the English and the Métis – and the Métis, importantly, are of both indigenous and French heritage. Thus the three groups of people that the Committee for a New Constitution desired to make the Canadian constitution
were those same three groups of people that were included within the "two
streams of heritage" of which Jack McClelland spoke in regard to Laurence's
novel. Laurence's vision in *The Diviners* of Canada as a country that brought
together English, French, and indigenous peoples was manifest in a collective statement that sought to change government policy. Her vision of
Canada as set forth in *The Diviners* was therefore aligned with a collective
vision of Canada as set forth by the Committee for a New Constitution.

By determining the "two streams of heritage" as English and Métis
rather than English and French in *The Diviners*, Laurence took a position
that resisted the hegemony of central Canada's "two solitudes" and replaced
those "two solitudes" with Western Canada's "two streams." Laurence foregrounded Aboriginal peoples in her work and situated them as equally
important as the two European founding nations. While she included
Aboriginal people in *The Diviners*, however, Canadian multicultural policy
did not. Smaro Kamboureli asserts that the Canadian Multiculturalism Act
is paradoxically constituted through both the presence of Aboriginal people
and a denial of that presence. The Canadian Multiculturalism Act in its very
form exposes the fact that there are two hegemonic cultures in Canada:
the two side-by-side French and English columns, each translations of the
other, exclude not only immigrant languages, but also the languages of First

Nations. Moreover, the Act explicitly excludes First Nations: in its "Interpretation" section, where it lists institutions that are in charge of implementing the multiculturalism policy, it states that it does not include First Nations institutions. As Kamboureli points out, it is unclear whether these institutions are excluded because First Nations do not fall under the mandate of the Act or whether they are excluded because they deserve separate and distinct treatment. In either case, the presence of First Nations is invoked in the Act at the same time that that presence is denied (Kamboureli 95–100). Ahead of her time, Laurence, both as part of the Committee for a New Constitution and in *The Diviners*, foregrounded rather than denied Aboriginal people in Canada and re-situated the "two solitudes" of central Canada, the English and French, as the "two streams" of Western Canada, the English and the Métis.

Laurence's *The Diviners* takes up not the history of First Nations in Canada, but, more specifically, the history of the Métis in the Red River area of Manitoba. Analyzing the history of Western expansionism in the area, Richard Day explains how the Canadian landscape in the 1800s came to be conflated with Aboriginal peoples. "Driven by visions of the glory of empire," he states, "those who identified with the new Dominion invoked the European dictum of *terra nullius* to construct the space they desired as empty, unstriated, and therefore fair game" (117). Of course, in Canada and elsewhere, the land was not empty but was occupied by First Nations peoples, and so, as Day notes, European colonizers set forth "to remove from the existing bodies their possession of full human subjectivity by setting them up as Others to the colonizer's Self" (118). The Red River settlement that the Métis occupied posed a particular kind of problem for colonizers, since the Métis there were, in the language of the colonialists, "too Savage to be tolerated and too European to be destroyed" (Day 118). Colonizers of the time thus constructed the British "half-breeds" and the French "Métis" as separate races, races that were made out to be inferior to British and Scottish immigrants.

Well before World War II, Canada was a nation of immigrants. However, not all immigrants were equally welcome in the country. As Troper explains, historically, "Canadian immigration policy was as racially selective as it was economically self-serving. Shaped during the 1920s, it reflected the widely held belief that the world's peoples were arranged in a racially drawn hierarchy" (1000). Regulations that barred immigrants from coming to Canada because of race began to loosen in 1948, and in 1967, all barriers to immigration due to race in Canadian policy were finally lifted (Troper 1001). Shortly after immigration law was loosened, official multiculturalism was implemented. When multiculturalism was first introduced by Trudeau in his address to the House of Commons in 1971, it had a direct relationship to the hegemony of the English and French in Canada. It was meant to appease the white ethnic vote, responding to immigrants such as Germans and Ukrainians, who were worried that their cultures would be subsumed into English or French cultures. In 1982, when multiculturalism was first written into the Canadian Charter of Rights, and in 1988, when the official Multiculturalism Act was established, multiculturalism addressed new immigrants coming from the so-called Third World through Canada's "open door" policy.

Laurence's *The Diviners*, then, came at a particularly interesting time in Canadian history. This period was concerned with separating from British cultural traditions and defining Canada as its own nation. Laurence's novel, ultimately, takes up this prominent concern in her own contemporary Canadian culture. Through Morag's relationship with Brooke in *The Diviners*, which can be read as an allegory for Canada's relationship with Britain, Laurence commented on Canada's need to break away from that imperial power. She exemplified a genuine humanitarian concern for the peoples of Canada, and specifically for Aboriginal peoples. She ultimately attempted to reach cross-cultural understanding in the coming together of the peoples of Canada and in the making of a multicultural Canadian nation.

Morag Gunn and Brooke Skelton: An Allegory for the Canadian Nation

Laurence suggested that Canada break from Britain and the practice of British cultural traditions through the characters of Morag Gunn and Brooke Skelton in *The Diviners*. Brooke, who is Morag's English professor at the University of Manitoba and eventually becomes her lover and husband, is of English descent but grew up in India, where his father was the headmaster of a boy's school (210). That Brooke grew up in a colonial family – where his father taught English values to Indian boys – suggests that he is aligned with English imperialism. Brooke is also named after two English poets, Rupert Brooke and John Skelton. Rupert Brooke was an English poet who was born in 1887 and died in 1915, early in World War I ("Brooke"). John Skelton was a London poet who was born around 1460 and died in 1529. He was a "Tudor poet and satirist of both political and religious subjects" ("Skelton"). Brooke's name suggests not only his English background, but also that he is aligned with and to some extent even represents the English literary canon. Morag represents a contestation of Brooke's alignment with English imperialism and the English literary canon for which he stands. When Brooke states that the passing of the British Raj in India "wasn't the answer" (235), for instance, she challenges his view: "But Brooke – surely you can't believe it was right for them, the British, even for you, to have lived there like that, in that way, house and servants, while – " (235). Likewise, Morag challenges the authority of the English canon by writing her own literature. Through her friend Ella's mother, Mrs. Gerson, who introduces her to Dostoevsky, Tolstoy, and other non-English writers, she comes to realize "that English is not the only literature" (203).

Just as Morag challenges the English literary canon, so too did Laurence in the writing of *The Diviners*. As Barbara Godard explains, with Morag's departure from the English Brooke Skelton and her engagement in a relationship with the Métis Jules Tonnerre, *The Diviners* invokes and revises William Shakespeare's *The Tempest*, positing Miranda as the lover of Caliban (55–62). In so doing, Laurence challenges the values implicit within an English canonical text. Laurence fought for the promotion of Canadian literature and the study of Canadian rather than solely English literature at the secondary and post-secondary levels. In a CBC interview in 1985 about a movement to ban her books from schools, she argued for the inclusion of Canadian literature in school curricula: "If our children are to have access in high schools as well as at the university level to some Canadian literature – serious novels and poems and so on – then we must speak out [against the banning of such books]" (McDonald). Morag's challenge to both the British Raj and the dominance of the English literary canon in Canada mirrors Laurence's challenge to British culture and her demand to recognize Canadian literature in Canada. As Troper has noted, after World War II, Canada began to search for a national identity and distinguish itself culturally from Britain. Creating and defining a Canadian literary canon, rather than a British one, was indeed a part of that search.

If, as Anne McClintock asserts in *Imperial Leather*, Western patriarchal narratives depict colonized countries as empty, and if, as she also argues, "the myth of the virgin land is also the myth of the empty land" (30), then the relationship between Morag and Brooke is an allegorical one: it represents the relationship between a colonized and a colonizing country. In *This Side Jordan*, as I discuss in chapter 1, the English character, Johnnie, views the African prostitute, Emerald, as a "virgin" who is "expressionless" and "blank" (*This Side* 231). Similarly, in "The Rain Child," the African child Ayesha has a mysterious or "empty" past, with no known language or home (*Tomorrow-Tamer* 114). Not surprisingly, then, in *The Diviners*, Brooke, following the discourse of such Western patriarchal narratives, construes Morag as a virgin (216) and determines that she has no history: when Morag asks, "What do you *like* about me?" Brooke replies, "Perhaps it's your mysterious nonexistent past" (212). In McClintock's discussion of H. Rider Haggard's map in *King Solomon's Mines* (1885), the "empty" land of the treasure map that is to be penetrated is also the body of a woman; in Brooke's assessment of Morag, likewise, Morag's "mysterious nonexistent past" might be likened to the "empty" land of the colonized. Moreover, Brooke's paternalistic attitude toward Morag ("My dearest love, you're very young" [215]) and his unwillingness to have a child with her, perhaps because he treats her like a child himself, is also the colonizer's attitude toward the colonized. As in "The Drummer of All the World," where Matthew's missionary father treats Africans as children, here, Brooke treats his wife as a child. Brooke's attitude toward Morag is at once the attitude of the patriarch toward his woman and the imperialist toward his subject.

To conflate the "empty land" with the "virgin body," and to suggest that foreign lands and women's bodies await discovery and penetration, is to define women and the colonized as material, the colonizer and men as spiritual. The colonizer and men, that is, bring "spirit" to that which passively awaits them, "matter." The word "matter" can be traced to a "set of etymologies which link matter with *mater* and *matrix* (or the womb)" (Butler 31). In *The Diviners*, Brooke defines Morag as a kind of empty but material land, passive, blank, without history. Ashamed of her past, Morag concedes to such a representation of herself. She wants to tell Brooke that "the state of original grace ended a long time ago" (213), but she does not. That "state of original grace" implicitly refers both to Morag's virginity and to the Western construction of colonized countries as pristine and untouched, like the Garden of Eden. Brooke assumes that Morag is a virgin, but because she is ashamed, Morag does not correct him (216). When Brooke first asks Morag where she comes from, she says, "'Oh – nowhere, really. A small town.... I don't have any family, actually. I was brought up by – ' By no one" (209–10). In *Decolonising Fictions*, Diana Brydon and Helen Tiffin state that "Both patriarchy and imperialism mask their aggression through language that ... infantilizes ... and that succeeds in making the colonized feel guilty for wishing to reject such 'love'" (102). In *The Diviners*, Morag plays into Brooke's infantilizing language as Brooke constructs her as an innocent child and a material, virginal body that is nevertheless void of history.

However, while Morag adheres to Brooke's construction of her, Laurence contests that construction. Laurence works within Western and patriarchal constructions of the colonized and women in order to challenge those very configurations. When Morag tells Brooke that she knows that child abuse happens, Brooke responds in a condescending and infantilizing way: "You know in theory, ... but you don't really know. My dearest love, you're very young" (215). Morag does not challenge Brooke, but Laurence reveals Morag's inward thoughts to the contrary: "She knows more than theory, about some things. Vernon Winkler, as a small boy, being beaten by Gus.

Eva crying in the dancehall" (215). Likewise, as we have seen, Morag does not correct Brooke's conception of her as a virgin, but Laurence challenges that view by revealing that "the state of original grace ended a long time ago" (213). Most interestingly, Morag states of her husband, "*I will never let him see the Black Celt in me*" (246). The phrase that Morag uses to describe herself here – "*the Black Celt*" – not only refers to her temperament, but also subtly suggests an alignment with "blacks" who have been colonized. Implicitly referring to the notion of the "Celtic savage," Morag posits herself as subordinate in both race and gender to the English colonizer.

McClintock explains that the English stereotyped the Celt as "a simianized and degenerate race" (52). She also notes that "English racism ... drew deeply on the notion of the *domestic* barbarism of the Irish as a marker of racial difference" (53). In *How the Irish Became White*, Noel Ignatiev explains that in nineteenth-century America, during Irish immigration there, the Irish were known as "white Negroes" and blacks were referred to as "smoked Irish" (101). Such references indicate that Britain and America constructed the Celt, historically, in racial terms. Although Morag and Laurence have Scottish rather than Irish ancestry, notions of the "Celtic savage" and the "Black Irish," especially in relation to Morag's identity as "Morag Dhu," are certainly implicit in *The Diviners*: Morag's Scottish lover, Dan McRaith, repeatedly refers to her as "Morag Dhu," black Morag (407, 412, 415). After Morag's adopted father, Christie Logan, dies, Morag finds among his belongings a book entitled *The Clans and Tartans of Scotland*. She looks in the glossary for the Gaelic word for black, and notes that "it says *dubh, dhubh, dhuibh, duibhe, dubha*, but omits to say under what circumstances each of these should be used" (427). "Morag Dhu," Morag muses. "Ambiguity is everywhere" (427). The "ambiguity" to which Morag refers is that which aligns her, at once, with the Black Celt and the Métis. Morag, that is, is here associated with Métis who were dispossessed as well as those immigrants of the British Isles who did that dispossessing.

When Morag is with the English Brooke Skelton, she refuses to let him "*see the Black Celt in [her]*" (246), denying her Scottish heritage and also her past, of which she is ashamed, as the adopted daughter of Christie Logan. When Morag is with the Scottish Dan McRaith, by contrast, she embraces her identity as "Morag Dhu." Her acceptance of this identity allows her to acknowledge rather than deny her Scottish heritage as well as her childhood past in Manawaka. But the term "Black Irish," as Ignatiev explains, was not only a phrase that was used to racialize the Irish. It was also a term used by the Catholic Irish to describe Protestants of Ireland who historically supported the British rule of Ulster (102). The term is a particularly ambiguous one, then, since it quite explicitly aligns Morag with those Celtic

Protestants who were with the British imperialists. Morag's and Laurence's ancestry as Scots-Presbyterian suggests that the histories of the character and the author alike are caught up in an alignment with the British.

In "(Grand)mothering 'Children of the Apocalypse': A Post-postmodern Ecopoetic Reading of Margaret Laurence's *The Diviners*," Di Brandt interprets "Morag Dhu" as Morag's dark moods, and argues that "the rising up of Morag Dhu, the 'Black Celt' in her," is an accurate and honest response to Laurence's and Morag's contemporary world (258). At such moments, Brandt explains, Morag contemplates the world's "spiritual impoverishment and the spectre of hard times ahead for her daughter and the generations to come (if indeed there will be a world for them at all)" (258). "Morag Dhu" comes to represent the "Black Celt," Morag's sense of darkness and despair, and both Morag's and the nation's sometimes dark and shameful history: that which Brooke misnames as Morag's "mysterious nonexistent past" (227). Despite Morag's deep understanding of the darker aspects of humanity, that which surfaces in "Morag Dhu," I would argue that both Morag and Laurence maintain a sense of hope. To understand Morag's despair in the world as definitive would be, as Brandt puts it, "to take Brooke's side in his argument with Morag" (262) that Morag and Brooke should not have a child because it is not the kind of world into which to bring a child (259). In an interview presented in the National Film Board production *Margaret Laurence: First Lady of Manawaka*, Laurence said, "Writers who maintain that they are totally in despair – I don't think they are, because … the reaction to total despair would be silence." This statement clearly suggests that Laurence maintained hope despite her clear understanding of the problems in the world, problems such as conflict between and among nations, racism and discrimination, and environmental concerns. Her awareness and activism regarding such problems are evident in her letters and her public stance against nuclear energy and war, in her support for the Public Petroleum Association of Canada (an environmentalist group), and in her affiliation with various women's groups.

Theorists have discussed how, in various historical contexts, the colonizer has felt desire, even love, toward the colonized. Brydon and Tiffin, for example, have suggested that both imperialism and patriarchy express a kind of "love" toward the colonized and women. According to post-colonial and psychoanalytic theories, this "love" is ultimately a narcissistic one. Homi Bhabha revises Freud's notion of the fetish and argues that the colonizer desires the colonized as his fetish object (74). Bhabha takes Freud's notion of the fetish from psychoanalysis back into the realm of colonial history. Freud disavows woman's sexual difference by positing her as one who is the same as man and yet not quite complete. In the same way, Bhabha suggests, imperial discourse disavows racial difference by positing colonized men as those who are the same as the colonizers and yet not quite complete because they are not European men (74–75). Both men and colonizers "love" that which is like them. Through women and the colonized, men and colonizers can see and "love" themselves. Within this discursive framework, men and colonizers posit women and the colonized as Others who make them whole.

Edward Said explains that the West feels desire for the Orient, perceiving it with "shivers of delight in – or fear of – novelty" (59). In both Bhabha's and Said's theories, the colonizer constructs the colonized as that which is familiar – woman and colonized as the same as man and colonizer, but not quite complete – in order to manage desire for the colonized. It is not surprising, then, that Laurence's allegory of the relationship between a colonizing and a colonized country is configured in the romantic relationship between a man and a woman. Just as the colonizer constructs the colonized, his object of desire, as familiar, so Brooke also constructs Morag, his object of desire, as that which is familiar – through tropes that depict both the colonized and women as passive, empty of history, and innocent. Allegorically, Morag's rejection of Brooke is Canada's rejection of Britain as that which makes it whole. Instead, Morag – and, implicitly, Canada – looks within, to herself and her own nation. Morag says of Jules Tonnere, "I guess I felt – feel – that he was related to me in some way" (254). Laurence posits Canada, rather than Britain, as the new centre. She foregrounds, re-situates, and re-figures, that is, the central and important historical and contemporary relation as that of the settler-descendant and the Aboriginal person, rather than the British or French and the Canadian settler-descendant.

Morag's departure from Brooke signifies a departure of Canada and Canadian literature from England and the English literary canon. As Gunilla Florby puts it, "Morag – the Canadian artist – must break loose from the shifting domination of English letters and write out of her own culture" (206). That the publication of Morag's first book instigates her departure from Brooke suggests that the book's conception is at once the conception of Morag as her own woman and the conception of Canadian literature apart from British cultural traditions. When the process of revising the novel is complete, Morag is "filled with the knowledge that this part of herself is really there" (280). Morag's publication of the book in her own name, and her final act in the novel, which is "to set down the title" (477) of her latest book, symbolically suggest that women and Canada have come into their own and can produce valuable literature. In "Where the World Began," an essay in her collection *Heart of a Stranger*, Laurence states, "We have only just begun to recognize our legends and to give shape to our myths"

(172). In *The Diviners*, Morag's departure from Brooke is the moment when she begins to value and give voice to herself, her abilities, and her myths.

Himani Bannerji argues that Canada's national imaginary is constituted, in part, upon a threat from outside itself. Always in danger of being subsumed and incorporated into an imperial power such as the United States or Britain, the argument goes, Canadians must identify and distinguish themselves apart from those imperial powers (80). Similarly, Eva Mackey states that "a constant theme in debates about Canadian identity ... is the notion that Canada is marginal to and victimized by various forms of colonialism, most recently American cultural imperialism" (9). In "Where the World Began," Laurence herself says that Canadians have lived "under the huge shadows of those two dominating figures, Uncle Sam and Britannia" (*Heart* 172).

Morag's departure from Brooke signifies both a woman's departure from a dominating man and Canada's departure from that dominating figure of "Britannia." Morag's inner response to Brooke's accusation that she is hysterical – "*I do not know the sound of my own voice. Not yet, anyhow*" (277) – refers not only to her voice as a woman within the institution of patriarchy, but also to the voice of Canada under the influence of Britain. Women and Canada, Laurence implies, must come to know "the sound of [their] own voice." Morag's realization that Brooke "has believed he owns her" (299) is the knowledge that, within the context of patriarchy and imperialism, men might believe that they own women just as imperialists might believe they own their subjects.

Such feminist implications in *The Diviners* are underscored by the fact that Laurence wrote the novel during the formation of the National Action Committee on the Status of Women (NAC) (1971), whose "goal was equality of opportunity for women" outside of the home and outside of the traditional marital and familial relations (Hamilton 55). Laurence also wrote the novel during a time of heightened Canadian nationalism. This nationalism is evident in the establishment of the Royal Commission on Bilingualism and Biculturalism ("the B & B Commission") (1969) and the introduction to state-implemented multiculturalism (1971), both of which began to imagine Canada in terms of diversity and multiculturalism rather than in terms of its relationship with Britain. Morag's departure from Brooke in *The Diviners* – especially when one notes that she moves directly from a romantic relationship with Brooke to a romantic relationship with her old schoolmate, Jules Tonnerre – allegorically signifies Canada's departure from "Britannia" and its turn toward an identification with the Aboriginal peoples of its own land. Canadian nationalism, for Laurence, is linked to an identification with Aboriginal peoples. At a time when Canada was distinguishing itself from Britain and would soon establish its own constitution to replace the BNA Act, Laurence imagined a reconciliation between white settlers and Aboriginal peoples.

This is not to say, however, that Laurence makes Morag indigenous to the land she inhabits. In this regard, I agree with Di Brandt: to say that Laurence's re-situating of Canada rather than Britain as central constructs Morag as indigenous is to "conflate racial identification and ethical cultural and land practices in simplistic and essentialist ways" (261). That Laurence does not conflate Morag's identity with an indigenous one is also evident in her treatment of the characters of Jules and Pique Tonnerre, a topic to which I will return later. Neil ten Kortenaar argues that nation is often established on the same foundations as empire: "anti-imperialism creates new centres where once there had been only margins" (11). In *Imagined Communities*, Benedict Anderson argues that the idea of the nation is based on a bringing together of a large, anonymous group and positing them as a community. According to Pierre Trudeau's multiculturalism, "acceptable cultural diversity must buttress the project of nation-building and national unity in Canada" (Mackey 66). *The Diviners* imagines Canadian unity on the basis of diversity, thus establishing a new centre in the bringing together of Canadians in the nation of Canada.

Catharine Parr Traill: British Settler-Subject and Canadian Woman

One of the ways in which Laurence contributed to a new vision of Canadian nationalism was through Morag's imagined relationship with the historical pioneer-settler, Catharine Parr Traill. Sister to fellow pioneer and writer Susanna Moodie, Traill emigrated from England to Canada in 1834, "faced disasters and family trials" in Canada, and wrote, among others, a book for Canadian settlers entitled *The Backwoods of Canada* (1836) (Gray x–2). In *The Diviners*, Morag invokes Traill as a spiritual ancestor and muse figure. Her choice of muse is apt, since Traill's book was essentially a handbook for future women settlers in Canada. As Sugars and Moss explain, Traill was "the author of some of the most practical, well-grounded, rational advice of any settler writer" (193). Morag situates herself alongside yet apart from an early and important Canadian feminist, pioneer, and writer.

Morag's invocation of Catharine Parr Traill as her muse figure enacts Anna Johnston and Alan Lawson's theory, in "Settler Colonies," that Canadian settlers and their descendants desired to be indigenous to the Canadian land they inhabit. Johnston and Lawson explain that settlers mimicked the country from which they were displaced, and yet, they could never quite mimic that culture exactly. Thus they created for themselves an indigenous identity. Such constructed indigenous Canadian identities, the authors assert, appear in idealized figures such as the Mountie, the pioneer, and the woodsman. If, as Johnston and Lawson explain, this "indigenization" of the settler effaced the presence of First Nations peoples and the violent history of the settlers' invasion of Canada, then one might argue that Morag's act of aligning herself with the pioneer Catharine Parr Traill in *The Diviners* establishes and secures Morag's Anglo-Canadian identity. But Morag does not disavow the indigene or usurp an indigenous identity. The complex, nuanced, and uneasy relations between Morag, Jules Tonnere, and their daughter, Pique, challenge that view. Furthermore, Morag's alignment with Traill is troubled, since she feels only an uneasy identification with her. More often than not, she feels inadequate in comparison to what she imagines to be Traill's expertise in gardening and domestic duties. Therefore, Morag's alignment with Traill and with Jules Tonnerre and Pique exemplifies a split subject position, a position divided between the old world and the new, England and Canada. This subject position, as we have seen, is prevalent in many of the settler-descendant protagonists in Laurence's work.

Imagining Catharine Parr Traill's plight and addressing her spirit, Morag states, "at least you wouldn't starve during the winter. You'd pick blueberries or something. Start a jam factory. Make pemmican out of the swayback which dropped dead of exhaustion on the Back Forty" (109–10). Traill's "Canadianness," it would seem, is grounded in her survival in the backwoods of Canada. Laurence creates Morag's character as one which identifies with and against this pioneer ancestor. That identity invokes both the idea that British settlers and their descendants were at one with the land they settled and the idea that it was this very oneness with the harsh northern Canadian landscape that made them distinct from "Uncle Sam," a presence, as Laurence asserts, "under the shadow" of which Canadians have lived for so long (*Heart* 172).

The invocation of Traill therefore allows Laurence to accommodate what Himani Bannerji argues were the two threats upon which Canada's national imaginary was based. On the one hand, Bannerji argues, Canada's national imaginary was constituted upon the idea of survival: *The Diviners* foregrounds Morag's perception of Traill's will to survive. Bannerji's view adheres to and perhaps draws from Margaret Atwood's argument, in her book *Survival*, that such was the prominent theme in Canadian literature to the 1960s. Threatened from within its own borders, the argument goes, early Canadians needed to endure the vast wilderness of Canada, perceived and interpreted as dangerous and empty. On the other hand, Canada's national imaginary was also constituted upon a threat from outside itself, a threat of being subsumed and incorporated into the United States. While the early settler's notion of being threatened from within Canada itself denied and ignored the presence of Aboriginal peoples, conflating them with the dangerous and threatening land they inhabited, the notion of being threatened from without, by U.S. powers, denied Canada's own imperial history and impetus. Canada's national imaginary emerged as it denied the presence of Aboriginal peoples and forgot its own history as an invader-settler colony.

By contrast, Laurence emphasized the difficult relationships between her settler-descendant characters and her Métis ones and exemplified instances of ongoing racism in Canada. She did not deny but rather exposed Canada's imperial history. She also demonstrated how this history, in the form of oppression and racism, was ongoing. For example, after Morag gives birth to Pique, her landlady, Maggie Tefler, upon seeing the child, immediately speaks a racist comment: "Did you get yourself mixed up with a Chinese or a Jap, dear? No? Well, I wasn't going to say halfbreed – I didn't think it *possible*. What's that? *Maytee?* I never heard *that* word. They're all halfbreeds to me, and I could tell you a thing or two, you betcha" (329). Such instances recur throughout the novel, indicating that Laurence sought to undo the notion that Canada's racist past is over. By exposing rather than denying moments of racism in Canada and by distinguishing Canada from the United States and acknowledging that Canada has a colonist history itself, Laurence enacts what she tells Graeme Gibson is the responsibility of any writer: "to try and tell as much of your own truth as you can bear to tell" (Gibson 190).

It is significant that Morag aligns herself with a historical figure who is not only a Canadian pioneer but also a woman. Interestingly, Morag calls on Traill as her muse at moments when she worries about her daughter, Pique, invoking her spiritual ancestor as a fellow Canadian and as a mother (107–10, 186–87, 374). In the context of Morag's invocation of Traill, then, that spiritual ancestor might be thought of as a mother to the Canadian nation. First-wave British feminists, according to Antoinette Burton in *Burdens of History*, constructed the notion of British motherhood as an imperial duty to aid Indian and African women. Such feminists spoke to the fear of degeneration by promising to maintain, preserve, and mother the white race. In the same way, some white Canadian feminists perceived themselves as superior to immigrants and attained the vote at the expense of Aboriginal peoples. Not only did Canadian suffragists pit themselves against non-English-speaking immigrants, securing "safe votes" for their male counterparts, but they also attained the vote between 1916 and 1922, well before Aboriginal peoples attained it in 1960.

Laurence revised and critiqued the notion that to mother the nation was to reproduce whiteness. Through the figure of Morag's Scots-Métis daughter, Pique, Laurence suggests that a child can legitimately be born outside of marriage and across race. She also suggests that a child can be raised legitimately without a father. Allegorically, she implies that a nation can be born without an imperial father – without the figure of Brooke Skelton, without England. Paradoxically, Laurence's novel situates Canada as apart from Britain even as it situates England's influence as integral to the forming of the nation. This positioning of Canada in relation to England is particularly relevant during a time when Canada was determining its own national imaginary apart from Britain. Morag – as the mother of a mixed-race child – symbolically gives birth to a new kind of nation, one that rejects imperial parenthood and situates the future of Canada in the possibility of confronting the conflicts between white settler-descendants and Aboriginal peoples.

Although Morag invokes Traill as a muse figure, she ultimately abandons her: "So farewell, sweet saint – henceforth, I summon you not" (431). As Christian Bök explains, *The Diviners* "argues that women who can be their own muse upset the phallocentric distribution of creative authority" (91). Laurence draws upon the notion of the muse figure, a figure that is traditionally embedded within the English literary canon. Laurence therefore "upset[s] the phallocentric distribution of creative authority" (Bök 91) not only by ultimately being her own muse figure but also by revising that very notion, by creating a muse figure for a female, rather than a male, writer. That Morag leaves Traill as she leaves Brooke Skelton earlier in the novel suggests that Morag becomes her own independent woman and is no longer defined by the system of patriarchy. Catharine Parr Traill, unlike Brooke Skelton, is not a patriarchal figure. As Bök implies, however, Morag's abandonment of her is nevertheless an abandonment of patriarchy, since, historically, the invocation of a muse for creative inspiration is a male tradition. By leaving Traill as her source of inspiration, Morag comes into her own as a woman and as a Canadian writer.

Karin E. Beeler states that "[Morag's] resistance to … Catharine Parr Traill functions as a … rejection of the authorities of colonialism" (31). Morag is implicitly aligned with the intertwining discourses of imperialism and first-wave feminism when she associates herself with Traill, and yet, she works against those very discourses when she ultimately outgrows her need for her. Furthermore, most of her inner discussions of and with Traill are preceded by contemplations of the Connor family, a family who lived in the pioneer house that Morag owns on McConnell's Landing. Catharine Parr Traill represents an ideal to which Morag unsuccessfully aspires – she often comments on Traill's perceived domestic faultlessness and compares her own "sloth" to Traill's productivity (108). Conversely, the Connor family, at least in Morag's imagination, is plagued by hardship and strife (106). Laurence's juxtaposition of these two "pioneer" stories challenges romanticized and idealized representations of settlers such as Traill and replaces them with stories, such as Sarah Connor's, that are about death in childbirth, madness, and despair (106–7). Laurence upset the national ideal of motherhood and domesticity. She maintained that settler women suffered, and she refused to take the ways in which women were represented as given.

We might read Laurence's inclusion of Catharine Parr Traill in *The Diviners* as gothic, and the novel itself as an example of Canadian Gothic Literature. Traill enters the novel as a ghost or spirit, and therefore haunts *The Diviners* just as Britain's and Canada's troublesome, colonial past haunts the Canadian nation itself. Justin D. Edwards argues that, in Canada, "stories of the past, stories that tell us who we are, tend to be haunted by a panic that the shared narrative might be an elaborate artifice, a social imaginary" (xiii). In Laurence's book, while Traill is invoked as the ghost of the past that haunts Morag's present, that ghost is revealed, at least in part, to be a fiction, an ideal that the imagined history of Sarah Connor exposes. Laurence's invocation of the ghost of Traill in *The Diviners* parallels Margaret Atwood's invocation of the ghost of Susanna Moodie, Catharine Parr Traill's sister, in *The Journals of Susanna Moodie*, a collection of poems that Atwood first published in 1970. That these two Canadian women writers returned to such pioneer women in their writing suggests a need to understand and correct a national history. If, as Edwards argues, "Canada is an in-between space. Caught between colonization and post-colonization" (xiv), then that "in-between" is represented by the figure of Traill's ghost in *The Diviners*. Neither fully in the present nor in the past, Traill haunts Morag's subjectivity until Morag can come into her own and put her history, both national and personal, to rest. Cynthia Sugars and Gerry Turcotte suggest that, in works of Canadian Gothic Literature, "there is an aura of unresolved and unbroachable 'guilt,' as though the colonial/historical foundations of the nation have not been thoroughly assimilated" (ix). This is certainly the case in Laurence's final novel: Morag's subject position is not secure but is shaken by her ancestor's settler-invader history. Exposing the fiction that the British were settlers rather than invaders, Morag remains "unsettled" throughout the book. Nor is she comfortable assuming a home, for which she searches throughout the novel. Instead, she comes to realize that "if she is to have a home, she must create it" (313).

Challenging Official Canadian Narratives:
Settlers of the British Isles and the Métis

Laurence wrote about the similarities between the nationalist Somaliland leader, the Sayyid, and the Métis leader, Louis Riel (*Heart* 31–57). She also drew a connection between the plight of the Scots during the Highland clearances and the plight of the Métis during the Riel Rebellions. In *The Diviners*, Laurence linked the histories of the Scottish and Métis peoples, but not by reinforcing what Eva Mackey calls "the Benevolent Mountie Myth," the placement of "a representative of the state and a representative of minority culture – colonizer and colonized – in a friendly, peaceful [collaboration]" (1). Rather, she reiterated how, as she stated in a CBC radio interview with Robert Fulford soon after the book was published, "the fate of these two peoples was interwoven and bounded together." Laurence brought forth this "interwoven and bounded" fate in the stories she relayed about each group of people throughout the course of the novel. While the novel presents various histories of the English, Scottish, and Métis battles in Canadian history, it does not present any of them as definitive. Instead, it juxtaposes various versions of the stories, giving none of them precedence over the others. When Morag finally goes to Scotland to visit her lover Dan McRaith and the land of her ancestors, she comes to the conclusion that "the myths are my reality. Something like that" (415). As Paul Hjartarson puts it, "Morag Gunn appears, on the one hand, to shape and give meaning to the life story she tells, and, on the other, to be entirely shaped, to be herself composed by the stories told" (43). The same could be said, we might note, of the nation of Canada itself, that Morag gives shape and meaning to histories of the nation as the nation itself comes into being by those very histories. The "myths" are "the reality" that make both Morag and Canada.

The Diviners works within and against the Scottish and Métis stories in order to demonstrate that they share a history of dispossession by the English and that the Scottish were problematically implicated in the dispossession of Métis peoples. During Morag's childhood and indeed throughout her life, Christie tells her stories about her Scottish ancestors. Christie's stories give Morag a sense of belonging in Canada as a Scottish descendent, since Christie creates for Morag an imaginary ancestor in Piper Gunn, an ancestor, as Morag later explains, who is based on the historical figure of "young Archie" McDonald (443). Archibald McDonald was born in Scotland and came to Red River in 1813. He became deputy governor of the Red River settlement, and, after the Red River Rebellion, he worked for the Hudson Bay Company and came to be chief in charge of Fort Langley (Woodcock 53). Christie's stories show how early Scottish immigrants were dispossessed from their own land by British colonialists. Referring to the 1746 Battle of Culloden, Christie explains that it marked the end of the Highland clan culture: "the clans stood together for the last time, and the clans were broken by the Sassenach cannons and the damned bloody rifles of the redcoat swine" (57). This dispossession is particularly meaningful to Morag, for, as Neil ten Kortenaar explains, "The ostracism Morag suffers because she is related to Christie the scavenger is related metonymically to the dispossession of the Highland clearances, and so becomes meaning-ful" (15). Laurence, however, through Morag, challenges Christie's glori-fication of the Scottish in relation to the Métis. When Morag asks, of the Métis, "Were they bad?" Christie "repeats the word as though he is trying to think what it means. 'No,' he says at last. 'They weren't bad. They were – just there'" (97). Christie's story regarding the dispossession of the Scot-tish at the Battle of Culloden demonstrates how the Scots and Métis people share a history of dispossession; his story regarding the Scots-Métis battle at Red River, and Morag's intervention in that story, conversely, show how the Scottish and the English share a history of dispossessing. Thus, through these stories, Laurence exemplifies Morag's divided subject position. As a Scottish descendent in Canada, Morag is aligned both with and against colonial histories.

Just as Laurence challenges and revises Christie's stories in order to show that the Scottish were dispossessed themselves and also dispossessed others, so she challenges official English-Canadian histories that con-structed Louis Riel, the Métis leader at Red River, from an English perspec-tive. Christie tells Morag stories about her Scottish ancestors, and, likewise, Jules Tonnerre's father, Lazarus, tells Jules stories about his Métis ances-tors. When Jules tells Morag Lazarus's story about Rider Tonnerre and the Prophet, Morag recognizes the Prophet from history class, and points out that he is Louis Riel. Jules's response indicates that his understanding of Riel opposes that of the history books: "Sure. But the books, they lie about him. I don't say Lazarus told the story the way it happened, but neither did the books and they're one hell of a sight worse because they made out that the guy was nuts" (161–62). By challenging the way in which Riel was constructed in official narratives, however, Laurence does not imply that Lazarus's and Jules's versions of the story are definitive. Morag says of Riel, for example, "I thought he was supposed to be a very short guy" and Jules responds, "No, very tall" (162). Laurence here juxtaposes the English and Métis versions of Riel as diminutive or glorified in order to demystify them and foreground the idea that there is no singular truth to the stories, but rather, versions and perspectives. As Morag herself puts it when she sees that the newspapers reporting about Dieppe are "full of stories of bravery, courage, camaraderie," "What is a true story? Is there any such thing?" (159).

Richard Day discusses how particular Canadian texts, especially those created for schools, efface the brutal history of the Canadian state (29). Laurence works against this effacement by setting the tales in *The Diviners* against official histories. By juxtaposing various stories regarding Scottish and Métis histories in Canada, she ultimately challenges any one version, thus working against the dominant representations of Others.

Referring to the beginning of *The Diviners*, when Morag studies photographs of her childhood, Nora Foster Stovel states that "Morag *reads* herself into the *Snapshots* ..., interpreting her unseen presence hidden behind the body of her dead mother, where she is 'buried alive, the first burial'" (*Divining* 106). The impending birth of Morag as a woman and a writer parallels the impending birth of Canada as a nation. The "dead mother" from whom Morag is severed, the novel implies, is also Britain, the "motherland" from which Canada must separate in order to be born. If, as Gunilla Florby asserts, Canadians are indeed severed from their collective histories (23), then Morag's position as an orphan parallels Canada's position as disengaged both from Britain and its own history in relation to Aboriginal peoples. Through the course of the novel, Morag rectifies her own position as an orphan, and metaphorically, Canada's position as such, by learning to divine personal and national meaning. Just as she divines personal meaning from the snapshots she reads, so she divines national meaning through the tales of Christie Logan and Lazarus and Jules Tonnerre. Just as she – through Christie – imagines her father's role in World War I in order to accommodate his seeming absence in the photograph of the Canadian Field Artillery (100–3), so she imagines the historical figure of Piper Gunn in response to the absence of her family name – Clan Gunn – in Christie's book on the Clans of Scotland (58–61). The stories that fill in the absences of Morag's and Canada's past are neither fact nor fiction, but both intertwined. Christie's story about Morag's father saving him during the war is later revealed by Prin to be a fiction (223–24). Prin says to Morag, "That Colin.... He never done that for my Christie. Saved him, like. Or maybe he done it. I dunno. He was a boy, just a boy, and that scared. Poor lamb" (224). As I have mentioned previously, Piper Gunn is actually based on the Canadian historical figure of Archibald McDonald, although he is a fictional ancestor of Morag's (443). For Morag's sake, Christie glorifies Morag's father's role in the war; Laurence, however, works against such glorification by revealing, through Prin, its possible fabrication. Laurence thus challenges histories, official or otherwise, that efface cultural domination as it is manifested in war. Ultimately, in *The Diviners*, Morag and Canada move from being orphaned from their histories to being reconnected with them by picking up the pieces of history – scavenging, divining, inventing, and creating.

Morag, the Tonnerre Family, and the Canadian Landscape

Eva Mackey makes the following statement regarding Canada's relation to First Nations peoples:

> Historically, in colonial discourse, links have been made between Native peoples and a purer state of nature.... Aboriginal peoples become equated with land and nature. They represent harmony between humans and nature, and the untouched and virgin natural land that comes to represent Canada's beginnings. Their presence constructs a historical connection to the land that helps make Canada a "Native land" to settlers and immigrants. (45, 77)

Laurence connects her Métis character, Pique Tonnerre, with nature. In the song that Pique writes, for instance, Pique says that "the mountain and the valley hold my name" (490). Unlike Morag, who, as a descendant of white settlers, is "native" to Canada "only insofar as she is 'foreign' to Natives" (Kamboureli 91), Pique, as part Native, is constructed as at one with the landscape in which she resides. Laurence also associates nature with "Canada's beginnings" (Mackey 77). She calls the weeds in the river "prehistoric" (379), for example, and she refers to the heron she sights as "ancient-seeming" (380). For Laurence, the Canadian landscape, the Aboriginal identity, and Canada's ancient past come together as one, and, in various descriptions throughout *The Diviners*, are intimately intertwined.

However, the novel not only associates Métis characters with landscape, but also settler-descendant characters. Morag's "Canadianness," for example, like Catharine Parr Traill's, is grounded in a survival of the elements: "[Morag] might just possibly survive the heat of summer after all. Then ... the battle to survive the godawful winter would begin. What a country, and how strange she cared about it so much" (378). Morag is Canadian, the novel implies, precisely because she "[cares] about" her country and survives its elements. Quoting Margaret Atwood's phrase, that Atwood's character in *Surfacing* is "on home ground, foreign territory," W. H. New states that the phrase "epitomizes what 'region' is all about: it's about people recognizing the degree to which they are shaped by others' maps of territory and possession – the degree to which they are all immigrants in the lands of the gentry" (*Land* 160). Morag negotiates her ambivalent position on the land that her ancestors have mapped and possessed; and yet, that land, for Morag, still somehow remains harsh, distant, "godawful" (378).

Laurence connects Morag to nature and landscape through Morag and Royland's sighting of a great blue heron. When Morag sees the heron, she is in awe, and she notes that it is "ancient-seeming, unaware of the planet's rocketing changes" (380). She speculates that it unknowingly moves "not only towards individual death but probably towards the death of its kind" (380). Her experience of sighting the heron recalls Donna Haraway's assertion that, after World War II, there was a Western desire to go back to nature in order to connect to an idyllic past. At the historical moment when the West was expanding and developing in science and technology, Haraway maintains, it imagined a recreation of the Garden of Eden, a reclosing of the broken globe. At the same historical moment, when Western progress and technology destroy nature and thus lead "towards the death of [the heron's] kind," Morag desires a spiritual connection to that which is about to be lost. After contemplating the heron sighting, she experiences a kind of epiphany: "That evening, Morag began to see that here and now was not, after all, an island. Her quest for islands had ended some time ago, and her need to make pilgrimages had led her back here" (380). Her epiphany is an awareness that she need not be dependent on those patriarchs of the British Isles, like Brooke, and also an awareness that Canada need not be tied to Britain. Her epiphany, moreover, suggests that the "here and now" is connected with an "ancient" past. This point is reiterated in the symbol of the river flowing "both ways" (11), past and present, and in the very form of the novel – in the way that Morag's present is narrated in the past tense, while her past is narrated in the present. For Morag as well as for Laurence, the white Canadian settler must break from the "island" of Britain and – through a connection with nature, the Canadian landscape, and one's own past – "make pilgrimages" that ultimately lead "back here," to home.

Read through the lens of ecocriticism, Morag's realization that the "once populous.... now rarely seen" (380) heron is nearing extinction could be a call to urgent environmental action. Indeed, Di Brandt explains how Laurence emphasizes "imminent cultural collapse in an ecologically stressed environment" (253), but Laurence critics generally have not highlighted environmental themes in the author's writing. Edwards argues that subjectivity "arises out of a haunting trepidation of losing one's self, of collapsing into the terrifying space of a void" (xvii); I would argue that Laurence's book demonstrates this fear of losing not only the self, but also the world. Morag remembers questioning the meaning of words when she was a child. Thinking about children of future generations, she says, "My grandchildren will say *What means Fish?* Peering through the goggle-eyes of their gasmasks. Who will tell old tales to children then? Pique used to say *What is a Buffalo?* How many words and lives will be gone when they say *What means Leaf?*" (187). Morag fears losing herself because of the importance of her role as a writer – keeping history and story alive – as is shown by her question, "Who will tell old tales to children then?" (187). She emphasizes how vital it is to retain Aboriginal history, specifically the fact that the settler-invaders killed off an essential part of the Aboriginal livelihood, the buffalo, when she says, "Pique used to say *What is a Buffalo?*" (187). And finally, she suggests a more global concern, a sense of the human destruction of the world itself, when she asks, "How many words and lives will be gone when they say *What means Leaf?*"(187).

Historically, in Western discourse, nature, the Canadian landscape, and the ancient past, as they are imagined, are conflated with Aboriginal peoples. Morag's desire to connect with nature and the land might also be a desire to connect with Aboriginal peoples. Conversely, her impetus to reconcile with the Métis characters Jules and Pique might be read as a desire to connect with Canada. Morag and Jules become romantically involved when Morag leaves Brooke: Morag, and implicitly, Canada, leave the colonial world of Brooke and Britain in order to reconnect with the local, the Aboriginal, and Canada's past. Laurence describes the lovemaking of Morag and Jules as not only a personal joining but also a joining of larger significance, a kind of unity of the Canadian nation:

> In her present state of mind, [Morag] doesn't expect to be aroused, and does not even care if she isn't, as though this joining is being done for other reasons, some debt or answer to the past, some severing of inner chains which have kept her bound and separated from part of herself. (292)

That Laurence describes their lovemaking as a debt suggests both Morag's personal past with Jules and Canada's national past with Métis people. On a personal level, Morag might feel that she and the people of Manawaka owe Jules and the Tonnerre family for their marginal treatment and especially for Jules's sister Piquette's tragic death by fire in the Tonnerre home. On a national level, Morag and Jules's lovemaking "answers" (292) the question of white settler-descendants' relation to Métis and is a gesture toward rectifying the separation between these two groups of people in Canada. The "inner chains," which, paradoxically, have kept Morag "both bound and separated from part of herself" (292), are those that have tied her to Brooke and Canada to Britain. The coming together of Morag, a descendant of white settlers, and Jules, a Métis, is, for Morag and for Canada, a letting go of that "part of herself" (292) that is tied to Britain and a welcoming of that which is just coming into being. Morag and the settler-descendants she represents come into being as they gain independence from the homeland

and move toward oneness with the place in which they reside. Just as Laurence creates a connection between Morag and the nature, land, and history that she negotiates, so too does she create a connection between Morag and the Métis people, who are historically associated with that very nature, land, and history.

The notion that Morag understands the joining of Jules and herself as "some debt or answer to the past" (292) is itself intriguing in relation to the concept of owing, a topic I address in chapter 3 in relation to *The Stone Angel*. The use of the word "debt" here implies that Morag's lovemaking to Jules is a kind of payment as well as a righting of a past wrong. Di Brandt, as I do, disagrees with Neil ten Kortenaar's and Frank Davey's argument that Morag dishonestly atones "for [her] colonial settler guilt by having a child with a Métis man, thereby acquiring Canadian indigenosity for her lineage by inauthentic means" (Brandt 261).This assumption, Brandt suggests, implies that "sexual union [is a] false or devious or dishonest means of social location," which is problematic, since "it was practically the only avenue of affiliation and advancement allowed to women for many centuries" (261). I prefer to think of the joining of Jules and Morag as an invocation to remember the injustice of the past and to correct it in the present. In *Payback*, Margaret Atwood postulates that debt and credit structures could not exist without a sense of fairness (12). Throughout that book, she emphasizes the strong connection between debt and memory: there can be no debt without memory. Referring to ancient goddesses of justice and scales of balance, Atwood says that the concept "that there is an underlying balancing principle in the universe appears to be almost universal" (*Payback* 27). Thought of in this light, Morag's understanding of her and Jules's lovemaking is acute. Through Morag, Laurence calls for us to remember the wrongs of history. She unsettles the past and challenges us to work toward a renewing of it in the present. This notion is reflected in the narrative structure of *The Diviners*, the intertwining of the past and the present, and the river that symbolically flows both ways. The act of balancing the weigh scales is also represented in the trading of the Currie plaid pin for the Métis knife: trades that criss-cross cultural and historical boundaries and move between Laurence's first and final Manawaka novels, *The Stone Angel* and *The Diviners*.

This coming together of settler-descendants and Métis people finds its ultimate expression in the character of Pique, the daughter of Morag and Jules. As Nora Foster Stovel explains, at the end of the novel, Morag passes "the torch to the younger generation embodied in Pique, who combines the words and music, Celtic and Métis myths, to celebrate her dual song that concludes *The Diviners*" ("(W)rites" 117). Pique's song, which includes both the written tradition of Britain and the oral tradition of Natives as well as her blending of Celtic and Métis myths, suggests that "the younger generation embodied in Pique" (Stovel, "(W)rites" 117) is no longer tied to patriarchy or Britain. Instead, Pique is at one with the Scots and Métis ancestors that are both part of Canada. The ongoing sexism and racism that Pique experiences, however, qualify that idea. Pique experiences overt sexism and racism when she is travelling through Manitoba, where some men throw beer bottles at her and cut her arm (118–19). That the police give Pique a warning for this incident, when it is clearly the men who are the abusers and Pique who is the victim, implies that such sexism and racism could be entrenched in the police system and thus the Canadian state. Pique experiences racism when a schoolmate calls her a "dirty halfbreed" (446). That this boy's father is on the school board, and that, as Pique says, "It wouldn't do any good to see the principal. He'd be sorry and all that, but he couldn't do anything" (447), both suggest that both sexism and racism could also be entrenched within the Canadian school system. While Laurence brings together Scots and Métis in Canada with the figure of Pique, positing a hopeful future for the next generation, she also quite powerfully exemplifies how that joining is not conclusively attained. Therefore, *The Diviners* posits a desire for a future nation while simultaneously exemplifying the systematic establishment of sexism and racism that remains.

The Diviners challenges moments when Laurence is aligned with Western imperial values. As in her writing about Africa, Laurence is both embedded within, and yet works against, values of the culture and nation within which she resides. The considerable presence of the Tonnerre family in the novel, for example, and especially the continual questioning of Morag's values by her Scots-Métis daughter, Pique, qualifies the notion that settler-descendants of the British Isles and Aboriginal people can easily come together. Such moments in the text also challenge the idea that Canada is for the settler-descendant of the British Isles. Pique, for example, explicitly contests Morag's Anglo perspective when she reiterates her treatment at school in Canada: "What do you know of it? You've never been called a dirty halfbreed" (446). Morag's subsequent realization that the school in England was preferable since it was "full of Pakistani and African and West Indian kids" (446), suggests that Canada, as a nation, is far from the celebrated multicultural ideal that, during the writing of *The Diviners*, it purported to be. Similarly, Morag's statement that "the old patterns" of discrimination (446) that the Tonnerres experienced when she was a child have resurfaced suggests that racism is still ever-present in Canada. Trudeau's new multiculturalism as set forth in 1971, Laurence subtly implies, did not go far enough to change the dominance of Western imperial and often racist values in Canada.

The circumstances that surround the death of Jules's brother Paul in *The Diviners* suggest that both the demise of Aboriginal peoples in Canada and the silences that surround that demise are ongoing. Importantly, Laurence calls for an end to that demise and that silence. Near the end of the book, Morag asks Jules about his family, and Jules makes the following reply:

> My youngest brother, Paul, he was drowned. He was working up north as a guide. His canoe overturned at some rapids. At least, that was the story. He just disappeared. Body never found. The tourists, coupla American guys, they got back all right after a few days in the bush, and reported it to the Mounties. Jacques tried to get an enquiry, but he never got to first base with it. They took the tourists' word for it. Paul was the best hand with a canoe I ever saw. They said he'd been out alone in it one evening. We won't ever know. (363)

That the tourists were a "coupla American guys" implies, perhaps, that Laurence does not want Canada to align itself with America. That the Mounties would not investigate the case, valuing the American tourists over the Métis, implies her belief that the Canadian state continued to condone the oppression and even annihilation of Aboriginal people in Canada. Laurence's *The Diviners* contests the denial of racism and the effacement of Aboriginal people in Canada. It is as if, through the Tonnerre family, the novel paradoxically challenges the very Western ideology within which Laurence herself was embedded.

✳ ✳ ✳ ✳ ✳

Laurence's novel works against Western values through the romantic relationship between Brooke Skelton, an imperial and patriarchal figure, and Morag Gunn. Brooke's past as a colonial in India and his infantilizing treatment of Morag reveal that Brooke and Morag's relationship is an allegory for the relationship between dominating and dominated countries. Morag's departure from Brooke signifies Canada's departure from the practice of British cultural traditions. Moreover, Morag aligns herself with the Canadian pioneer woman, Catharine Parr Traill. Since Traill is of British heritage, Morag's alignment with her might also imply an alignment with the colonial history of which Britain was a part. Importantly, however, Morag abandons Traill as she abandons Brooke Skelton earlier in the novel, suggesting a severing of Morag's and Canada's ties to Britain. Ultimately, then, Laurence suggests that Canada depart from the inheritance of solely British values by recreating various Canadian histories and by interweaving fact and fiction with regard to those histories. She reimagines history as a meld-ing of different perspectives and life views.

Clearly a nationalist, Laurence posited a unified Canada by bringing together the settler-descendant, Morag Gunn, with nature, Canada's past, and Aboriginal peoples. While Laurence hoped for a united nation, how-ever, that hope is not conclusively realized in *The Diviners*. The author pos-its the future nation in the Scots-Métis character of Pique, but also points out the "old patterns" (446) of discrimination against her. Essentially, the novel is a call for cross-cultural understanding and the coming together of all peoples in the nation, even as it realizes the difficulty of that unification and shows the entrenchment of racism there.

The Diviners is particularly important when read in relation to Cana-dian nationalism in the late 1960s and early 1970s, and in relation to emerg-ing multiculturalism in Canada. Laurence presented the historical stories of Christie Logan and Jules and Lazarus Tonnerre as counter to official Canadian narratives. She addressed Métis history and worked against the idea, set forth in the Indian Act, that Aboriginal people should be assimi-lated into Anglo-Canadian society. Influenced by the European dictum of *terra nullius* (Day 117), she posited the Métis as at one with the Canadian landscape, while also challenging that construction. Working within and against nationalist discourses of the time, Laurence resisted an alignment with Britain as she established a new centre in the nation of Canada. Her protagonist, Morag Gunn, remains in an ambivalent, divided position – between the old world and the new – even as she finally comes home to Canada. Ultimately, Laurence's *The Diviners* divines the Canadian nation in order to imagine and create it anew.

Conclusion

Essays, Letters, and Politics

"I always think that writing is only partly an act of will; it is so much more an act of faith and even in some way an act of love. Probably this sounds like a bunch of platitudes – but I do believe this is all true, however difficult it may be to verbalize without clichés" (Laurence, letter to Ian and Sandy Cameron). The faith and love with which Laurence wrote is evident in her writing about Africa and Canada. It is also evident in her essays and letters, which are both personal and political. In a letter to her college friend, Helen Warkentin, written during the summer of 1945, Laurence referred to "imaginary friends" – future fictional characters that were already beginning to take shape in her mind. Fascinatingly, one of those "imaginary friends" seemed to be an early creation of two future characters: Christie, the garbage collector, and Royland, the diviner, from *The Diviners*. Laurence's "imaginary friend," like Royland, was a "River Man," who "came out West with La Verendrye." Like both Royland and Christie, he was a spiritual guide, "guarding ancient treasure near the river; showing nightwanderers the way home." His physical appearance as Laurence described it in her letters matched Christie's: "His face is well-moulded and tanned ... and his eyes are blue and kindly" (Laurence, Letter to Helen Warkentin, "Monday").

The letters from Laurence to Helen Warkentin were acquired by the Clara Thomas Archives at York University in 2004; written in 1945, they are the earliest writings by Laurence acquired by the archives. Until then, Laurence's early imaginings of the characters of Royland and Christie from

The Diviners were unknown. Similarly, her early writing of the characters of Chris and Michael in *A Bird in the House* was discovered. As I explain in chapter 3, her letters to Helen Warkentin reveal that the characters were based in part on Laurence's boyfriend during World War II, Derek. *Margaret Laurence Writes Africa and Canada* is the first critical study to discuss these letters and make the connection between the author's imagined characters in the letters and some of her characters in *A Bird in the House* and *The Diviners*. That she envisioned these characters years before she wrote books about Africa and Canada shows the importance, to Laurence, of coming home. In her writing, she returned to early versions of her characters, her creativity, her ancestors' history, and her place: the Canadian land and nation.

While Laurence ultimately returned home in her writing, however, she remained always aware of her complex subject position. As a Westerner, she was privileged and mobile, not always aligned with Aboriginal peoples and the lands they inhabit. She felt unease with regard to her subject position, as we can see in her writing about Africa and Canada. Paradoxically, both her unease with her subject position and her sense of knowing where she belonged – of coming home – are also evident in her non-fiction writing, and specifically, in three essays published in her collection of essays, *Heart of a Stranger*: "Sayonara, Agamemnon," "Open Letter to the Mother of Joe Bass," and "A Place to Stand On." Each of these essays represents her beliefs against the oppression of Others in the wake of globalization, but each of them also addresses a different aspect of and context for her politics: "Sayonara, Agamemnon" discusses the problem of Western development in foreign lands; "Open Letter to the Mother of Joe Bass" addresses her nationalist belief that Canada must distinguish itself from the imperial power of America; and "A Place to Stand On" exemplifies her sense of self as a Canadian prairie person with Scots-Presbyterian roots. That essay also demonstrates her important and complex centring of herself and settler-descendants in Canada as particularly Canadian. In *Heart of a Stranger*, Laurence "offers a radically new framework for the reading of Canadian identity" (Szamosi 281).

"Sayonara, Agamemnon" was originally published in the American travel magazine *Holiday* in 1966, and then in 1976 in *Heart of a Stranger*. The essay is a travel narrative in which Laurence recounted her and her husband's journey on a tour bus through Greece. In many ways, the essay comments more on the "culture of the tour bus" than on Greek culture itself. The title of the essay encapsulates the juxtaposition of the tourists on the bus and the ancient places they visit: "Sayonara" refers to the salutation, which is taught by a Japanese family in the group to their fellow travellers, and "Agamemnon" refers to the legendary Greek figure whom Laurence considers as she views the place where he fell. Laurence explains how the tourist industry presented the people of Greece and certain sites within it as unchanging and ancient. In so doing, she emphasizes the mobility of the Westerner, and she critiques the very culture of which she was a part. Most interestingly, she addresses the problematic and deliberate separation between the tourists and the local people upon whom the tourists gazed. She draws our attention to the ways in which the tourist industry at once intruded upon and remained distinct from the lives of the local people.

Her description of the tour bus as it moved through Greek villages highlights the separation between tourists and locals. Laurence emphasizes the constant presence of Western tourists in the locals' daily lives when she states, "People did not bother to look up as we passed, for the tour buses zoomed along here every few minutes" (17). Yet she also foregrounds the imposed separation between tourists and locals when she calls the tour bus "our metal-and-glass bubble" (17) and contrasts the "ease and speed" of the bus with "the local farmers' way of travel, which was by donkey" (13). She thus demonstrates that the tourists' comfortable lifestyle was largely unavailable to the locals, even though the tourists were ever-present in the locals' lives. Most interestingly, she discusses how tourists attempted to take photographs that would render the local life absolutely separate from the tourism that infiltrated it. She relates, for example, how her husband, Jack, attempted to take a picture of the stadium arch at Olympia, but could not because a "denim-clad American boy" was in the way (17). When she told her husband to take the picture anyway, to capture the juxtaposition of the modern boy and the ancient stadium, the boy turned around. "Today was facing Today," Laurence remarks, "and they were both holding cameras aimed at each other" (17).

In "White Privilege and Looking Relations: Race and Gender in Feminist Film Theory," Jane Gaines states that "some groups have historically had the license to 'look' openly while other groups have 'looked' illicitly" (301). The encounter between Jack and the "denim-clad American boy" at the Olympic arch is particularly intriguing in relation to Gaines's statement, since the Westerner is in the privileged subject position of being able to "look openly" (301). The photographs that tourists desire in "Sayonara, Agamemnon" do not include Westerners or other tourists. Laurence highlights the fact that the American boy is in the way of Jack's view of the arch. She therefore challenges the unwarranted perception of Greece as ancient and unchanging. Similarly, as we have seen in her writing about Africa, she challenges these same unwarranted beliefs about Africa. Laurence highlights the fact that the American boy turns around and points his camera back at Jack. She therefore suggests that the boy refuses to be the object of the tourists' gaze – the boy looks back in confrontation. To look back in confrontation is to expose the presence behind the camera. It is to reveal that the photographers construct the objects of their gaze. It is to reveal, in essence, that the object of the tourists' gaze is, at least to some extent, fabricated. With her reference to this incident, then, Laurence draws our attention to the tourists' failure to recreate a Greece that existed apart from the infiltration of modern tourism. This moment relates to the overall argument I have presented in *Margaret Laurence Writes Africa and Canada*. Laurence here foregrounds not only the separation of the tourist from the local, but also the privileged and mobile position of the tourist, who is allowed, in Gaines's terms, to look openly at Others. In this essay, Laurence also self-identifies as a tourist herself. She therefore exposes her own privileged position. As in both her writing about Africa and her writing about Canada, she sympathized with the local but was at one with the tourist. She was at home in neither subject position.

In her essay "Road from the Isles," in *Heart of a Stranger*, Laurence makes the following statement about Highlanders and the tourist industry:

> What he [the Highlander] really was, in the past, is not comprehended by anyone outside his own tribe, but he has been taken up and glamourized and is expected to act a part. The Dance of the Ancestors – slicked-up, prettified, and performed forever in the same way.... The tourists are paying to be provided with an embodiment of their own fantasies. The local populace must surely sometimes want to say, "Look, it's not that way, not at all." (120)

In "Sayonara, Agamemnon," as we have seen, Laurence critiques the tourist industry's tendency to deny its intrusion into local lives and landscapes. In the above quotation from "Road from the Isles," she explicitly states how tourism constructs the local populace as that which they are not. Laurence condemns tourism's fabrication of local landscapes and peoples as apart from the destructive forces of development.

If Laurence argued that the tourist industry constructed locals in a particular, fabricated way, then she did so by separating herself – at least in part – from those who did that constructing. Just as Laurence viewed herself as separate from the British colonialists in *The Prophet's Camel Bell*, so she viewed herself as separate from the other tourists in Greece. In the introduction to "Sayonara, Agamemnon," for example, Laurence states that she had "seldom been a tourist," and that, in Africa, she and her husband, Jack, had been "outsiders, strangers," but not tourists (11). Moreover, she begins the piece ironically by poking fun at the title of the tour they are about to take, "the Four Day Ultra Classical Tour" (11). Unlike the other tourists, Laurence implies, she and Jack are aware of the absurdity of the construction of Greece as such. Throughout the essay, Laurence mocks the other tourists, who are preoccupied with their own comfort in a foreign land. This preoccupation with one's own comfort is particularly evident in Laurence's description of Mrs. Webster, an American woman who travelled to Africa and was appalled by the state of the roads there (13). Her husband, Mrs. Webster states, "did not mind the discomfort one scrap.... For thirty years he had been mad to see Africa, and now thank goodness he had seen it" (13).

While Laurence clearly distinguishes herself from the other tourists, however, there are moments in the essay where she realizes that she cannot do so completely. In her discussion of Nick, the tour guide, for instance, she says, "In the winter he painted watercolours of ruined temples, which his wife sold to the January foreigners (12). She draws attention to Nick's statement that such foreigners "didn't like to consider themselves tourists," even though they were. She therefore demonstrates awareness that the Laurences, despite their resistance to the label, are also tourists by virtue of their privileged presence as mobile Westerners in a foreign land. At the end of the essay, she imagines and attempts to align herself with ancient Greek women and the Greek landscape, recalling the myth of Agamemnon and Clytemnestra, and seeing the "red poppies" in the field as the "newly spilled blood" of Clytemnestra's daughter. Ultimately, however, as she is jolted back to the present day by the call of a fellow tourist, she cannot exempt herself from the tour's intrusion into the land. "Our initiation was over," she states. "We were qualified tourists" (21).

The essay "Open Letter to the Mother of Joe Bass" was published in 1968 in *Maclean's* magazine, and in that same year it was also included in a collection of essays about Canadian perspectives on Americans that was edited by Al Purdy and entitled *The New Romans*. It was also published in 1976 in *Heart of a Stranger*. I discuss this essay in my article "Margaret Laurence's Correspondence with Imperial Oil." As I explain there, in "Open Letter to the Mother of Joe Bass," Laurence discusses two newspaper photographs in order to critique American police who shot Joe Bass, an African-American boy, and the American military that bombed Vietnamese civilians during the Vietnam War. The first newspaper article on the shooting of Joe Bass states that the boy was shot directly in the neck and that the police were aiming at Bass's friend, whose only crime was stealing a six-pack of beer. Addressing Joe Bass's mother, and speaking from the perspective of a mother, Laurence here calls for an end to such acts of violence and racism by the state. The newspaper article and photograph of Joe Bass remind Laurence of another newspaper photo. This photo is that "of a North Vietnamese woman trying to wipe napalm from the face of her child" (Stovel, *Divining* 77). Speaking again from the perspective of a mother who is moved by this photograph, Laurence criticizes the violence and racism that the American state and its military employ (Davis, "Margaret" 71).

Catherine A. Lutz and Jane L. Collins explain that "all war photography can potentially suggest parallels between gun and camera" (100). Such a parallel between gun and camera is evident in Laurence's description of the newspaper photograph of Joe Bass, whose face was photographed straight on immediately after he was shot dead by police: "He was lying on the sidewalk, and his eyes were open.... He was bleeding, and one of his hands lay languidly outstretched in a spillage of blood" (158). While absent from the photograph themselves, the killer, the photographer, and the reader are aligned in subject position. The killer and the photographer foreground Joe Bass's dead body while making themselves absent from view. A similar vantage point is evident in Laurence's description of the photo of the Vietnamese woman and child. Just as the killer and the photographer are absent from the photo of Joe Bass, so the American military is absent from the photograph of the Vietnamese woman and child Laurence describes. The photograph elides the power relationship between the American military and the Vietnamese people and replaces it with a focus on the relationship between mother and child. This elision is particularly interesting in light of Lutz and Collins's argument that in 1968 – which was the same year that "Open Letter to the Mother of Joe Bass" was published in *Maclean's* and *The New Romans* – "popular American protest against participating in the Vietnam War reached a critical point" (206). Magazines such as *National Geographic*, Lutz and Collins point out, stopped including Westerners in photographs of Vietnam because the public did not support the American presence there (206). In "Open Letter to the Mother of Joe Bass," it is precisely this absence of the perpetrator that Laurence critiques. The elision of the presence and power of the American police force and military in such photographs alleviates such organizations from responsibility. As Laurence puts it, "The wheels turn, but no one admits to turning them.... The fantasy is taking over, like the strangler vines of the jungle taking over the trees. It is all happening on TV. Except that it isn't" (159). Laurence's essay, then, critiques the oppression of Others both between nations (as in the photograph of the Vietnam War) and within nations (as in the photograph of the dead African-American boy, Joe Bass). Laurence was culturally and historically aligned with the white, Western oppressor. Yet she also dissociated herself from that oppressor, both politically and nationally.

Thus "Open Letter to the Mother of Joe Bass" might be read as nationalist. The essay was published in a collection of essays by Canadians about America, *The New Romans*, implying that Canadians must take a stand, as peacekeepers, in relation to America's oppressive practices. Donna Bennett explains how, throughout the 1970s, the view that Canada must affirm itself as a nation was being challenged by the idea that Canada must embrace pluralism and not adhere to a singular identity. As Neil Besner and Smaro Kamboureli point out, however, this view was problematic, since it situated Canada as superior to other nations – as a nation, that is, that matured from a colony of Britain to an independent country and, finally, to a multicultural country that must help others achieve tolerance and cross-cultural understanding (40, 44). On the one hand, we might read Laurence's essay as implicitly suggesting that Canada is a progressive country that has achieved a kind of tolerance that America has not. On the other hand, however, it is clear throughout the Manawaka series that Laurence does not believe that Canada has achieved that tolerance. As we have seen in my discussions of *The Stone Angel* and *The Diviners*, for example, characters experience ongoing oppression and racism by the Canadian state. Laurence worked to end such violence and its manifestations both at home and abroad.

Laurence's stance against certain aspects of American police and military systems is evident not only in the essays of *Heart of a Stranger*, but also in documents concerning her political activism. In a newspaper article entitled "Call for Halt to Missile Parts Manufacture, Author Urges," appearing in the *Toronto Star* on 3 October 1982, columnist John Munch reported her statement that "Canadians should pressure the federal government to ban test flights of the U.S. cruise missile in Canada and to halt production of parts for the missile here." Likewise, in a panel statement for a conference called "Operation Dismantle" in 1982, Laurence wrote, "Social services are being cut drastically in America, and may soon be cut in our own country," while "550 <u>billion</u> dollars are spent world-wide on armaments including nuclear arms, and the sum is increasing." With regard to that kind of government priority, Laurence said that, for her, "this is not only insanity … it is brutality."

In her statements in the *Toronto Star* article and in the "Operation Dismantle" panel statement, Laurence demonstrated how Canada was dominated by America. She drew attention to the use of Canadian soil as a testing ground for American missiles, and she disagreed with Canada's permitting the United States to conduct such tests. Exemplifying nationalist beliefs, she voiced the concern she later articulated in her essay "Ivory Tower or Grassroots? The Novelist as Socio-Political Being," published in 1978. Here she worried that Canada "is now under the colonial sway of America" ("Ivory

Tower" 24). She also reiterated the notion that Canada must assert its independence and its stance toward cross-cultural understanding. She asserted her sincere humanitarian belief that war and violence against peoples must end.

Laurence was concerned not only with America's dominance over Canada, but also with Canada's exploitation of its own people. As a letter from Christine Judge of the Socialist Rights Defense Fund to Laurence reveals, she stood against certain aspects of police systems in Canada as well as in America. The letter thanks Laurence for her support "for the legal initiative of Ross Dowson in his suit against the Royal Canadian Mounted Police." As an article in the April 1978 issue of the New Democratic Party newspaper, *The Commonwealth*, explains, Ross Dowson took the RCMP to court for slander "arising out of that force's secret spying activities in Canada, and, specifically, [on] the New Democratic Party" ("Slander Action Launched"). Once again, Laurence stood not only against the domination of peoples of one country over peoples of another, but also against the domination of peoples within a single nation.

Laurence's "A Place to Stand On" was published in the Canadian literary journal *Mosaic* in 1970, and again in *Heart of a Stranger*. In the essay, which takes its title from a line from Al Purdy's poem entitled "Roblin Mills, Circa 1842," Laurence located her own world vision in her roots in a small prairie town. "Whatever I am was shaped and formed in that sort of place [Manawaka]" (9), she states. "My way of seeing, however much it may have changed over the years, remains in some enduring way that of a small-town prairie person" (9). Her emphasis on small-town Canadian life is prevalent in her work, and yet she rarely idealized that life. The Reverend Jim Penhale addressed the significance of the small prairie town in Laurence's writing. In a sermon to his congregation at Margaret Laurence's own United Church in Neepawa, Manitoba, at the time of the author's death, he stated,

> As Margaret held up a mirror to reflect life in a small prairie town, we found that the images were not always flattering. Sometimes they were brutal, sometimes crude, and frequently frightening. We identified sometimes too closely with the characters in the novels. And through her stories, we saw parts of our own nature that we would rather avoid acknowledging.

Laurence wrote out of the place from which she came, not in order to glorify it, but in order to demonstrate its reality: its racism, for example, as exemplified in some of the Anglo-Scots characters' treatment of the Tonnerre family; and its violence, for example, as exemplified in her exposure of the child abuse Eva Winkler and her brother experience in *The Diviners*.

Although Laurence located her world vision in her roots as a prairie person, she also believed, as she said in "A Place to Stand On" through a quote by Graham Greene, that the writer must "illustrate his private world in terms of the great public world we all share" (5). Such a viewpoint is evident in the essays of *Heart of a Stranger*, in her writing about Canada, and also in her correspondence. In a letter to Marian Engel written on 19 September 1978, she explained how angry and hurt she was that author Rudy Wiebe, in a *Maclean's* article about him, stated that Laurence "hasn't lived on the prairies since she was a kid":

> Is he saying that my work, and [Robert] Kroetsch's, have no "presence," no "range of experience," and that we write with the viewpoint of "a child, an adolescent," and that this interesting state of affairs is because we have lived away from our native birthplaces? Ye gods!! I really cannot believe that my years in England and Africa did anything but give me somewhat a broader view into what one might term the human dilemma. And what else are novelists writing about? It doesn't matter <u>where</u>.

In a subsequent letter to Marian Engel (20 September 1978) about her "row with Rudy Wiebe," Laurence noted that Wiebe said he was misquoted in the *Maclean's* article, and that Laurence believed him. Laurence also made the following statement: "I suppose in my letter I attacked him when I should have reassured him, but Marian, I did not do it in public print, and how long must women reassure and not protest when we ourselves are ostensibly attacked?" Laurence insisted not only that her history on the Canadian prairies was tied to who she was, but also that her time away from the prairies made her more open-minded, more able to understand people. Yet the land of the Canadian prairies, she asserted in "Where the World Began," "still draws [her] more than other lands" (173). Canadian settler-descendants must, she implied, reconcile with Aboriginal peoples and therefore work toward cross-cultural understanding (*Heart* 166).

Laurence clearly articulated how she felt at one with the place from which she came. In "A Place to Stand On," for instance, she states, "Writing, for me, has to be set firmly in some soil, some place, some outer and inner territory" (9), and in "Where the World Began," she asserts that the prairie landscape "formed [her]" (*Heart* 174). Laurence's insistence that one must remember and return to one's past countered a forgetting of the genocide of Aboriginal peoples in Canada as it countered a forgetting of life before modernization. While a return to one's past in a small prairie town might be a return to that which is configured in the Garden of Eden, Mother Earth, and, quite literally, childhood innocence, in Laurence's case, it was not exclusively so. In some instances, Laurence did idealize the prairies and the history there. Just as Matthew, in *The Tomorrow-Tamer* story "The Drummer of All the World," desires a return to the old Africa and his lost childhood, so Laurence, in many of the *Heart of a Stranger* essays and in her fiction, returned to the pioneer life of a small town and her childhood experiences there. Matthew's old Africa is "the giant heartbeat of the night drums. The flame tree whose beauty is suddenly splendid" (*The Tomorrow-Tamer* 19), just as Laurence's Canadian prairie includes the northern lights that "[flare] across the sky ... like the scrawled signature of God" (*Heart* 170). But she predominantly exposed small-town prairie life for what it was. As she puts it in "Where the World Began," "The town of my childhood could be called ... agonizingly repressive or cruel at times, and the land in which it grew could be called harsh.... But never merely flat or uninteresting. Never dull" (170).

If, as Laurence says in "A Place to Stand On," her writing, as well as the writing of many others, "involves an attempt to understand one's background and one's past, sometimes even a more distant past which one has not personally experienced" (6), then it addresses not only her own background in a prairie town, but also that of her pioneer ancestors. Thus, just as Matthew, in "The Drummer of All the World," engages in what Renato Rosaldo calls "imperialist nostalgia," a Western longing for, ironically, that which the West has destroyed, so too, to a certain extent, does Laurence. In essays such as "A Place to Stand On" and "Where the World Began," Laurence desires to return to a fleeting past that is always already reconstructed and nostalgic.

The essays of *Heart of a Stranger* are important in order to understand the connection between Laurence's writing about Africa and her writing about Canada. In "A Place to Stand On," Laurence connects her return to her ancestors' pioneer past with African writers' return to their pasts. Many African writers, she asserts, return to their pasts "in order to recover a sense of themselves, an identity and a feeling of value from which they were separated by two or three generations of colonialism and missionizing" (6). Similarly, in "The Poem and the Spear" a *Heart of a Stranger* essay about Somaliland leader Mahammed 'Abdille Hasan, she compares that historic figure with the Métis leader Louis Riel. She understood different imperial situations in relation to one another. In "Sayonara, Agamemnon," the author critiques Western development and challenges the notion that it is separate from "ancient" lands and peoples. In "Open Letter to the Mother of Joe Bass," she urgently states that people must work together to end oppression, and she strongly asserts that Canada must take a stand apart from its American neighbour. In "A Place to Stand On," Laurence situates herself as a Canadian with small-town prairie roots, a Canadian who, it may be noted, remembered and recounted a pioneer past that included the histories of settlers and Aboriginal peoples. In the essays of *Heart of a Stranger*, Laurence essentially exemplified her strong political beliefs against imperialism as it manifested in America, Canada, and many parts of the world.

Nowhere is Laurence's life view clearer than in her unpublished letters to the African writer Chinua Achebe. As a literary figure in the world, Achebe is of no small significance. In two letters written from Laurence to Achebe in 1984 and now housed at the William Ready Special Collections and Archives at McMaster University, Laurence expressed her compassion for all humans. These letters help us to understand the connection between Laurence's writing about Africa and her writing about Canada. In a letter to Achebe dated 3 June 1984, for example, Laurence wrote,

> As you know, I have long felt a great affinity with your writing, and have felt that in many ways, out of our very different cultures, we have been aiming at some of the same things – the relationship with the ancestors and family; the necessity of continuing to try to communicate, however difficult this may be; the sense of social injustice, an outrage that has to be communicated in fiction through the dilemmas and tragedies of human individuals and not in any didactic way.

In a subsequent letter to Achebe dated 26 June 1984, Laurence stated, "It was a great pleasure to talk with you – I have long felt a similarity in our 'aims' (if they may be called that) in writing, and it was reassuring to me to know that you, too, had been trying to cope with some of the same problems of writing fiction in this terrifying world." In these letters, Laurence communicated to Achebe the notion that their writing is similar in its underlying principles. Though Laurence and Achebe were from different parts of the world, and though they came from different ancestral and historical pasts, Laurence felt that she understood Achebe's writing and his impetus toward cross-cultural understanding. At the same time, a sense of dismay at the oppression of people in the world comes through in these letters, and this dismay is quite explicit in the last few sentences of Laurence's 26 June letter, where she wrote, "You are absolutely <u>right</u> that this [the corruption of governments and affiliation of governments with corporations] creates a climate of non-caring for honesty and decency. Most of our politicians do indeed speak with forked tongues. It is hard not to despair – but we <u>must not</u>."

Laurence felt an affinity with Achebe's writing spiritually as well as politically. In the letter dated 3 June 1984, for example, Laurence wrote about her own religious views and aspects of her own religion with which she did not agree. At the same time, however, she recognized how much her religion was a part of her own heritage:

> I disagree deeply with many of the concepts in some of the old hymns of the Protestant churches, (Onward, Christian Soldiers, for example … terrible), but they are in some ways noble hymns and I suppose they are also so deeply a part of my childhood and my heritage, so I love them and frequently change some of the words when I go to church (United Church of Canada), which I don't do all that often. "Praise, my soul, the King of Heaven," e.g., a truly noble hymn, with a wonderful melody, becomes, in my parlance, sometimes, "the Queen of Heaven" and I substitute "Her" for "Him" every other line. It seems only fair.

In such sentiments, it is clear that Laurence was aware of, and perhaps dismayed by, her own divided subject position. On the one hand, she "love[d]" the hymns and felt connected to her Protestant heritage; on the other hand, as a pacifist, she resisted hymns that glorified war. Moreover, she believed, as she explicitly stated to Achebe, that "the female principle in the Holy Spirit must be recognized." In fact, in a turn from discussing her own religion to discussing religions of Africa, Laurence explained in the letter that she came to an awareness of the importance of the female principle by "reading the indigenous faiths of Ghana (especially the Akan)." Her reverence for and affinity with Achebe's writing demonstrate a connection between her own writing about Africa and her writing about Canada. The letters Laurence wrote to Achebe also clearly exemplify her political beliefs against the oppression of Others, and her belief that religions of the world are deeply connected by the spirituality underlying all of them.

∗ ∗ ∗ ∗ ∗

In Africa, Laurence worked to resist the violent colonial domination of African peoples. She took up the Gold Coast's impending freedom from Britain in both her African novel and her African stories, and she was both optimistic about that freedom and wary of ongoing Western development there. In Canada, she worked against the predominance of British cultural traditions and the ongoing oppression of Aboriginal peoples. The protagonists of Laurence's Manawaka cycle – in particular, Hagar Shipley in *The Stone Angel*, Vanessa MacLeod in *A Bird in the House*, and Morag Gunn in *The Diviners* – identify with their Anglo-Scots ancestors as they simultaneously negotiate their changing multicultural country. Laurence took up the historical and contemporary relationship between Scots-Presbyterian settlers and Métis peoples in her final Manawaka novel, *The Diviners*, confronting the violent imperialist actions of the British and the Scots. Her life work, as exemplified by her literature and correspondence, shows how she fought forcefully against the oppression of peoples, even as she was limited by her entanglement within Western imperial ideology.

In *The Prophet's Camel Bell*, Laurence is acutely aware that she cannot exempt herself from Western ideologies. She admits, for example, the problem of her ambivalent subject positioning outright (10). She also shows how she was distraught precisely because she was at an impasse and there was, seemingly, no way out. Such is the case in *The Prophet's Camel Bell*, when she meets the Somali women who ask her for medicine, and the child prostitute, Asha, whom she cannot help. In *This Side Jordan*, she plays into the Western trope of the African landscape as feminine and maternal, and she works within and against the problematic notion that the West is "progressive" and Africa "traditional." Also in *This Side Jordan*, she critiques ideas of Africa held by the English character Johnnie Kestoe. As a sympathetic outsider, she represents Africa and Africans within the confines of Western discourse, even as she adamantly refuted that very discourse.

In *The Political Unconscious*, Fredric Jameson argues that the novelistic genre can provide imaginary resolutions to irresolvable social issues. Jameson's notion relates to Laurence's work insofar as it speaks to Laurence's account of Asha, in her memoir *The Prophet's Camel Bell*, and Ayesha, in her story "The Rain Child." Unlike Asha, the fictional Ayesha is rescued from her plight as a child prostitute and resides peacefully in a Ghanaian village. Haunted by her encounters with Asha and her inability to help her, perhaps, Laurence created a fictional character that is taken out of her oppressive situation. While Laurence might have been limited, in her African memoir, by the conventions of the genre itself, her fiction, at times, gave her the freedom to imagine and work toward an overcoming of violence that resulted in suffering.

Laurence's African stories in *The Tomorrow-Tamer* take up Ghana's movement toward independence in the 1950s, and they critique ongoing Western development there during decolonization. "The Pure Diamond Man" demonstrates how colonized subjects, represented in the character of Tetteh, resist empire through appropriation, working within and yet against the Western discourses that inscribe them. In that story, Laurence challenges the idea that Africans are solely victims and do not have the agency to resist imperial domination and exploitation. "The Drummer of All the World" and "The Rain Child," unlike "The Pure Diamond Man," are narrated by Westerners in Africa. Both stories delineate the difficulty of being "a stranger in a strange land"; and, yet, they also critique the violence implicit within the colonial enterprise. In "The Drummer of All the World," Matthew's African friend, Kwabena, becomes increasingly Westernized: he decides, for example, to become a Western-style doctor rather than a "ju-ju man" (15). Laurence here demonstrates not only how imperialism violates peoples and landscapes physically, but also how it affects the ideals and values of the colonized. Further, she challenges the notion that the West is more progressive than Africa and shows that, in 1950s Ghana, much cultural production, to use Karin Barber's words, "cannot be classified as either 'traditional' or elite' … because it straddles and dissolves these contradictions" (2). In "The Rain Child," the character of Violet Nedden, much like Laurence herself, sees the absurdity and the decay of the glorified imperial enterprise. Nedden mocks the English empire within which she is implicated by describing her cane as an "ebony scepter" (112), her "rattan chair" as a "throne" that is decaying – the red on it "subdued by the sun," the "gilt … flaking" (112). Laurence is highly critical of her own position – and the position of the English empire – as "enthroned" in a place that is not her own.

Just as Laurence's African characters and herself in her memoir about Africa exemplify a divided subject position, so too do her characters that reside in the fictional Canadian prairie town of Manawaka. In *The Stone Angel*, Hagar Shipley, an elderly woman, moves back and forth in her mind between her present and her past; similarly, Laurence implies, the Canadian nation moves back and forth between its present and its past in order to negotiate a complex and troubling history. In *The Stone Angel*, it is only when Hagar comes to terms with her past that she is released from its oppressive power; and in the same way, Laurence implies, it is only when the Canadian nation can confront its history of racism and domination over Others that it will truly become a multicultural and humanitarian country. Unlike *The Stone Angel*, *A Bird in the House* is narrated by a young girl, Vanessa MacLeod. This collection of short stories examines Vanessa's relationship to the female role models in her family, the patriarch of her family – her grandfather Connor – and her ancestral and communal past. Vanessa's ancestry and her community, Laurence suggests, are equally important in Vanessa's development of herself, and it is only when she works to understand them that she comes into her own. Even though this work, uniquely, is a collection of short stories rather than a novel, it can still be understood as a *Bildungsroman*, since it traces Vanessa's growth and her growing awareness of herself in relation to her community. In a sense, Vanessa MacLeod – much like Hagar Shipley in *The Stone Angel* and Morag Gunn in *The Diviners* – learns to listen as well as to speak her own voice as she comes to understand her relationship with her family and ancestors, the people in her community, and, ultimately, the Canadian nation itself.

The Diviners, Laurence's final and most lengthy Manawaka book, addresses the history of Scots-Presbyterian settlers and Métis peoples in

Western Canada. Laurence wrote and published the book in the early 1970s, when immigration policy in Canada was loosening, and when Canada was just beginning to define itself as "multicultural." Laurence recognized that the Scots contributed to the dispossession of First Nations and Métis people in Canada, even as she distinguished Scottish highlanders from the British: the Scots were themselves colonized by the English. The novel was clearly influenced by historical events such as Canada's impending constitution and Canada's introduction of multiculturalism in the 1970s. In addition, the novel addresses cross-cultural understanding and forces its readers to recognize how intertwined the history of settler-descendants and Aboriginal people is. Moreover, it begins to address how people of different races and cultures might come to understand one another in Canada. While paying heed to ongoing and systematic racism in Canada, Laurence desired not to deny but to overcome conflict. She worked against oppression and hoped, as she put it in "Man of Our People," that we will "reach a point when it is no longer necessary to say Them and Us" (*Heart* 166).

Like Laurence, Nuper Chaudhuri and Margaret Strobel, in *Western Women and Imperialism*, understand imperialism as the relationship of dominance and subordination between nations. In Africa, Laurence was particularly interested in the decolonization that was happening at the time that she resided there. But Laurence's understanding of imperialism changed during her time in Africa: she initially understood it simply as the English colonialist occupation and exploitation of Africa; after she spent time in Africa, she began to understand it as inclusive of ongoing Western economic development there. For example, in *The Prophet's Camel Bell*, Laurence does not, at first, see the construction of the *ballehs* and her presence in Somaliland as imperialist. She comes to realize, however, that the Somali people "were by no means convinced that the project [of constructing the *ballehs*] was designed to help them" (44). Laurence was concerned not only with the relationship of domination and subordination between nations, but also with the relationship of domination and subordination *within* nations. This was clearly the case with the history of Scots-Presbyterian settlers and the Métis in Western Canada, a history that Laurence addressed in *The Stone Angel*, *A Bird in the House*, and *The Diviners*. Laurence foregrounded Britain's historical and cultural domination over Canada, and she desired a break from Britain. She also foregrounded British and Scots settlers' historical and ongoing domination of Aboriginal peoples, and she worked against such domination. Laurence resisted white Westerners' violence against Others and was concerned, in a broad sense, with domination and exploitation of lands and peoples in various historical and contemporary locations.

Just as Laurence understood and worked against the violent and literal domination of Others by Western peoples, so, too, she understood and worked against powerful and insidious Western *representations* of Others. In *This Side Jordan* and "The Drummer of All the World," for instance, Laurence employs and critiques the trope of land-as-woman in the characters of Emerald and Afua, respectively. Likewise, in *This Side Jordan*, Laurence works within the trope that defines Africans as ancient and traditional. At the same time, however, she counters that trope by suggesting that the African drums, much to Johnnie Kestoe's dismay, are persistent in their threat to disrupt what is Western and modern. Johnnie's possession of the African woman, Emerald, in *This Side Jordan*, is also, allegorically, the English colonizer's possession of Africa. In the same way, Brooke's possession of Morag, in *The Diviners*, is also England's possession of Canada, both symbolically and culturally. The intertwinement of the discourses of imperialism and patriarchy represented in these instances is epitomized in the map of H. Rider Haggard's novel, *King Solomon's Mines*, which, as Anne McClintock points out, is both a treasure map and a diagram of a female body (3). Although Laurence did not specifically contest the intertwinement of these two discourses, she did counter both the possession of the colonized by the colonizers and the possession of woman by man. Her anti-imperialism and her feminism were each a part of the other.

Laurence's beliefs and values were influenced by the history of first-wave feminism in both Britain and Canada. Problematically, some British feminists during colonialism considered themselves superior to Indian and African women. Also problematically, in Canada, some first-wave feminists fought for the vote at the expense of ethnic minorities and Aboriginal peoples. Laurence directly stated that she was influenced by two of Canada's most famous first-wave feminists, Nellie McClung and Emily Murphy ("Books" 241). Laurence's work against the oppression of African and Aboriginal peoples by Western countries did not always align her with feminists in Britain and Canada, and yet, her stated support for such feminists, and her strong support for feminist issues in Canada, suggests an affiliation with them. Thus, once again, Laurence exemplified a divided subject position that was not quite at one with her ancestors and predecessors, such as McClung and Murphy, and not quite apart from them either.

In *A Writer's Life: The Margaret Laurence Lectures*, Margaret Atwood explains the cultural milieu and historical circumstances within which Laurence was embedded as an emerging Canadian writer. She explains that, in 1964, when Laurence's "breakthrough book," *The Stone Angel* (*Writer's Life* 315), was published, "there were only a few publishers.... There was no Writers' Union. There was no Writers' Trust. There were no agents to speak of" (317). She also suggests that "the postwar years – the late '40s, the '50s – were the most male-dominated period in international English-language literature since the eighteenth century" (319). With regard to Laurence's entrance into the literary scene at this time, Atwood comments,

> Here comes Margaret Laurence, then – determined to be a writer. This is the world she stepped into. A Depression childhood, a dead mother, then a dead father, then a war that wiped out a lot of the young men she knew; then a literary world in which it was commonplace to say that women couldn't write, and neither could Canadians, and any woman or any Canadian who tried was likely to meet more than one big slap-down. It's hard to imagine the sheer guts or perhaps obsessiveness that it must have taken to persevere in what must have seemed a futile and indeed a loony endeavour. (319)

Atwood's comment here – in which her utmost admiration for Laurence is clear – makes evident Laurence's great success under challenging circumstances. As a writer, Laurence entered into a culture that valued English rather than Canadian literature. Indeed, Canadian literature did not yet exist as a field of study in its own right. I hope that I have shown, in *Margaret Laurence Writes Africa and Canada*, how Laurence not only entered into such a culture, but helped to form and shape it. According to Atwood in *A Writer's Life*, Laurence certainly opened the door for women writers in Canada. She showed that it was possible for women to write successfully *in* Canada and *about* Canada. Atwood explains that she felt this possibility when she read *The Stone Angel* for the first time:

> It could be done, then. The impossible, dreamed-of-thing could be done. You could write a novel about Canada – which at that time did not exist as a force in the international literary world, and pretty much did not exist as a force in Canada itself. You could write a novel about Canada that was real, and strong, and authentic, and smart, and moving. It was like watching an albatross take off from a cliff top for the first time, and spread its wings, and soar. (316)

Laurence clearly remains one of Canada's most important literary figures. As *Margaret Laurence Writes Africa and Canada* demonstrates, she was a contributor to the changing and developing arts and culture scene in Canada: she marked Canada's literary place on the map; she contributed to Canada's understanding of itself as a country that stands against the oppression of Others – even as she showed how racism was still prevalent during Canada's re-envisioning of itself as a multicultural country; she sought to define Canada itself through her service on the Committee for a New Constitution; and she took part in helping to shape Canada's place in the world by working against the dominance of multinational corporations such as

Imperial Oil. Laurence was a writer who helped conceptualize and determine our current understanding of the nation itself.

Margaret Laurence Writes Africa and Canada examines both Laurence's African and Canadian work in relation to the history and politics within which it is embedded. I have discussed how Laurence addressed culture and nation in her work. Her essays and correspondence are testaments to the fact that her writing was not produced apart from the cultural and historical milieu of Canada, nor was it produced apart from ongoing colonization that she worked to contest. Thus the British withdrawal from Ghana, at the time that she was writing about that country, was highly significant to her outlook on Britain's domination. Likewise, Canada's loosening of its immigration policies in the 1960s and 1970s, its movement toward multiculturalism in the 1970s and 1980s, and its creation of a new constitution in 1982 are highly relevant to Laurence's writing about Canada and her politics in general. She sought to go beyond the boundaries and limitations that caused Westerners and Canadians to view "us" in relation to "them." As a kind of "Drummer of All the World" – one who "drums" or sends a message to the readers of her works – Laurence's work asks people to pay heed to one another's difference and yet to come together in mutual understanding, respect, and reciprocity.

Notes

1. When the new constitution was being written, there was controversy over whether there needed to be provincial agreement to its legislation. The Supreme Court of Canada deemed that the majority of provinces should agree to its legislation. Quebec did not sign its agreement to the constitution, and so the Meech Lake Accord, in 1987, was an attempt to secure Quebec's agreement, with provisions that would be of interest to the province. The Meech Lake Accord failed to pass, due to the delays initiated by the Oji-Cree Member of the Legislative Assembly (MLA) Elijah Harper.
2. The term "memsahib" was a title for English colonial wives by Indian and subsequently African peoples. Laurence rejected the term on two counts: first, because it implied that she was a colonialist, by virtue of her Anglo heritage and her marriage to a white man; and second, because it foregrounded her role as a wife, rather than as an independent woman. The term, however, was used to describe white married women in the colonies, and as such, Laurence could not ultimately refuse it.
3. It is noteworthy that the description of Africa as a woman and more specifically as a prostitute occurs in other white women's writings about Africa. In her autobiographical work, *West with the Night*, for instance, the white Kenyan writer, Beryl Markham, describes a brothel keeper in terms of Western tropes of Africa. The language in Laurence's and Markham's descriptions of the women is extraordinarily similar: Emerald and Johnnie have "no language in common" (233), just as Markham's African woman speaks a language Markham has "never heard" (267); and Emerald's face is blank and expressionless in the same way that Markham's brothel keeper's face is unreadable: it "held the lineage of several races, none of which had given it distinction" (267).
4. Laurence repeated this technique in her later novel, *The Fire-Dwellers*. In one scene of that novel, she juxtaposes a television newscast of world events with the protagonist Stacey's conversation of everyday things with her children.
5. In "Three Essays on the Theory of Sexuality," Freud speaks of the fetish as an object that is "substituted for the sexual object," and he states that "such substitutes are with some justice likened to the fetishes in which savages believe that their gods are embodied" (249). For Freud, the fetish is that which involves a delusion, since, in his theory, the young boy upholds his belief that his mother has a penis so that "the mutilated woman can be restored to imaginary wholeness" (McClintock 190).

Works Cited

Acoose, Janice. "Fenced In and Forced to Give Up: Images of Indigenous Women in Selected Non-Indigenous Writers' Fiction." *Essay Writing for Canadian Students, with Readings*, 6th ed., edited by Kay L. Stewart et al., Pearson, 2008, pp. 218–27. Reprinted from *Iskwewak—kah' Ki Yaw Ni Wahkomakanak: Neither Indian Princesses nor Easy Squaws*, Women's Press, 1995.

Anderson, Benedict. *Imagined Communities: Reflections on the Origin and Spread of Nationalism*. 1982. Verso, 2006.

Appiah, Kwame Anthony. *In My Father's House: Africa in the Philosophy of Culture*. Methuen, 1992.

Atwood, Margaret. *Payback: Debt and the Shadow Side of Wealth*. Harper Collins, 2008.

——. *Survival: A Thematic Guide to Canadian Literature*. Anansi, 1972.

——. *A Writer's Life: The Margaret Laurence Lectures*. McClelland and Stewart, 2011. 25th Anniversary of the Lecture Series, presented by the Writers' Trust of Canada.

Bannerji, Himani. *The Dark Side of the Nation: Essays on Multiculturalism, Nationalism, and Gender*. Canadian Scholars P, 2000.

Barber, Karin. Introduction. *Readings in African Popular Culture*, edited by Barber, Indiana UP, 1997, pp. 1–12.

de Beauvoir, Simone. *The Second Sex*. Translated and edited by H. M. Parsley, Vintage, 1989.

Beckman-Long, Brenda. "Nationalism and Gender: The Reception of Laurence's *The Diviners*." *West of Eden: Essays on Canadian Prairie Literature*, edited by Warren Cariou, CMU P, 2008, pp. 157–73.

——. "*The Stone Angel* as Feminine Confessional Novel." *Challenging Territory: The Writing of Margaret Laurence*, edited by Christian Riegel, U of Alberta P, 1997, pp. 47–66.

Beeler, Karin E. "Ethnic Dominance and Difference: The Post-Colonial Condition in Margaret Laurence's *The Stone Angel*, *A Jest of God*, and *The Diviners*." *Cultural Identities in Canadian Literature*, edited by Benedicte Mauguiere, Peter Lang, 1988, pp. 25–37.

Bennett, Donna. "English Canada's Postcolonial Complexities." *Essays on Canadian Writing*, vol. 52, 1994, pp. 164–210.

Besner, Neil. "What Resides in the Question, 'Is Canada Postcolonial?'" *Is Canada Postcolonial? Unsettling Canadian Literature*, edited by Laura Moss, Wilfrid Laurier UP, 2003, pp. 40–48.

Bhabha, Homi. *The Location of Culture*. Routledge, 1994.

The Bible. Authorized King James Version, Oxford UP, 1998.

Blodgett, Harriet. "The Real Lives of Margaret Laurence's Women." *Critique*, vol. 23, no. 1, 1981, pp. 5–17.

Bök, Christian. "Sibyls: Echoes of French Feminism in *The Diviners* and *Lady Oracle*." *Canadian Literature*, vol. 135, 1992, pp. 80–93.

Brandt, Di. "(Grand)mothering 'Children of the Apocalypse': A Post-postmodern Ecopoetic Reading of Margaret Laurence's *The Diviners*." *Textual Mothers/Maternal Texts: Motherhood in Contemporary Women's Literatures*, edited by Elizabeth Podnieks et al., Wilfrid Laurier UP, 2010, pp. 253–69.

"Brooke, Rupert." *Merriam-Webster's Encyclopedia of Literature*, Merriam-Webster, 1995, p. 176.

Bruce, Harry. "Doing Something! A Working Plan to Save Canada." *Montreal Gazette*, 4 June 1977.

Brydon, Diana, and Helen Tiffin. *Decolonising Fictions*. Dangaroo, 1993.

Burton, Antoinette. *Burdens of History: British Feminists, Indian Women, and Imperial Culture, 1865–1915*. U of North Carolina P, 1994.

Burton, Richard Francis. *First Footsteps in East Africa*. 1856. Routledge, 1966.

Buss, Helen M. "Reading Margaret Laurence's Life Writing: Toward a Postcolonial Feminist Subjectivity for a White Female Critic." *Margaret Laurence: Critical Reflections*, edited by David Staines, U of Ottawa P, 2001, pp. 39–58.

Butler, Judith. *Bodies That Matter: On the Discursive Limits of "Sex."* Routledge, 1993.

Carolan-Brozy, Sandra, and Susanne Hagemann. "'There is such a place'—Is There? Scotland in Margaret Laurence's *The Diviners*." *Studies in Scottish Fiction: 1945 to the Present*, edited by Hagemann, Peter Lang, 1996, pp. 145–58.

Chaudhuri, Nuper, and Margaret Strobel, editors. *Western Women and Imperialism: Complicity and Resistance*. Indiana UP, 1992.

"Chinese Canadians." *The Canadian Encyclopedia*, http://www.thecanadianencyclopedia.ca/en/article/chinese-canadians/. Accessed 6 Aug. 2016.

Clara Thomas Archives and Special Collections (Margaret Laurence Fonds). York University, Toronto.

Collu, Gabrielle. "Writing about Others: The African Stories." *Challenging Territory: The Writing of Margaret Laurence*, edited by Christian Riegel, U of Alberta P, 1997, pp. 19–32.

Committee for a New Constitution. "Committee for a New Constitution Criticizes Trudeau's Constitutional Proposals." Press release, 23 June 1978. Margaret Laurence Papers, 1980-001, Box 15, File 32, Item 1971. York University Library Archives, Toronto.

Cooper, Frederick, and Ann Laura Stoler, editors. *Tensions of Empire: Colonial Cultures in a Bourgeois World*. U of California P, 1997.

Davis, Laura K. "Margaret Laurence's Correspondence with Imperial Oil: An Anti-Imperialist at Work." *Journal of Canadian Studies*, vol. 44, no. 1, 2010, pp. 60–74.

Davis, Laura (Strong). "Creating a New Multicultural Canada: Motherhood and Nationalism in Margaret Laurence's *The Diviners*." *(M)Othering the Nation: Constructing and Resisting National Allegories through the Maternal Body*, edited by Lisa Bernstein, Cambridge Scholars P, 2008, pp. 88–98.

Day, Richard. *Multiculturalism and the History of Canadian Diversity.* U of Toronto P, 2000.

DelFalco, Amelia. "'And then—': Narrative Identity and Uncanny Aging in *The Stone Angel*." *Canadian Literature*, vol. 198, 2008, pp. 75–89.

Demetrakopoulos, Stephanie A. "Laurence's Fiction: A Revisioning of Feminine Archetypes." *Canadian Literature*, vol. 93, 1982, pp. 42–57.

Desai, Gaurev. *Subject to Colonialism: African Self-Fashioning and the Colonial Library.* Duke UP, 2001.

Dobson, Kit. *Transnational Canadas: Anglo-Canadian Literature and Globalization.* Wilfrid Laurier UP, 2009.

Dopp, Jamie. "Win Orr Lose: Searching for the Good Canadian Kid in Canadian Hockey Fiction." *Canada's Game: Hockey and Identity*, edited by Andrew C. Holman, McGill-Queen's UP, 2009, pp. 81–97.

Edwards, Justin D. *Gothic Canada: Reading the Spectre of a National Literature.* U of Alberta P, 2005.

Eustace, John C. "African Interests: White Liberalism and Resistance in Margaret Laurence's 'The Pure Diamond Man.'" *International Fiction Review*, vol. 30, nos. 1 and 2, 2003, pp. 20–26.

Fabre, Michel. "From *The Stone Angel* to *The Diviners*: An Interview with Margaret Laurence." *A Place to Stand On: Essays By and About Margaret Laurence*, edited by George Woodcock, NeWest P, 1983, pp. 193–209.

Fagan, Kristina. "Adoption as National Fantasy in Barbara Kingsolver's *Pigs in Heaven* and Margaret Laurence's *The Diviners*." *Imagining Adoption: Essays on Literature and Culture*, edited by Marianne Novy, U of Michigan P, 2004, pp. 251–66.

Fanon, Frantz. *Black Skin, White Masks.* Translated and edited by Charles Lam Markmann, Grove P, 1968.

Florby, Gunilla. *The Margin Speaks: A Study of Margaret Laurence and Robert Kroetsch from a Post-Colonial Point of View.* Lund UP, 1997.

Freud, Sigmund. "Three Essays on the Theory of Sexuality." *The Freud Reader*, edited by Peter Gay, Norton, 1995, pp. 239–91.

Friedan, Betty. *The Feminine Mystique.* 1963. Norton, 2001.

Frye, Northrop. *The Bush Garden: Essays on the Canadian Imagination.* Anansi, 1971.

Fulford, Robert. "Margaret Laurence Pens *The Diviners*." *Sunday Supplement*, CBC Radio, 19 May 1974. *CBC Digital Archives*, http://www.cbc.ca/archives/entry/margaret-laurence-pens-the-diviners. Accessed 20 Nov. 2016.

Fyfe, Christopher. "Race, Empire, and the Historians." *Race and Class*, vol. 33, no. 4, 1992, pp. 15–30.

Gaines, Jane. "White Privilege and Looking Relations: Race and Gender in Feminist Film Theory." *Feminist Film Theory: A Reader*, edited by Sue Thornham, New York UP, 1999, pp. 293–306.

Gibson, Graeme. *Eleven Canadian Novelists*. Anansi, 1973.

Gikandi, Simon. *Maps of Englishness: Writing Identity in the Culture of Colonialism*. Columbia UP, 1996.

———. "Reason, Modernity and the African Crisis." *African Modernities: Entangled Meanings in Current Debate*, edited by Jan-Georg Deutsch et al., Heinemann, 2002, pp. 135–57.

Gilman, Sander. *Difference and Pathology: Stereotypes of Sexuality, Race, and Madness*. Cornell UP, 1985.

Godard, Barbara. "*The Diviners* as Supplement: (M)Othering the Text." *Open Letter*, vol. 7, no. 7, 1990, pp. 26–73.

Gray, Charlotte. *Sisters in the Wilderness: The Lives of Susanna Moodie and Catharine Parr Traill*. Penguin, 1999.

Green, Gayle. *Changing the Story: Feminist Fiction and Tradition*. Indiana UP, 1991.

Greer, Germaine. *The Female Eunuch*. Bantam, 1970.

Grosz, Elizabeth. *Jacques Lacan: A Feminist Introduction*. Routledge, 1990.

Hamilton, Roberta. *Gendering the Vertical Mosaic: Feminist Perspectives on Canadian Society*. Copp Clark, 1996.

Haraway, Donna. *Primate Visions: Gender, Race, and Nature in the World of Modern Science*. Routledge, 1989.

Hjartarson, Paul. "'Christie's Real Country. Where I Was Born': Story-Telling, Loss and Subjectivity in *The Diviners*." *Crossing the River: Essays in Honour of Margaret Laurence*, edited by Kristjana Gunnars, Turnstone P, 1988, pp. 43–64.

hooks, bell. *Feminist Theory: From Margin to Center*. 1984. Routledge, 2015.

Ignatiev, Noel. *How the Irish Became White*. Routledge, 1995.

Jameson, Fredric. *The Political Unconscious: Narrative as a Socially Symbolic Act*. Cornell UP, 1982.

Johnson-Odim, Cheryl. "Actions Louder Than Words: The Historical Task of Defining Feminist Consciousness in Colonial West Africa." *Nation, Empire, Colony: Historicizing Gender and Race*, edited by Ruth Roach Pierson and Nuper Chaudhuri, Indiana UP, 1998, pp. 77–93.

Johnston, Anna, and Alan Lawson. "Settler Colonies." *A Companion to Postcolonial Studies*, edited by Henry Schwarz and Sangeeta Ray, Blackwell, 2000, pp. 360–76.

Judge, Christine. Letter to Margaret Laurence on behalf of the Socialist Rights Defense Fund. 1 June 1978. Margaret Laurence Papers, 1980-001, Box 15, File 32, Item 1953. Clara Thomas Archives and Special Collections, York University, Toronto.

Kamboureli, Smaro. *Scandalous Bodies: Diasporic Literature in English Canada*. Oxford UP, 2000.

King, James. *The Life of Margaret Laurence*. Knopf Canada, 1988.

ten Kortenaar, Neil. "The Trick of Divining a Postcolonial Canadian Identity: Margaret Laurence between Race and Nation." *Canadian Literature*, vol. 149, 1996, pp. 11–33.

Kristeva, Julia. "From One Identity to Another." *Critical Theory since Plato*, edited by Hazard Adams, revised ed., Harcourt Brace, 1992, pp. 1162–73.

Kroetsch, Robert. *The Lovely Treachery of Words: Essays Selected and New*. Oxford UP, 1989.

Kuester, Hildegard. *The Crafting of Chaos: Narrative Structure in Margaret Laurence's* The Stone Angel *and* The Diviners. Rodopi, 1994. Cross/Cultures: Readings in Post/Colonial Literatures and Cultures in English 13.

Laurence, Margaret. *A Bird in the House*. 1970. McClelland and Stewart, 1989.

———. "Books That Mattered to Me." *Margaret Laurence: An Appreciation*, edited by Christyl Verduyn, Broadview, 1988, pp. 239–49.

———. *Dance on the Earth: A Memoir*. McClelland and Stewart, 1989.

———. *The Diviners*. 1974. McClelland and Stewart, 1988.

———. *The Fire-Dwellers*. 1969. McClelland and Stewart, 1988.

———. *Heart of a Stranger*. 1976. Edited by Nora Foster Stovel, U of Alberta P, 2003.

———. "Ivory Tower or Grassroots? The Novelist as Socio-Political Being." *A Political Art: Essays and Images in Honour of George Woodcock*, edited by W. H. New, U of British Columbia P, 1978, pp. 15–25.

———. *A Jest of God*. 1966. McClelland and Stewart, 1988.

———. Letter to Chinua Achebe. 3 June 1984. Margaret Laurence Papers, Accrual 1, Box 10. William Ready Division of Archives and Research Collections, McMaster University, Hamilton, Ontario.

———. Letter to Chinua Achebe. 26 June 1984. Margaret Laurence Papers, Accrual 1, Box 10. William Ready Archives and Special Collections, McMaster University, Hamilton, Ontario.

———. Letter to C. J. Martin. 12 May 1962. Margaret Laurence Papers, 1980-001, Box 19, File 132a. Clara Thomas Archives and Special Collections, York University, Toronto.

———. Letter to Gordon R. Elliott. 10 Mar. 1963. Margaret Laurence Papers, Box 9. William Ready Archives and Special Collections, McMaster University, Hamilton, Ontario.

———. Letter to Helen Warkentin. "Monday" (Postmarked 15 May 1945). Margaret Laurence Papers, 2004-040, Box 1, File 1. Clara Thomas Archives and Special Collections, York University, Toronto.

———. Letter to Helen Warkentin. "Tuesday" (Postmarked 6 June 1945). Margaret Laurence Papers, 2004-040, Box 1, File 1. Clara Thomas Archives and Special Collections, York University, Toronto.

———. Letter to Ian Cameron. 12 May 1970. Cameron Family Fonds, 2005-001, Box 49, File 02. Clara Thomas Archives and Special Collections, York University, Toronto.

———. Letter to Ian and Sandy Cameron. 15 Oct. 1969. Cameron Family Fonds, 2005-001, Box 49, File 2. Clara Thomas Archives and Special Collections, York University, Toronto.

———. Letter to Marian Engel. 19 Sept. 1978. Marian Engel Papers, Box 36. William Ready Division of Archives and Research Collections, McMaster University, Hamilton, Ontario.

———. Letter to Marian Engel. 20 Sept. 1978. Marian Engel Papers, Box 36. William Ready Division of Archives and Research Collections, McMaster University, Hamilton, Ontario.

———. Letter to Willis Kingsley Wing. 8 June 1962. Margaret Laurence Papers, 1980-001, Box 19, File 132a. Clara Thomas Archives and Special Collections, York University, Toronto.

———. *Long Drums and Cannons: Nigerian Dramatists and Novelists 1952–1966*. 1968. Edited by Nora Foster Stovel, U of Alberta P, 2001.

———. "Mask of Beaten Gold." *Tamarack Review*, 1963, pp. 3–21.

———. Panel Statement for "Operation Dismantle" Conference. 22 Oct. 1982. Margaret Laurence Papers, 1984-004, Box 5, File 137. York University Library Archives, Toronto.

———. *The Prophet's Camel Bell*. 1963. McClelland and Stewart, 1988.

———. Statement for Women's Petition for Peace. Apr. 1982. Margaret Laurence Papers, 1984-004, Box 6, File 149. York University Library Archives, Toronto.

———. *The Stone Angel*. 1964. McClelland and Stewart, 1988.

———. *This Side Jordan*. 1960. McClelland and Stewart, 1991.

———. "Time and the Narrative Voice." *A Place to Stand On: Essays by and about Margaret Laurence*, edited by George Woodcock, NeWest P, 1983, pp. 155–59. Reprinted from *The Narrative Voice*, edited by John Metcalf, McGraw-Hill Ryerson, 1972.

———. *The Tomorrow-Tamer*. 1963. McClelland and Stewart, 1993.

———. *A Tree for Poverty: Somali Poetry and Prose*. 1954. McClelland and Stewart, 1993.

Laychuk, Riley. "Manitoba-born Author Recognized as 'Person of National Historic Significance.'" *CBC News*, 26 Feb. 2016, http://www.cbc.ca/news/canada/manitoba/margaret-laurence-recognized-historic-significance-1.3464664. Accessed 4 Nov. 2016.

Leney, Jane. "Prospero and Caliban in Laurence's African Fiction." *Journal of Canadian Fiction*, vol. 27, 1980, pp. 63–79.

Lennox, John, and Ruth Panofsky, editors. *Selected Letters of Margaret Laurence and Adele Wiseman*. U of Toronto P, 1997.

Li, Peter S. "Chinese." *Encyclopedia of Canadian Peoples*, edited by Paul Robert Magosci, U of Toronto P, pp. 355–73.

Lutz, Catherine A., and Jane L. Collins. *Reading National Geographic*. U of Chicago P, 1993.

MacFarlane, Karen E. "'A Place to Stand On': (Post)colonial Identity in *The Diviners* and 'The Rain Child.'" *Is Canada Postcolonial? Unsettling Canadian Literature*, edited by Laura Moss, Wilfrid Laurier UP, 2003, pp. 223–37.

Mackey, Eva. *The House of Difference: Cultural Politics and National Identity in Canada*. U of Toronto P, 2002.

MacLennan, Hugh. *Two Solitudes*. 1945. McClelland and Stewart, 2009.

Mannoni, Octave. *Prospero and Caliban: The Psychology of Colonization*. Translated by Pamela Powesland, Praeger, 1950.

Margaret Laurence: First Lady of Manawaka. Directed by Robert Duncan, National Film Board of Canada, 1978.

Markham, Beryl. *West with the Night.* 1942. North Point P, 1983.

McClelland, Jack. *Imagining Canadian Literature: The Selected Letters of Jack McClelland.* Edited by Sam Solecki, Key Porter Books, 1998.

McClintock, Anne. *Imperial Leather: Race, Gender and Sexuality in the Colonial Contest.* Routledge, 1995.

McDonald, Marguerite. "Margaret Laurence's Books Banned." *The National*, 25 Jan. 1985. *CBC Digital Archives*, http://www.cbc.ca/archives/entry/margaret-laurences -books-banned. Accessed 20 Nov. 2016.

McNeil, Bill, and Maria Barrett. "Margaret Laurence's First Novel." *Assignment*. CBC Radio, 19 Dec. 1960. *CBC Digital Archives*, http://www.cbc.ca/archives/entry/ margaret-laurences-first-novel. Accessed 20 Nov. 2016.

Millett, Kate. *Sexual Politics.* 1969. Simon and Schuster, 1990.

Minh-Ha, Trinh T. "Not You/Like You: Postcolonial Women and the Interlocking Questions of Identity and Difference." *Dangerous Liaisons: Gender, Nation, and Postcolonial Perspectives*, edited by Anne McClintock et al., U of Minnesota P, 1997, pp. 415–19.

Mudimbe, V. Y. *The Idea of Africa.* Indiana UP, 1994.

———. *The Invention of Africa.* Indiana UP, 1988.

Munch, John. "Call for Halt to Missile Parts Manufacture, Author Urges." *Toronto Star*, 3 Oct. 1982. Margaret Laurence Papers, 1984-004, Box 5, File 136. York University Library, Toronto.

New, W. H. *Land Sliding: Imagining Space, Presence, and Power in Canadian Writing.* U of Toronto P, 1997.

———. "Margaret Laurence and the City." *Margaret Laurence: Critical Reflections*, edited by David Staines, U of Ottawa P, 2001, pp. 59–78.

———. Introduction. *Margaret Laurence: The Writer and Her Critics*, edited by New, McGraw-Hill Ryerson, 1977, pp. 1–16.

Ogunyeme, Chikwenye Okonjo. "Womanism: The Dynamics of the Contemporary Black Female Novel in English." *Signs: Journal of Women in Culture and Society*, vol. 1, no. 1, 1985, pp. 63–80.

Osachoff, Margaret. "Colonialism in the Fiction of Margaret Laurence." *Southern Review*, vol. 13, no. 3, 1980, pp. 222–38.

Palmateer Pennee, Donna. "Looking Elsewhere for Answers to the Postcolonial Question: From Literary Studies to State Policy in Canada." *Is Canada Postcolonial? Unsettling Canadian Literature*, edited by Laura Moss, Wilfrid Laurier UP, 2003, pp. 78–93.

———. "Technologies of Identity: The Language of the Incontinent Body in Margaret Laurence's *The Stone Angel.*" *Studies in Canadian Literature*, vol. 25, no. 2, 2000, pp. 1–23.

Pell, Barbara. "The African and Canadian Heroines: From Bondage to Grace." *Challenging Territory: The Writing of Margaret Laurence*, edited by Christian Riegel, U of Alberta P, 1997, pp. 33–46.

Penhale, Rev. Jim. Sermon. Neepawa United Church, Neepawa, Manitoba, 10 Jan. 1987. *Manawaka Peggy: A Portrait of Margaret Laurence*, produced by Craig Boyd and

Kelly Dehn, written by Kelly Dehn. Video recording available at the Margaret Laurence Home, Neepawa, Manitoba.

Powers, Lyall. *Alien Heart: The Life and Work of Margaret Laurence*. Michigan State UP, 2003.

Pratt, Mary Louise. *Imperial Eyes: Travel Writing and Transculturation*. Routledge, 2007.

Purdy, A. W., editor. *The New Romans: Candid Canadian Opinions of the U.S.* Hurtig, 1968.

Riegel, Christian. "Recognizing the Multiplicity of the Oeuvre." Introduction. *Challenging Territory: The Writing of Margaret Laurence*, edited by Riegel, U of Alberta P, 1997, pp. xi–xxiii.

———. *Writing Grief: Margaret Laurence and the Work of Mourning*. U of Manitoba P, 2003.

Rimmer, Mary. "(Mis)Speaking: Laurence Writes Africa." *Challenging Territory: The Writing of Margaret Laurence*, edited by Christian Riegel, U of Alberta P, 1997, pp. 1–18.

Rosaldo, Renato. "Imperialist Nostalgia." *Representations*, vol. 26, 1989, pp. 107–22.

Roy, Wendy. "Anti-Imperialism and Feminism in Margaret Laurence's African Writings." *Canadian Literature*, vol. 169, 2001, pp. 33–57.

———. *Maps of Difference: Canada, Women, Travel*. McGill-Queen's UP, 2005.

Said, Edward. *Orientalism*. Vintage Books, 1978.

Schipper, Mineke. "Mother Africa on a Pedestal: The Male Heritage in African Literature and Criticism." *African Literature Today*, vol. 15, 1987, pp. 35–54.

Shakespeare, William. *A Midsummer Night's Dream*. *The Norton Shakespeare*, edited by Stephen Greenblatt et al., Norton, 2015.

———. *The Tempest*. *The Norton Shakespeare*, edited by Stephen Greenblatt et al., Norton, 2015.

"Skelton, John." *Merriam-Webster's Encyclopedia of Literature*, Merriam-Webster, 1995, p. 1039.

"Slander Action Launched on RCMP 'Subversion Charge.'" *The Commonwealth*, Apr. 1978. Margaret Laurence Papers, 1980-001, Box 15, File 32, Item 1953. Clara Thomas Archives and Special Collections, York University, Toronto.

Sparrow, Fiona. *Into Africa with Margaret Laurence*. ECW P, 1992.

Stoler, Ann Laura. "Making Empire Respectable: The Politics of Race and Sexual Morality in Twentieth-Century Colonial Cultures." *Dangerous Liaisons: Gender, Nation, and Postcolonial Perspectives*, edited by Anne McClintock et al., U of Minnesota P, 1997, pp. 344–73.

Stovel, Nora Foster. *Divining Margaret Laurence: A Study of Her Complete Writings*. McGill-Queen's UP, 2008.

———. Introduction. *Heart of a Stranger*, by Margaret Laurence, edited by Stovel, U of Alberta P, 2003, pp. xi–xxxiii.

———. "Talking Drums and Dancing Masks." Introduction. *Long Drums and Cannons: Nigerian Dramatists and Novelists 1952–1966*, edited by Stovel, U of Alberta P, 2001, pp. xvii–liii.

———. "(W)rites of Passage: The Typescript of *The Diviners* as Shadow Text." *Margaret Laurence: Critical Reflections*, edited by David Staines, U of Ottawa P, 2001, pp. 101–20.

Sugars, Cynthia, and Laura Moss. *Canadian Literature in English: Texts and Contexts*. Vol. 1, Pearson, 2008.

Sugars, Cynthia, and Gerry Turcotte, editors. *Unsettled Remains: Canadian Literature and the Postcolonial Gothic*. Wilfrid Laurier UP, 2009.

Szamosi, Gertrud. "Mapping Canadian Identity in Margaret Laurence's *Heart of a Stranger*." *Contested Identities: Literary Negotiations in Time and Place*, edited by Roger Nicholson et al., Cambridge Scholars Publishing, 2015, pp. 269–82.

Tapping, Craig. "Margaret Laurence and Africa." *Crossing the River: Essays in Honour of Margaret Laurence*, edited by Kristjana Gunnars, Turnstone, 1988, pp. 65–79.

Thomas, Clara. *The Manawaka World of Margaret Laurence*. McClelland and Stewart, 1975.

Topor-Constantin, Andreea. *Racial, Ethnic, Gender and Class Representations in Margaret Laurence's Writings*. Cambridge Scholars Publishing, 2013.

Troper, Harold. "Multiculturalism." *The Encyclopedia of Canada's Peoples*, edited by Paul Robert Magocsi, U of Toronto P, 1999, pp. 997–1006.

Ware, Tracy. "Race and Conflict in Garner's 'One-Two-Three Little Indians' and Laurence's 'The Loons.'" *Studies in Canadian Literature*, vol. 23, no. 2, 1998, pp. 71–84.

White, Anne. "The *Persons* Case, 1929: A Legal Definition of Women as Persons." *Framing Our Past: Constructing Canadian Women's History in the Twentieth Century*, edited by Sharon Anne Cook et al., McGill-Queen's UP, 2001, pp. 216–21.

William Ready Division of Archives and Special Collections at McMaster University, Hamilton, Ontario.

Woodcock, George. *Gabriel Dumont: The Métis Chief and His Lost World*. Hurtig Publishers, 1976.

Xiques, Donez. *The Making of a Writer: Margaret Laurence*. Dundurn, 2005.

Young, Robert J. C. *Colonial Desire: Hybridity in Theory, Culture, and Race*. Routledge, 1995.

Index

abjection, 41–42, 77, 78–79

Aboriginal peoples: Canadian nationalism linked to identification with, 119–20; colonization of, 14–15; conflation with land and nature, 112, 128, 130; critique of depictions of, 98; cultural displacement, 95; displacement in Canada's creation, 84–85; "dying race" narrative and dispossession, 96–99; foregrounded in *The Diviners*, 111, 112, 119–20; Laurence's resistance of oppression of, 7, 10, 11, 15; and multiculturalism policy, 111–12; reconciliation with settlers, 8–9, 130–32, 143; role in nationalist myths, 10–11. *See also* Métis

Achebe, Chinua, 2, 45, 71, 145–46

Acoose, Janice, 97, 98

Africa: African philosophy and African crisis, 57; expatriate mourning of, 59, 60–61; pan-Africanism, 3, 5, 12, 46; womanism, 69–70

Africa, and Laurence: introduction, 2; approach to Africa and colonialism, 4, 43, 146; books on Africa, 2; connection between African and Canadian writings, 44, 144, 145, 146; contestation of Western ideas of Africa, 6–7, 40–41, 46–47, 48–50; on independence movements, 3–4; position in Africa, 29; on viewing Africans as individuals, 64. *See also The Prophet's Camel Bell* (Laurence); *This Side of Jordan* (Laurence); *The Tomorrow-Tamer* (Laurence)

Africa, Western ideas about: African art, 37; as ancient and traditional, 61–62, 147, 150; city *vs.* rural as modern *vs.* traditional, 36–38; colonized as domesticated, 37; contestation of, 6–7, 40–41, 46–47, 48–50; feminization of Africa, 6–7, 39–40, 41, 61–62, 67, 147, 150, 153n3; history of, 5, 46; impasse on how to deal with, 56–58; as land of childhood, 55; as mysterious, primitive, and savage, 48–50, 52; rationality of Africans, 68; sexualization of African women, 66; Western origins sought in Africa, 67; Western self sought in Africa, 71

Africanization, 35, 55

Afua (fictional), 7, 58–59, 61–62, 63, 67, 150. *See also* "The Drummer of All the World" (Laurence)

alternative energy activism, 2, 15

Anderson, Benedict, 18, 120

anthropology, 53–54, 70

anti-nuclear activism, 15, 16, 102, 117, 141